10 Seasonal magic spells and rituals for the whole year

GOLDEN TAROT
by Kat Black

FANTASTIC SUBSCRIPTION OFFER!
PAGE 182
DON'T MISS OUT!

185 Weekly astrological planner for the year

contents

INSIDE

Editor: Marion Williamson
Assistant Editor: Jemma South
Art editor: Alexandra Bourdelon
Designers: Sophie Harwin, Kathryn Slack, Mark Brewster
Sub editor: Emma Bartlett
Illustrator: Annie Rudden at www.annierudden.com

All correspondence to: Prediction Magazine, Leon House, 233 High Street, Croydon CR9 1HZ. Price £7.99 from all good newsagents and bookshops.© Copyright IPC Media Limited 2008. All rights reserved.
Distributed by Marketforce, 5th Flr, Low Rise Buildings, King's Reach Tower, London SE1 9LS (020 7633 3333).
Distributed to the book trade by BookSource, 50 Cambuslang Road, Cambuslang, Glasgow, G32 8NB. Telephone Number: 0845 370 0067 Email: ipc@booksource.net

prediction
life-lines

Prediction bring the best psychics, astrologers and fortune-tellers together to advise and answer your most personal questions

LOVE TAROT

Call one of our specialist Tarot readers to help sort out any relationship or love-life dilemmas that might be spinning around in your mind.

CALL
*0906 344 0762

LOVE PSYCHIC

Our love and relationship psychic will answer questions such as 'When will you meet the right partner?' and 'Am I with the right person?'. Ask our love psychics for their expert advice!
Includes a CD of your reading
TEXT
PLOVE (space) and your question to 86655
CALL
*0906 344 0744

HOROSCOPES

For your fantastic weekly and monthly cash, career and romance forecasts!

ARIES **0905 515 0037**
TAURUS **0905 515 0038**
GEMINI **0905 515 0039**
CANCER **0905 515 0040**
LEO **0905 515 0041**
VIRGO **0905 515 0042**
LIBRA **0905 515 0043**
SCORPIO **0905 515 0044**
SAGITTARIUS **0905 515 0045**
CAPRICORN **0905 515 0046**
AQUARIUS **0905 515 0047**
PISCES **0905 515 0048**

SP: Eckoh, Herts, HP3 9HN Starlines updated every Tuesday. BT calls cost 60p per minute and last approx. 3 minutes. Costs from other networks may be higher.

RUNES

Discover your mystical destiny with a fabulous rune reading!
CALL
*0906 344 0751

LIVE MEDIUM

The Spirits are an invaluable source of information – is there a message waiting for you?
CALL
*0906 174 1514

or pay by Credit/debit card
0800 063 0628

TEXT A PSYCHIC

What's in store for 2008, are you with the one?
Text your burning question...
text PSYCHICS (space) then your question to
*86655

* BT calls/Credit Card readings cost £1.50 per minute. Cost from other networks may be higher. Callers must be 18+. Cost includes a CD of your reading upon request. Lines are open from 7am-2am every day. Maximum length for calls is 20 minutes/Credit Card readings 40 minutes. Text readings costs £1.50 inc. VAT. All replies take up to two messages. Standard operator rates apply for all messages you send. Psychics will promptly reply to all messages. When you text a Psychic, you will get marketing messages from IPC Media Ltd and Prediction magazine. However you can reply NO at any time to unsubscribe from marketing messages. Helpline: UK 0800 140 9049. Service provider: Pronto Media Ltd, PO Box 199, Selby, YO8 1BP. All calls are recorded. Readings are for Entertainment purposes only. This service is regulated by PPP.

numerology

The year ahead, 2009 is a '29', '11', '2' year, which symbolises exciting new opportunities for all of us. Numerologist **Sonia Ducie** looks closely at the number magic for the months ahead

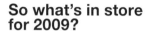

The potent little digits in the date influence us all. Numbers highlight truth. If we tap into their hidden wisdom they will give us clear messages that can help us lead happy, healthy and inspirational lives. Each of the numbers 1 to 9 contains strengths, challenges and hidden unexplored potential. Numbers, patterns or cycles repeat themselves so that we can learn from the past. They can also open us up to whole new ways of experiencing our lives.

So what's in store for 2009?

2009 = 2+0+0+9= 29; 2+9 = 11; 1+1 = 2.
So 2009 is year 29/11/2
Number 29 highlights the qualities of love, wisdom, compassion and understanding; it is extremely uplifting. Number 11 is the great spiritual transformer – it's offering us a wake-up call and a big reality check, and is helping us to gain clarity. We are truly emerging into the light in order to uplift humanity, and hearing the call to do what we can to serve the greater good of the planet. Number 2 highlights balance, decision-making, peace and wisdom.

We are in the process of forming an inspired society, and the 29/11/2 with its bright energy is illuminating new opportunities for us to lift ourselves out of our daily toils and improve life for all.

During this 29/11 year we need to be very realistic when aiming for our personal goals, and stay true to our beliefs and our values.

Whatever avenue we explore in life, we will always live and learn; our soul is always the winner. With the new energy coming in this 29/11/2 year we can learn to be open to life, and to be accepting that we, and others, can really only ever do our best.

Lifestyle changes
There are a number of lifestyle decisions we need to make in 2009 and they should include:
■ Learning to lead a simple life on a daily basis and choosing to make decisions that are harmless, that will keep the peace and keep us anchored in the world.
■ Learning to listen can create more harmony in our own lives and in the world. With a million external distractions (including our own emotions and mind), actually learning to hear what is being said can help save time and enhance all our relationships.

Jacaranda Designs
Individually Designed CRYSTAL GEMSTONE & Glass Jewellery

Gemstones Listed A to Z
with Healing Properties

Modern & Classic Styles
Jewellery for ALL Occasions

FREE Pair of HEMATITE
Earrings with
Your 1st Order

Tel : 07957 869 577

email : jacaranda-designs@blueyonder.co.uk

www.jacaranda-jewellery-designs.co.uk

BRITISH ASTROLOGICAL & PSYCHIC SOCIETY
(Founded 1976 by Russell Grant)

Certificated Correspondence Courses

(Full Member of A.P.A.E.)

*Send 6 X 1ˢᵗ Class Stamps
for Courses & Registered
Consultants Booklets*

**BAPS Dept, PR
PO BOX 5687
SPRINGFIELD
MILTON KEYNES
MK6 3WZ
TEL: 01908 201 368**

info@baps.ws— www.baps.ws

LIVE Tarot Readings & Spiritual Life Coaching

ASK THE ANSWER

With Anne-Marie
"My team of trusted readers will guide you"

Text 'PREDICT' to
82768
T A R O T

Credit Card FREE Phone
0800 028 1692
Calls cost £16 for 30 mins or £29 for 1 hour

On Your Phone Bill
0906 890 8672
Calls cost 60p/min Live calls recorded

18+ Only. Text Msgs cost £1.50 for each message recieved, some messages may be up to two messages long (£3.00). Helpline 08704 541000 www.asktheanswer.com

Republic of Ireland Callers: 1580 932 851

18+ Calls cost €2.40/min. Mobile calls may cost more. Live calls recorded. Helpline 08704 541000 Pacific Tel Co. PO Box 384, Cambs. CB22 5NE.

---

psychicswitchboard.co.uk
Our sincere & gifted readers can guide you 24/7

55p
per min

0905 355 0417

CREDIT CARD FREEPHONE – £21 for 40 mins or £29 for 1 hour – 0800 075 6360

18+ only. 0905 = 55p per min from a BT landline, other ntwks & mobiles may vary. Calls recorded. PS Ltd helpline 0844 944 3094.

Wendy & Lee

*Psychic Mediums
Genuine, Honest, Accurate,
Caring Spiritual readings.
Tarot also available.
We are not an agency.
£35-Unlimited time.
For professional guidance, please ring
01935 815 607 Mid-day until 1 am.
All major credit/debit cards accepted.*

Lotus Moon
Caring, Gifted, Psychic & Witch

Offers accurate insight, guidance and spells
for all areas of your life:
Love - Health - Wealth

Let me work with you to help resolve your
problems and be happy

Tel: 02920 564507
Mob: 07747 153193

Credit card payments & cheques accepted

■ Learning to see the bigger picture means we are able to step aside from our own desires and view the real purpose of a situation.

■ Learning to use our creative gifts can raise our spirits and inspire others to do the same.

■ Learning to compromise is a gift because it can help to bring peace, love and stability into everyday life.

■ Learning to be kind and thoughtful towards others means we are acting in a helpful way.

Health

The number 29/11/2, may highlight unresolved issues and feelings relating to grief, sadness, or hopelessness. We may even feel intense emotions at times when we're clearing through old emotional baggage, and bringing issues to the surface to be healed. Simple breathing exercises, yoga or meditation may help us to stay calm and help us to process these feelings internally so they can be transformed.

Career

It's a big year for us all to grow up and make those all-important decisions. Yes we may need to spend time deliberating indecisively, but if we follow our passions, be true to ourselves, and aim to do the work we love, we will know what to do and decisions will come easily. This year is a great time to start giving something back to humanity, like getting involved with charities. We can all make a difference.

Loved-ones

This is a great year to open our hearts to love, to get closer to loved ones, or to meet the love of our life. On another level this 11-year is asking our 'little selves' (our personality) to bond with our soul (our 'higher self') so that they can live, work and make more love together, and so we can fulfil our greater potential.

Finances

The 29/11 energy can at times bring intense highs and lows, and feel a little precarious. Financially it may help us to keep an eye on our destination or goals, and keep up with the book keeping to so we can keep our account balanced. Living simply with our available resources can go a long way, whatever our financial status.

Soul work

It's a good time to give to others – that's food for the soul. Visiting cathedrals, beautiful gardens or photographic or art galleries, or even reading about them, can help to stimulate the abstract part of our brain

Spraysmudge – Magic in a Bottle!

Spraysmudge is the no-mess alternative to the smudgestick, created with powerful crystal essences of black tourmaline, smokey quartz and herkimer diamond, to ground, protect and clear, together with a blend of essential oils, including sage. Simply spray and smudge away any negative or unwanted energies! Spraysmudge is also great for therapists and readers to use in between clients to clear the space.

**You can order Spraysmudge by phoning
020 8504 1803**

All major credit and debit cards accepted.
Take a look at the website for other products from www.spraysmudge.com

Live Psychics

LOVE · HEALTH · MONEY

0906 160 2626

Credit card payments call:

0845 053 0825

'I was amazed at the quality of your readings!'
- S.M, Leeds

Calls Cost 60p/min from BT landline, MS PO Box 332. M60 3ZS

KUMAR

World famous leading Indian Psychic who can prove to be working in London since 1968 with thousands of satisfied clients. He can help and advise you on your problems in love, marriage, job, immigration, bad luck, examination, infertility, business or any other problems of life can be solved with guarantee and confidentially. Ring **0208 802 0457** for an appointment at:- **289, High Road, Tottenham, LONDON N15 (One minute from Seven Sisters Tube)** Mobile **07956 830626** Fax:- **0208 802 4837** or Email:- surinderbatra@aol.com

Information from the Spirit Guides

Discover how the spirit world works positively for us all

dreams • positive energy
hauntings • healing

Gazelle Book Services   tel: 01524 68765
www.lealodgebooks.co.uk £9.99

YOU'LL KNOW I AM THE REAL THING WHEN I NAME YOUR REAL LOVER?

I will read your mind and your partners, then tell you if their love is for real, what will happen next, if you will travel, receive money, find new love. What's more I will tell you the one that loves you the most. You will receive names, dates and places.

You won't be disappointed.

Call us now, you'll be surprised.

realpsychiclover.com

**CALL: 0905 009 0535
CREDIT CARDS: 0870 249 1522**
£1.50/min. Infodial. Customer Service: 0870 9222 220.
Readings for guidance only. All Calls Recorded. 24 Hours.

⊛ Children of Artemis ⊛ and Witchfest

Join the largest Witchcraft and Wiccan organisation in Europe. Membership, magazine, web forums, events, courses, shops and far more For details see:
**www.witchcraft.org
www.witchfest.net**

Stepping Stones

Cambridge House and 4 Cambridge Place, Farnham New Age Holistic Shop

Readings and Mediumship
Full range of holistic Therapies
Workshops and evening talks/
Demonstrations on a variety of subjects

Tel. 01252 821616
info@steppingstones.biz
www.steppingstones.biz

and help us to tap into the subconscious world.

World issues

Issues regarding values and beliefs are being aired and discussed openly in the public domain. Those who continue to cling to rigid mindsets will render themselves impotent. Collectively we are adapting to a brand new world that welcomes everyone as equals. More people are turning towards religion and spirituality than ever, perhaps to find something they believe in.

World trade

Originally we ate the food we grew in our own backyards and now we are spoiled for choice. Food crops can easily be introduced back into our local environment with foods that suit our climate. Food shortages have occurred throughout history and we need to learn to be more adaptable with resources.

Education

Education and training is high on our agenda. It's the key to success that offers everyone the ability to earn a living, take responsibility and make a contribution. Education also places the spotlight on Human Rights issues. We need to inspire co-operation to enable help to go to those who cannot help themselves.

Economics

Following the economic explosion in China, Africa is the next frontier to be conquered. It's a rich country with much virgin territory. As world resources run low, many world economies will want to ally with Africa, ensuring it also remains the focus as a political hotspot. Gold prices may peak, as much more of this precious commodity is unleashed onto the market especially from North-West Australia.

Environment

Yes! We have woken up to the serious challenges facing humanity regarding the weather; intense heat, fires, winds and earthquakes around the world – but we're on to it! This 29/11-year is offering us the best chance yet to make a concerted effort and do our bit. The lungs of the planet, the rainforests, need protecting, and this is also a good time for replanting trees.

Now the environmental situation also makes us think about how we are contributing to world health, and makes us aware of what it is we truly need in order to lead a simple life.

Overview 2009/2010

In 2008 much breaking down of old structures and ideas occurred in order to make way for the new energy in this 29/11/2 year. An enormous wake up call has been sounded. Our collective soul has been highlighting areas needing change.

In 2010, year 30/3, there will be a natural expansion that allows us to let go of the past, make the most of our present and be optimistic about our future.

We must remain focused on what's important. It's an opportunity for us to recognise what we have been doing, what we are trying to achieve, and to put thoughts into action. ❖

further info

For courses, workshops and readings, visit: www.numerology. org.uk. Or read, *Do It Yourself Numerology* (Watkins, £10.99) and *Power Pendants; Wear Your Lucky Numbers Every Day* (Connections, £5.99). By Sonia Ducie the author of this article.

Magical seasons

Amanda Samson shows you how to use the transformative power of the changing seasons

Following the magical year offers a great way to celebrate the changing seasons. When you are in harmony with the natural world, it helps you to connect magically with everything around you. You can use the energies of each season to find balance, enhance your sense of flow and deepen your important relationship with yourself, with others and with the wider Universe.

Each season has traditional festivals with their own special magic. You can tap into this energy using certain colours, eating dedicated foods and focusing in a particular way when you do any magical or spiritual work. The suggestions on these pages for celebrating each magical moment in the year can be adapted to suit your own beliefs and intuitive reactions at the time.

The magical year ends at Samhain and begins at Yule, but you can start using the energies at any seasonal ritual you choose. Maybe you are drawn to Imbolc in February or perhaps Lammas in August.

Try to think about why this festival in particular resonates more with you than any of the others. It's also important at each celebration to make sure you take some time out, both before and after, to reflect on its meaning for you personally.

Magical seasons for the Northern Hemisphere

Name	Date	Symbolism
Samhain	31st October	Transformation
Winter solstice	21st/22nd December	Renewal
Imbolc	2nd February	Inspiration
Ostara	21st/22nd March	Growth
Beltane	1st May	Creativity
Litha	21st/22nd June	Love
Lammas	1st August	Abundance
Mabon	21st/22nd September	Generosity

Samhain

Known as Samhain or Halloween, 31st October signifies the end of the old summer and the transition to winter. Samhain marks the beginning of space between the old year and new. It's a time to embrace the mysteries of life and death, and honour the past and the spirit world.

Release the past so you can move towards the future. Find pumpkins, apples and other spirit

talismans to decorate your house. Hold a party or ritual to honour death and transformation, serve apple cider, pomegranates and pumpkins to connect with the festival.

Burning myrrh and patchouli incenses, as well as orange and black candles represents the energy of Samhain. Bury an apple or pomegranate to honour the spirits.

Transformation ritual

Light a black candle and say, "I accept my faults, hurts and pain, I consign my weakness to the flames." Write the lessons you have learned or the hurt you've caused over the year. Reflect on these and then burn the paper.

Light an orange candle and say, "Blessed be the year past, may what is good and useful last." Write or draw what you achieved over the year. Fold and seal with wax.

Light a white candle and say, "The light defines the darkness and connects me to what is beyond. I am connected to all and within me." Ask what the next year will bring and meditate on the answer. Write down any intuitions. Fold and seal. Open at the next Samhain.

Winter solstice

The winter solstice around the 21st December heralds the new solar year. Fires and candles are lit to welcome the return of the Sun god. It welcomes the new year and wishes health and peace to all.

People would go from door to door singing and offering blessings or gather in fields to bless the livestock and the coming year's crops.

Rituals at this time focus on peace and well being. It's time to bring forward the plans discerned at Samhain. What will you

'give birth' to as the wheel of the year begins to turn towards the warmth and light of the Sun?

Decorate your house with anything green, red and gold. Deck your halls with holly, mistletoe, ivy and pine cones. A tree with trimmings and gift giving are ancient traditions.

Consecrate your tree by sprinkling it with salt water, weaving incense smoke around it and lighting a candle. Make a yule log; carve three holes to place green and red candles in.

Hang bells to bless the fairies and spirits. Make a

modern version of Wassail; a drink to celebrate the Sun, usually of honeyed and spiced wine or ale.

Renewal ritual

In the quiet dark of the solstice morning, wake early and step outside into the cold. Let your feet touch the Earth and feel the chill, then wrap yourself warmly and wait for the sky to lighten. Use this time to meditate on what you would like to take root in your life or in the world this year. It could be a state of mind, a change or something you make. ☞

Imbolc

Halfway between the winter solstice and the spring equinox is the Fire festival of Imbolc. Celebrated as the first signs of spring begin to appear, this festival is all about hope and healing.

There are many celebrations to the goddesses at this time, with Brigid and Cailleach being popular.

In magical work Imbolc heralds the return of the maiden aspect and is a time of purification and initiation. It's time to invite healing and purification into your life.

Leave buttered bread in your kitchen for the fairies, and make a broomstick and dream pillows filled with lavender. Other seasonally appropriate rituals include burning sandalwood incense and anointing candles with vanilla oil. Fill your home with white flowers and place candles outside to banish the darkness.

Cleansing ritual

A purification and dedication ritual resonates with this time of year.

Make a herb bag of muslin or cheesecloth using lavender, rosemary and camomile. Place it in a bath and allow the herbs to steep into the water.

Decorate the bathroom with white flowers and candles and burn frankincense. Then, when you're in a relaxed frame of mind, get into the bath and focus on inviting positive and uplifting energies into your space.

This is the best time to let go of any negative thoughts and feelings. Dedicate yourself to walking your own path.

Ostara

The length of sunlight and darkness are in perfect balance and from now until the summer solstice the light will grow. Taking its name from the fertility goddess Eostre, the promise of fertility and growth is symbolised by the giving of eggs and the images of rabbits. It is a time of nurturing as small creatures are born and the Earth's gifts begin to grow and flourish. The astrological calendar begins now with Aries, a symbol of energy and drive. All the careful planning of the winter months can be released into action. This is a time of great power where the promise of spring enables you to focus on your goals and dreams.

Decorate your house with yellow flowers and green candles to symbolise the union of Earth and Sun, goddess and god, female and male; potent energies of growth.

Light jasmine incense to wave farewell to winter and bake buns or cakes decorated with the solar cross to welcome the spring. Leave small gifts in the garden for the fairies. It's a time to celebrate the feminine energy of birth and nurture.

Ostara 13 Moons ritual

Create a circle of 13 white candles that represent each of the lunar months of the year. Ask your inner self what you need to nurture to move forward. This will help you to enhance your personal development and solve problems in all areas of your life.

Perhaps a relationship is troubled, your work is unsatisfying or a project seems stalled. By accessing what lies deep within you and bringing it out into the light you are more able to move forward. Enhance this ritual by using astrological signs and ask each for help as you light the candles.

Beltane

The beginning of May is celebrated as Beltane, an ancient Fire festival of fertility. The Pagan summer starts with rituals of purification and the celebration of life. Maypoles, bonfires, the hanging of hawthorn and rowan around the doorways and windows are all May time events.

Beltane honours life and the celebration of all that represents. Just as Samhain, this is a time where the passage between this world and the next is open and many rituals ask for the blessings of the otherworld for good harvests and all that sustains life.

Beltane is best celebrated with exciting colours and festivity - and maybe some sneaking off to the woods with a lover!

Make paper baskets filled with seasonal flowers to offer to friends, make flower or bead chains and decorate yourself and others. Dark green candles and sweet, flowery incense are best as you celebrate happiness and life.

Creative focus ritual
Rituals that open you to sensuality and creativity are appropriate at Beltane. These enable you to feel connected with the Earth and your body; honouring the power of fertility within.

Use this time to manifest an idea, relationship or project that you've had in mind for some time. Or bathe yourself in water rich with rose oil and petals to honour your sensual, creative nature.

Litha

The 21st or 22nd of June heralds the summer solstice, Litha. Celebrate all night with rituals to greet the morning Sun!

The energies of love and health remind us of protection, prosperity and empowerment. It's the birth month of the nine muses so music, dance and theatrics are in order.

Litha sends us out into nature; seek fairy folk in the woods and remember to count and honour your blessings. Decorations for the home can include blue candles, lavender or musk incenses and oils, and an abundance of summer fruits and flowers.

Just as the warm Sun nurtures the maturing earth, you can think about ways to care and nurture those you love. Creating protection amulets and healing talismans or psychic dream pouches are all Litha activities.

Collect your own herbs as this time signifies heightened healing powers. Weave a 'witches ladder' to hang for protection by braiding red, black and white yarn to represent the triple goddess and decorate with nine feathers or charms to represent the nine muses.

Midsummer ritual
Use this ritual to celebrate life and make a wish for the future. On the dawn of the solstice day have a floating candle and a large bowl of water, unless you can find yourself beside a stream, lake or sea.

Stand facing the dawn and chant the following words in the box below... ☞

"Greetings to the dawn, air and mind
May [your wish] be mine to find."
Light your candle and say,
"With Fire to inspire and empower
May my wish flourish and flower."
Place the candle on the water and say,
"Deep within let the water flow
May [your wish] in my life grow."
Clap your hands and say,
"With Air, Fire, Water and Earth
I celebrate with light and mirth,
To [your wish] let my energy flow
As above so below."

Lammas

Early August brings the festival of bread and berries with the celebration of Lammas. Passion, abundance, feasts and fetes are all offerings at this time. It is a good time for hand fasting and unions of all types!

This time reminds us to appreciate all we have and all the potential within, but it also reminds us that loss and death walk with life and love. We must attend to our creations to ensure they ripen and flourish.

Create a magical picnic with berry pies and fresh bread. Use golden and yellow candles, burn frankincense and use lots of summer flowers such as sunflowers and gerberas. Consider how abundance manifests in your life. Do you take the time to enjoy the fruits of your labours or are you busy rushing on to the next thing?

Make time to stop and enjoy what you have and honour what nourishes you. The energy of abundance reminds us that without tending, what we have will die.

Abundance ritual
Celebrate abundance by recognising your gifts. Plan a feast and ask each of

your friends to contribute something that represents their own gifts. This may be food, organising, music, decorations and so on. Before the feast begins, acknowledge each others' gifts and the blessings they bring.

Mabon

The final harvest feast takes place at the autumn equinox when day and night are equal, before the dark of winter creeps up. Prepare for the darkening days and enjoy the final feasts of summer. It is

a time for honouring all you are and all you've achieved. The energy of Mabon reminds us to honour the generosity and the abundance of the summer harvests.

Be mindful of the balance of the cycle of life. Use rich browns, oranges and golds for candles and acorns, leaves and autumn flowers to decorate. Cook using beans and squashes with smoked meats and honeyed wine.

Prepare for the end of the year by clearing out and donating possesions to others. Give thanks to life and the energy that flows around you.

Blessing ritual
Light a yellow candle and face East, then say, "Of dawn and Air, of soul and mind, wisdom gained and offered in kind." Light a red candle and face the South, "Of Fire and heat, of passion and desire. Energy flows through me to inspire." Light a blue candle and face West, "Of Water and flow, of heart and emotion. Love, the guide, directing all motion." Light a green candle, face North, "Of nature and Earth, of yours and mine. Prosperity shared equals the divine." ❖

Raven

Weird and wonderful magical stuff to tickle your imagination.

Spell Kits, Tarot Cards, Temple Equipment, Witchy Stuff, Voodoo, or High Magic—you name it, we probably stock it.
Send 2 first class stamps for our fab catalogue—so huge we can hardly get it in the envelope!
Unlock your magic with
Raven 17 Melton Fields, Brickyard Lane, N Ferriby, East Yorks HU14 3HE

Elizabeth Rose - International Clairvoyant, Medium & Psychic NOW ONLINE!
As featured on GMTV & with over 35 years experience

NEW - TEXT A PSYCHIC

Simply text the word FORTUNE and your question to 88818
Each reply costs £1.50. Callers must be 18+

or call **0906 500 0618**
Pay using your Phone Bill @ £1.50 /min. All calls recorded. Live 24/7. PO Box 7154, Mansfield, Notts

or call **01623 423 444**
ALL MAJOR CREDIT/DEBIT CARDS ACCEPTED

www.Elizabeth Rose.co.uk

Psychic Proof
The Proof Is In The Reading

Genuine live readings about love & relationships, career, money & future happiness

0906 119 4082
1580 106 815 (Eire)

Calls £1.50 per min BT land line (€2.40 ROI) & recorded. Helpline 0800 915 2343

0800 915 2343
Credit Card £29.95 for 20 mins

www.psychicproof.com

Text **PROOF** and your question to **84184**

Text replies £1.50 each, some answers may take more than one text

30 YEARS EXPERIENCE
Kalyani
GIFTED
INTERNATIONAL
CLAIRVOYANT

Psychic/Crystal Ball/Palm Reading by
KALYANI
Kalyani will help you deal with love Worries, stress, disappointment, relationship, doubts & problems, in life. For an appointment or a reading call

07958 451 202
After 7p.m. Mon. - Sun. or visit at M30 New Shephards Bush Market, London W12 8DE. on Saturday 11-5p.m.

"Under the new legislation, for entertainment purposes only"

Alexia
Traditional clairvoyant and occultist

Accurate readings from by post & e-mail £10

Powerful Spells cast contact for details

www.psychic-reading.co.uk

Box A369 Prediction, Leon House 233 High St Croydon. CR9 1HZ
All major debit/credit cards are accepted

THE
BRITISH ASSOCIATION
OF
CLAIRVOYANTS & MEDIUMS

We uphold the **highest** professional standards for **authentic** clairvoyant consultations

01843 871111
Exclusive Credit & Debit Card Service

0906 111 4491
Convenient Pay By Telephone Service (24hrs)

Text ESP & any question to 84184 to know your future!

www.britishclairvoyants.com
Calls @ £1.50 per minute from BT Land line & recorded.
PO Box 287, CT10 1XQ

Live Spiritual and Tarot Readings

kooma
spiritual you

75p per min
0906 758 1306

Credit Card **0800 075 9007**
£14 for 20 mins or £27 for 40 mins

Over 18's. 0906 = 75p per min from a BT landline, other ntwks & mobiles may vary. Calls recorded. 24hr helpdesk 0844 944 3044.

Talk to the professionals ...

Live astrology readings ...
... top qualified astrologers

Consultant Details & Schedules
www.astrolivelink.com
0800 834 861

Dial 0906 1111 618

Calls cost £1.50 per minute. Maximum call length 20 minutes. All calls are recorded.
Alternatively, for easy access and better value, call the helpline to pay by credit card.

From Ireland: 1580 92 73 78 €1.90 p.m. Australia: 1902 265 001 $5.50pm USA: 1-888 476 2188 (Toll free booking)

Astro*Live*Link Ltd., PO Box 4114, London W1A 6TF Helpline: 0870 125 00 11

Fantastic *Prediction Magazine* astrologer, **Rick Hayward**, provides a month-at-a-glance guide to the year ahead for all the zodiac signs. Read here for predictions for love, home, travel, money and health. Simply find the page that marks the start for your sign's year to discover what 2009 has in store for you!

2009

your astro guide

CONTENTS

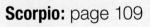

For your fantastic weekly & monthly cash, career and romance and forecasts

Call 0905 515 0037

Starlines are updated every Tuesday. BT calls cost 60p per minute and last about 5 minutes. Cost from other networks may be higher. SP: Eckoh Herts HP3 9HN

Aries
march 21 to april 20

Zodiac fact file

Planetary Ruler: Mars

Quality & Element: Cardinal Fire

Colours: Bright Reds

Metal: Iron

Wood: Mahogany

Flower: Nasturtium

Animal: Ram

Gem: Ruby

Fabric: Wool

January

The arrival of the New Year sees you in a dynamic frame of mind, more determined than ever to achieve your goals and make your mark on the world. Mars, your fiery ruler, rides high in your solar chart and you'll be inclined to be decidedly proactive rather than reactive. As you'll be aware, the key to your character and destiny is initiative and an instinctive need to push forward and take the lead. Put simply, you are a pioneer and are happiest at the heart of the action. From the very start of the year it looks as if you're going to be in the driving seat and therefore in your natural element. Seize the initiative and start 2009 ready to succeed in all your put your mind to.

LOVE

There's absolutely no need to feel rejected, neglected or dejected if not much appears to be happening in January.

Prevailing cosmic trends suggest that it's what's going on in the background that ultimately puts the love light back in your eye. However, throughout January this is where your natural desire for instant gratification may prove frustrating.

Time is of the essence and this calls for patience. You need to allow things to happen. The Fates are moving in mysterious ways, so you won't be doing yourself any favours by interfering or attempting to impose your preconceived ideas on what you want.

If you have an established relationship it's unlikely there will be any cause for complaint. Both from an emotional and a material point of view, everything points to a steady enrichment and a feeling of increasing contentment throughout 2009.

MONEY

There's a decidedly friendly feel surrounding a journey early in the month, and though business is likely to be the keynote it looks as if there'll be a pleasant spin-off in terms of new friendships and an extra dimension to your social life. The lines of communication are buzzing and the people you are in contact with will have a inspiring influence on your mind.

However, do try to be more organised in planning any business trips in the second half of the month rather than leaving anything to chance.

Have your plan B worked out in readiness otherwise you risk being left in the lurch.

Use your initiative and make the situation work for you

presents itself in the early weeks of the year. Career and finance are under a progressive trend, and the ball is in your court if you wish to raise your game and improve your status. The only proviso is to watch out that you don't take on more responsibilities than you can comfortably handle, especially after the 21st when any minor mistakes could develop into major problems.

Towards the end of the month you should be prepared to re-think aspects of your objectives. In particular, any corporate endeavours may need examining, updating and re-structuring.Use your initiative and make the situation work for you.

TRAVEL

In your dynamic frame of mind it's unlikely you'll be wasting much time if an opportunity

Lucky dates
6th, 14th, 16th, 24th

February

A decision that's been hanging in the balance since early January falls into clearer focus this month, and at last you'll begin to feel a forward momentum in your current aims and objectives. Two pivotal dates are the 5th and 9th, when you're likely to experience a change of pace at a very practical level. You need not fear as this will not create a major crisis. However, you may feel strongly pulled between the security of your familiar routines and the potential for striking out in a brand new direction. If in doubt, it's wise to stick with what you know best. On the whole, however, February's happenings will live up to your hopes and expectations.

MONEY

If you're beginning to feel that there's a growing gap between effort and reward, now is the time to do some serious thinking. You might not meet with any major financial hassles, but it would do no harm to take careful stock of your work situation and look into the possibilities of change.

You have it in your power to win friends and influence people at this point, so don't be afraid to get out there and make the right noises, especially if you want to improve your earning power and put your career on a more lucrative course.

LOVE

If your love life has recently been a tale of woe, the presence of Venus in your sign from the 3rd onwards throws a happier light on the situation.

It could be that a romantic attachment you had almost given up on takes a turn for the better. The background to this scenario is likely to be rather complex, but now that the situation is becoming clear the original source of misunderstanding will fade into the background. Taking a longer view, it seems that events taking shape in the first half of the month will have satisfying reverberations well into the future. The potential for meeting someone very special, perhaps a future marriage partner, is greatly enhanced at this time. With Venus set to spend an unusually lengthy sojourn in your sign, 2009 promises to be a year when your cherished hopes and wishes are realised.

HEALTH

A rather tense combination of Saturn and Uranus warns you to ease the pace and cultivate a more laid back approach in your lifestyle.

Work pressures are liable to build and before you know it you're lumbered with more responsibility that you can comfortably deal with.

Remember there are only 24 hours in a day, and you owe it to yourself to take some time out if it's getting to be a case of all work and no play.

Be warned – if you attempt any heroics when you are feeling slightly off colour, you'll only have yourself to blame if you end up a nervous wreck!

Lucky dates
8th, 12th, 17th, 27th

March

Although you are the kind of person who likes to cut your own path and are not inclined to take too kindly to those who see things differently or wish to take a slower pace, you must realise that this is something that could work against you in March. Throughout the month you'll make your best progress by co-operating with others and working as a team. This doesn't mean that you need to take a back seat, but you will need to watch out that you don't tread on other people's toes or make out that only you know best. You have a chance to build valuable friendships at this time, so don't blow it by being too pushy. Take it easy and let others recognise your strengths.

LOVE

Venus continues to grace your own sign throughout the month, throwing a pleasant light on romantic affairs and ensuring that existing ties of love remain sweet.

This planet inclines you to focus on the enhancement of your personal image and to cultivate a wider circle of social contacts, but even without any conscious effort, your personal magnetism is increased and you'll find yourself in greater demand socially. The upshot of all this is that you not only find yourself attracting new friends into your orbit but, more significantly, an attachment of a more intimate nature. What takes place around the New Moon later in the month is sure to put the love on the agenda.

However, as Venus is moving through a retrograde cycle, this isn't the time to force issues or to expect instant bliss. Don't be anxious, time is on your side.

> *March is a good month to sign up for a new class or club*

HEALTH

Provided you heed Saturn's warning to slow the pace and not treat your physical body like a perpetual motion machine, then there's no real threat to your general well being. In the latter half of March you may feel that your energy levels have dropped into a lower gear, which could be a warning signal if you have been driving yourself a little bit too hard recently. With this in mind it's an excellent month for focusing more attention on health, seeking out appropriate therapies and maybe even re-organising your diet if you are beginning to feel a bit out of shape.

Your best policy is to cultivate a relaxed attitude to life and there's no doubt that you'll reap the rewards.

TRAVEL

Take advantage of the energising trends early in the month if you are aiming to drum up support for a campaign or wish to organise a special social event.

It might mean putting in a lot of mileage but the extra effort should bring satisfying results. It promises to be a socially interesting month ahead, and at times you're likely to be whizzing about all over the place in an attempt to keep in close touch with what's going on.

If you're interested in local politics and wider social issues, a meeting along these lines is where you are likely to meet up with people who are on the same spiritual wavelength as you. This could be a good time to join a club or sign up for that adult education class you fancy.

Lucky dates
4th, 13th, 17th, 26th

April

Until Mars pushes into your own sign on the 22nd it would be unwise to take any fresh initiatives without first having prepared the ground carefully. Mistakes can easily be made by attempting to carry on regardless of consequences and in the hope that things will all turn out right in the end. The fact is, they probably won't, and in the process you stand to upset certain people who are otherwise favourably disposed towards you. So, make sure you know all the pros and cons before moving into action. By late April situations that may have been vague will become clarified and any awkward obstacles will fade into insignificance leaving you ready to forge ahead.

MONEY

Lively trends coming into force from the second week onwards throw a helpful light on all business and commercial activities. Not only will transactions run on oiled wheels, but you'll be in a position to put new ideas into action and streamline existing projects.

For those intent on starting up a new business, the omens are favourable, so waste no time in gathering relevant info and making useful contacts. If a lack of funds has been a stumbling block in the past, what takes place later in the month puts you firmly in the driving seat and gives you the necessary confidence to move forward.

LOVE

You may be under the impression that everything is hunky-dory as far as current romantic attachments are concerned, but don't take too much for granted. With Venus backtracking into a rather secretive area of your solar chart feelings change and wishful thinking is revealed for what it is. The more rational you can be, the less likely feelings will be hurt. The trouble is that rationality is usually a scarce resource when romantic emotions are stirred. Look at the situation a little more objectively rather than letting negative emotions drive you around in ever-decreasing circles. The good news is that Venus re-enters your sign late month, signalling a fairly swift change from negative to positive. An old affair may be in for a re-run and there is much to suggest that it will be happier and longer lasting the second time around.

HEALTH

The Aries temperament is rooted in the need for action and the urge to move forward. While this does give you an edge, it can backfire on you. This is something you need to be aware of in April.

With your ruling planet (Mars) at odds with Saturn on the 6th, and with Uranus on the 15th, impatience and haste could lead to mishaps and accidents. Be particularly careful at work, especially if you handle machinery. Above all, don't do anything too strenuous on these dates. If you're into sports, don't say you haven't been warned!

Lucky dates
2nd, 9th, 22nd, 28th

May

It's likely that your experiences in the first four months of the year have taught you some valuable lessons in the art of waiting for the right moment. At times you probably felt trapped in a repeating cycle of negative events, and the more you tried to get it right the more everything seemed to go pear-shaped. At last this negative pattern changes and from this month onwards you'll start to get the feeling that you have found the right groove. The presence of both Mars and Venus in your sign gives you the power to draw into your orbit what you most desire. It's a month when the right moment presents itself as if by magic so reach for the stars!

LOVE

In view of what's just been said it almost goes without saying that your amorous desires will find plenty of scope for expression during these weeks. New romance is likely to crash into your life, take you by surprise, and open your eyes to just how powerful the force of attraction can be.

If you're sceptical about the possibilities of love at first sight, perhaps you should suspend your disbelief until later in the month. What happens on the 1st, 10th and 21st is almost certain to change the picture. This is, admittedly, the best-case scenario, but one thing is for sure – it's unlikely there'll be any dull moments as far as amorous encounters are concerned. The only proviso where such powerful energies are in force is that it could all turn out to be one of those mad infatuations that doesn't last. On balance, though, the portents are looking good.

> A new romance is likely to crash unexpectedly into your life

TRAVEL

Just when you were beginning to feel that everything is on track, a minor glitch on or soon after the 7th could throw a spanner in the works. This applies especially if you have arranged an important journey, meeting or interview. Be prepared for last-minute changes and adopt a flexible policy when making any further plans for later in the month. It seems that there'll be some catching up to do in regard to business affairs. Maybe you find that certain details have been overlooked and you are obliged to cover the same ground again. It's a case of double-checking and not leaving anything to chance. Taking the time to correct things now will save you valuable time in the future.

MONEY

With Mercury sidling back into the money area of your solar chart mid month you are advised against taking risks or putting your faith in verbal promises and agreements you've been given.

Careful attention is needed in dealing with anything of a legal or official nature. If you have any doubts, get a second opinion and don't allow yourself to be too easily persuaded by slick-talking dealers. You can make the best of this trend for sorting out essentials from inessentials and apply it to overhauling your budget.

Much to your delight, you may discover several ways in which savings can be made. Take the opportunity to examine your outgoings and see where you can cut back, leaving cash for new projects.

Lucky dates
1st, 12th, 21st, 27th

June

The month divides fairly neatly down the middle, on either side of which your approach to life will take a different slant. At the beginning of June it looks like matters of a very practical nature are your main centre of gravity. Unfinished business needs to be dealt with, and this is where your energy and initiative will get speedy results. If you're in process of re-aligning the infrastructure of your personal economy, you're guaranteed to have good progress. From the middle of the month onwards you'll experience a welcome variation in your daily routines and find greater scope for diversifying your activities and discovering new opportunities.

MONEY

As already hinted matters of practical significance take precedence in your current scheme of things during these weeks. Although cash flow is liable to heat up, it seems that you have a firm handle on the situation and may even be able to turn a potentially difficult situation to good account. If your expenses seem heavy, don't be alarmed, because it looks as if the demands on your resources will be quickly restored.

Towards the end of the month an added bonus is promised, giving you the green light for splashing out on treats that will make your life more pleasant and stylish.

LOVE

Established ties of love and friendship come under favourable trends, bringing a feeling of increased contentment as well as confidence to those who plan to take the plunge into marriage.

Helpful developments at a practical level play an important part in your destiny at this time, and you will no longer feel that you're running faster just to stay in the same place. At last there will emerge a feeling that you are getting to where you want to be. Meanwhile, if you're single but hoping to find love, the prospects are getting brighter all the time. What takes place around the 21st could make all the difference in the world to hopeful Ariens

who have been languishing in limbo since the start of the year.

A more meaningful and lasting relationship is likely to develop from what seems like a very insignificant beginning so don't rule anyone out!

TRAVEL

As the pace of your life is set to increase in the second half of June, you'll need to be more adaptable to make the best possible use of your time and energy. People you meet, either by chance or prior arrangement, will have a stimulating influence on your mind, and it will be in your interest to take notice of ideas offered later in the month.

If you're into education and self-development, put these interests on a more serious level. Duty should come before pleasure if someone needs your help later in the month.

Lucky dates
7th, 9th, 19th, 28th

July

The rapidly changing cosmic picture makes this a potentially breathtaking month, a time when you will find it hard to keep pace with everything that's going on. However, there's no need to panic. Everything seems geared to carrying forward your main aims and objectives. Even your spare time interests and hobbies are likely to gather a more lively and productive momentum this month, making you realise that perhaps you are not making the most of your special abilities. This is not a time to hide your light under a load of misplaced modesty. If you feel you have something special you can contribute, get out there and make sure you get yourself noticed!

LOVE

There is more than just a hint that a journey provides the key to your heart's desires in the coming month. This doesn't necessarily mean that you have to travel far, and it may be that a short trip arranged at a moment's notice throws you together with someone you find immediately attractive. This feeling is most likely to be mutual and above all instantaneous. The odd thing is that it is just when romance is furthest from your mind that it enters your orbit in a surprising and delightful way.

From a different angle, you need not be so surprised if a relative or close friend announces a wedding before July is out. Also expect to receive good news and an invitation towards the end of the month.

Meanwhile, established couples should have more leeway for creating more quality time together. If you're planning on taking a holiday, so much the better!

HOME

The swift dash of Mercury through the lower sector of your solar chart signals a lively state of affairs on the domestic scene. Between the 3rd and 17th there may be times when you find it hard to prevent the situation falling into chaos. A whole spate of visitors is forecast, so make sure you are well prepared. It's likely that children and youngsters will be very much in evidence, and maybe you'll be obliged to mind other people's children for a day or two around the middle of the month. Generally speaking, you'll find the whole thing delightful, but watch out for trouble spots around the 6th and 7th.

> Expect to receive good news and an invitation at the end of July

It might suit you to already have made plans these days!

MONEY

Until the middle of July it is essential that you keep close tabs on your finances. In one way or another money is liable to slip through your fingers and believe it or not you'll hardly be aware of it.

Everything depends on keeping a firm hold on the situation and avoiding extravagance in any form. At best the trend is highly progressive, but it won't be until the third week of the month that you'll finally be able to gage how the tide of your fortunes is flowing.

You'll find the going much easier from the 22nd onwards, especially in areas that have to do with loans, mortgages and longer-term investments. Take time to examine these closely.

Lucky dates
2nd, 16th, 19th, 28th

August

There's a kaleidoscopic quality to your experience during the coming month, with a fairly equal balance between practical and leisurely activities. Other people may find you hard to pin down, so maybe it would be a good policy to set out a fairly organised agenda for yourself as early as possible. A strange kind of push-pull combination of Mars, Saturn and Jupiter during the second week of August suggests there's a need for you to go backwards in order to move forwards. You're in an enterprising mood and impatient to push ahead with change, but remember it's essential to keep your plans structured rather than to simply go plunging ahead.

HOME

Although this is a traditional holiday month, it seems that matters closer to home will be an important focus of your attention. Venus, the planet of beauty and harmony, sheds a pleasant light on family and filial ties, ensuring easy relations between Aries parents and offspring (and vice versa). Existing emotional tensions and differences of opinion are unlikely to persist and you'll find it easy to establish a better understanding within the family circle. At a practical level, this is an excellent month to focus on the enhancement of your living space. A change of décor will be excellent therapy.

LOVE

Until later in the month single Ariens may feel that romance is a receding dream and that your cherished wishes are showing no signs of fulfilment. However there can be little doubt that existing ties of love and friendship benefit greatly under the gentle influence of Venus.

For those married or living in partnership, home and family affairs are a source of increasing happiness and good feeling. Psychologically it is as if you are putting down deeper roots and feeling increasingly secure, both within yourself and in your surroundings. This is bound to reflect favourably in the quality of your intimate life.

Getting back to the possibilities of new romance, it's not an entirely hopeless case, because once Venus changes signs later in the month the situation begins to offer something more promising. A happy ending could be in sight, so don't despair.

TRAVEL

If a vacation is planned you can be sure that everything meets your expectations. Avoid starting a journey on the 11th, when there's a greater potential for delay. Apart from this small warning, this is a good month for travel. In the first couple of weeks you'll make friends in unfamiliar territories, and in the second half of August you can pull out all the stops and be self-indulgent. If travel has to do with business, contacts you make will prove productive.

Lucky dates
6th, 13th, 20th, 27th

September

You may have to accept the fact that there's going to be a disjunction between what you hope to achieve and what circumstances actually dictate during September. A feeling that certain important objectives have come to a standstill may cause you impatience or even a sense of injustice. However, it would be unwise to throw everything overboard just yet or let yourself be panicked into abandoning a course of action. Unless you can see a productive alternative, hang on in there, because it looks as if the whole situation begins to turn around once Jupiter turns direct in about six weeks time. In the meantime, sit back and take a breather.

LOVE

For those who have felt out in the cold recently or suffered disappointment in love, there is more than just a hint that this is soon to become a thing of the past. In view of the changing cosmic pattern, the chances of meeting a genuine soul mate are greatly enhanced as Venus traverses a heart-warming sphere of your solar horoscope. It could be something promised earlier in the year finally gets off the ground and a time of doubt and uncertainty gives way to something a little more flourishing.

An added bonus with Venus smiling on your personal affairs comes in the shape of increased social life and greater ease in establishing new friendships at all levels. In fact it's a time when anything that somehow expresses and enhances your joie de vivre

finds greater scope and brings a feeling that you're a riding the crest of a wave.

TRAVEL

From a practical point of view you need to take note of Mercury's retrograde shift from the 7th onwards. Between this date and the 18th be sure you double-check any special arrangements, whether this has to do with travel, appointments, meetings or anything that depends on a well timed schedule.

> The chances of meeting a genuine soulmate are greatly enhanced

Taking too much for granted will be sure to land you with a lot of unnecessary irritations, so don't allow your attention to slip and make sure other people mean what the say (and say what they mean).

Watch out for any ambiguous messages around the 11th. Appearances can be deceptive so make sure you keep your wits about you around this time.

HOME

After the relative peace and quiet of Venus, you now have something of a contrast as the fiery planet Mars transits the home area of your solar chart.

This is not to imply that disasters are imminent, but there may be times when you have to deal with minor emergencies – probably of a very mundane and practical nature. Tricky dates are the 13th and 27th, when you should definitely avoid tackling complicated DIY jobs around the house.

Attempts to mend faulty gadgets could cost your dear, so be prepared to call in the experts if essential household items go on the blink.

If you're house hunting or about to move, take extra care during this period and make sure you check out every detail, no matter how small.

Lucky dates
1st, 4th, 22nd, 29th

October

After several months of hanging in the balance it looks as though you are finally beginning to see your way ahead more clearly and will feel confident that your aims and objectives are definitely moving in the right direction. What you have achieved in the past will provide you with the right kind of platform to move forward, and from now onwards opportunities for expansion and enrichment are likely to come through your ability to co-operate closely with other people. If you've been campaigning for a special cause, but without much success so far, this is where it all begins to turn around. Your patience is about to be rewarded so hang in there!

LOVE

Lunar trends in your own sign early in October could mean that sensitivities are on a knife-edge. It's probably just a passing mood and maybe you're feeling a bit stressed due to work pressures. It could mean that an existing romantic attachment is put in jeopardy simply because your partner happens to be the nearest person to you. Something quite trivial could flare up into an epic row, with all the usual melodrama of stomping out and slamming doors. Forewarned is forearmed, so if you're feeling tetchy try not to automatically blame your lover or spouse. From the middle of the month onwards it's a complete contrast, as Venus throws an aura of harmony and understanding over all close ties of love and affection. This is especially good news, not only for established relationships, but particularly for those taking the plunge into marriage at this time.

TRAVEL

Unlike the previous weeks when trying to keep in touch with certain people was an uphill struggle, you can expect all communications to go like a dream in October. Business and commercial transactions present no problems and you'll find it easy to swing negotiations in your favour. You'll get the most positive and speedy response while Mercury activates your opposite sign from the 10th onwards. Other people will be more ready to listen to what you have to say and all your discussions, interviews and exchanges of ideas are guaranteed to come up with the goods.

MONEY

Of great significance is the departure of Saturn from the area of your chart focusing on employment and occupational goals. Over the past couple of years you've been content to plod along in a fairly routine way, while building up a store of valuable experience. From now on the horizons begin to widen and you'll not be quite so content to go round in the same old circle. What happens in the coming weeks is almost certain to change the parameters and open doors. Efforts to improve your work style and income will succeed.

Lucky dates
4th, 10th 17th, 20th

November

As Jupiter begins to pick up a more positive momentum in November, performance in the areas that are most important to you not only meets your expectations, but could also close the gap between your ideals and reality. You can expect your circle of friends to expand, and as your social life becomes more interesting you'll be drawn together with people on your own mental and spiritual wavelength. For those involved in wider social issues, political affairs and humanitarian schemes, the prevailing trend could not be more supportive. Now is your chance to make a real difference so take your skills and expertise and make it happen.

LOVE

Your emotional learning curve is likely to be pushed to a new level during these weeks, with the result that you gain greater insight into your own deeper desires and motivations.

If a romantic attachment is going through a tricky phase, maybe this is your cue to reflect on your own reactions and ask yourself what it is you are really seeking through intimate attachment to another person. Remember that if we don't learn from past mistakes and negative experiences we are condemned to repeat the same old pattern over and over again. Psychologically you are going through a phase of transformation and inner growth, and it is how you experience love in both its positive and negative phases that finally takes you to a more mature level. What you'll realise more than ever is that what you receive depends upon what you give.

TRAVEL

There seems to be a lot of intense dialogue going on in the early part of the month. If you're interested in the deeper realms of the mind, occultism, spirituality and psychology, contact with like minded individuals is sure to bring you a great deal of fresh insight at this time. The first half of November is excellent for all kinds of detective work and research. What this means is that new light is shed on something that has puzzled you and important information you receive will prove invaluable.

Later in the month a message from afar calls for a change of plan and a lengthy journey. Grasp this and embrace the opportunities such travel awards you.

> The greatest rewards often come from taking the highest risks

MONEY

Now that you have a firmer handle on your finances and can see your way further ahead, you'll be feeling more confident about taking fresh initiatives geared towards improving your fortunes and your worldly status.

It is as if you are now tapping into a fresh source of creative energy and are able to generate your own opportunities. For those interested in the creative arts, entertainment or sports, this is a month when things could really begin to take off.

Prevailing trends favour those who are not afraid to strike out in a more independent direction and perhaps take a few risks. The greatest rewards often come from the highest risks so take these challenges and you could bask in the results.

Lucky dates
5th, 9th, 19th, 26th

December

The recent highly significant move of Saturn into your opposite sign signals important changes in your attitude to work. But more importantly, it means that partnerships of one sort or another will become a major centre of gravity in your life during the next couple of years. Traditionally, Saturn is associated with Fate, or with the kind of events and encounters that open a new window on the world. Although you might not notice much at all just yet, the fact is that certain people you meet in the near future could have a profound and far-reaching influence on your destiny. Be open to new contacts and friendships and you will thrive.

LOVE

Saturn does of course have a rather gloomy reputation according to the old astrologers, but this is only because there are times when we have to get real, rather than being driven by wishful thinking and immature emotions. It doesn't mean that amorous experience is about to become heavy-weather, but it does mean that if you wish to realise genuine happiness through intimate association with a partner, a shallow and frivolous attitude is not going to get you anywhere. To put it simply, if you want love to be interesting you must first make yourself an interesting person.

People who flit from one affair to another are simply expressing deep insecurity and are in fact coming from a level that can be described as the spoilt brat syndrome. You'll need to take all this to heart now that Saturn presides over your House of Partners.

TRAVEL

As the season of festivities approaches, a wider horizon beckons and far-flung excursions suddenly take on a higher profile in your world. Maybe you'll be planning to get away from familiar surroundings towards the end of the month or will receive an invite from a friend overseas. This is indeed a great idea, because there's a close link between travel and pleasure during these weeks.

Alternatively, it could be that one or two people you've not seen for years will be paying you a visit, all of which adds up to something truly delightful later in the month.

MONEY

The urge to broaden your range of influence now that certain restrictions have eased is sure to have a favourable impact on your personal economy, both now and in the coming year. However, rather than forge ahead with any new projects, this is a good month for careful reflection on what is and what is not realistically possible.

Your ruling planet Mars switches to retrograde mode on the 20th, warning you to slow down the pace, take your time, and consider your actions carefully if you are intent on taking a more creative direction in the coming months.

Lucky dates
8th, 11th, 16th, 26th

For your fantastic
weekly & monthly
cash, career and
romance and forecasts
Call 0905 515 0038
Starlines are updated every Tuesday.
BT calls cost 60p per minute and last about
5 minutes. Cost from other networks may be
higher. SP: Eckoh Herts HP3 9HN

Taurus

april 21 to may 20

Zodiac fact file

Planetary Ruler: Venus

Quality & Element: Fixed Earth

Colours: Green, cream

Metal: Copper

Wood: Cherry

Flower: Carnation

Animal: Bull

Gem: Jade

Fabric: Satin

January

The New Year arrives on a lively and optimistic note as Jupiter moves into the topmost sector of your solar chart. This expansive planet provides the key for developments in your life in the coming months and signals a phase of increasing opportunity and success. Events taking shape as early as the second week of January will give you a clue to future developments so be sure to take notice of any new contacts or offers. Chances are that a new door will open and you'll receive an offer that is hard to refuse. Quite simply, all efforts to improve your status and enrich your life are under a lucky trend, and if you're feeling ambitious the sky is the limit!

LOVE

Venus draws you into congenial social circles from early January onwards, promising new friendships and the realisation of romantic hopes and wishes. In fact, there is an element of serendipity connected with a friend, who may quite unwittingly play the role of matchmaker in the development of a new amorous attachment.

Watch out for special effects around the 9th and especially the 23rd, when something quite unexpected puts the love light in your eye. Even if there's no sign of any wild passions developing, there is certainly tremendous scope for weaving sympathetic links and finding a truly kindred spirit. From a different angle, it could be that a friend needs some emotional support due to a romantic affair that's threatening to turn into a soap opera – or a farce.

TRAVEL

Prevailing trends suggest that a great deal of your energy is being directed towards broadening your range of experience, socially, mentally and through travel. You're likely to be feeling adventurous and out-going throughout January, perhaps focusing your mind on important journeys and places you wish to visit in the months ahead. Indeed this is an excellent time to organise a far-flung excursion or vacation, and this is where friends are likely to give you much encouragement and inspiration.

In the meantime, long distance contacts and communications keep you at the cutting edge.

MONEY

Although 2009 contains exciting prospects, there are times when decisions need to be faced to make the best of a potentially very expansive trend. If you are free of ties and not afraid to move around, there's no problem. Be prepared for some tactful negotiations with loved ones if a job offer entails changes in your circumstances.

The Solar eclipse in late January marks a difficult transition, but with Jupiter riding high, determination and luck will pull you through.

Lucky dates
7th, 9th, 19th, 30th

February

A message arriving early in the month clarifies an ambiguous situation and gives you the green light for pushing ahead with a current project. After several minor but irritating delays and setbacks, the way ahead becomes clear and you can focus on the things that really matter to you. There's a continuing and increasing accent on worldly aims and ambitions in February. This means it's unlikely you'll be wasting any time if an opportunity to advance your interests presents itself, which is, in fact, highly likely. It's your own initiative that has the right impact and gets you where you want to be, so don't underestimate

MONEY

A powerful accent on matters of a very practical nature makes this a month when you'll be very much in your natural element.

It's a continuing story of success for ambitious Taureans. Not only are you in a position of increasing strength, but you can be sure that persons of power and influence are well disposed towards you. Don't be afraid to stick your neck out if you can pull a few strings.

Even if the competition is heavy, your willpower and determination (with a bit of stubbornness thrown in for good measure) enables you to raise your game and improve your fortunes.

LOVE

Events taking shape in the background are likely to be weaving the right kind of magic for the romantically inclined. Something you hear through the grapevine around the 8th or towards the end of the month makes you realise

that you are not being left completely out in the cold. Someone you chanced to meet, maybe only briefly, a few weeks back has perhaps been hovering around in your thoughts and reflections. Anyway, the upshot of this is that a spark was lit at the time, and before long it's likely to grow into a steady flame. There's no need to force any issues or get anxious that not much appears to be happening. Towards the end of February all will be revealed, and what you had almost given up as a wistful dream begins to materialise in a most delightful way. Love grows in its own time, so let it be.

HOME

As the pattern of events is likely to be pulling you away from home at present, this could contain potential for a build up of tensions either with

your spouse or with other members of your household.

Career interests and other outside commitments might be at a crucial stage and may be demanding a large slice of your time and attention. However, don't let this cause you to lose sight of matters closer to home. Above all, be careful that you are not taking other people too much for granted. Don't treat them as if they are there simply for your own convenience. This is the time to do something to show those close to you that you really do care. Think about organising a special event or maybe a trip away. Your success in other areas this month may depend on it.

Now is the time to show those close to you that you do care

Lucky dates
3rd, 8th, 17th, 27th

March

A key to what you experience in March focuses on the retrograde movement of your ruling planet, Venus. This highlights matters of a rather private or secretive nature, and it could mean that what you need is a phase of relative peace and quiet. This is an excellent trend for pursuing interests such as meditation and anything that you feel is good for your soul. Psychologically, this important trend suggests a period of inner growth and a need to reflect more carefully on what you really and truly value in your life. A short retreat or escape from usual routines may be needed now. Take time out to order your mind.

LOVE

Of course Venus is the planet of love, and it is especially in this area that an element of secrecy is indicated. As Venus is on the whole well placed, it is unlikely that such secrecy will contain anything of a negative nature – for instance, the temptation to get involved in something potentially scandalous or deceitful.

At best, Venus enhances your sensitivities and enables you to cultivate deeper empathy with your nearest and dearest. It is as if there's a deep exchange of energies going on between lovers, giving rise to a closer rapport and greater intimacy. If you're able to spend some time away from usual routines and the demands of work, this would certainly be the best kind of mutual soul therapy.

For singles, a secret admirer is indicated, though it would be unwise to jump to conclusions. You'll know when the right moment arrives.

TRAVEL

Be prepared to act quickly if a problem crops up early in the month. You may find that a misunderstanding between friends or colleagues can be headed off by taking diplomatic action. If you are taking part in high profile discussion and negotiations, the going could get tough. You will only make matters worse if you stubbornly cling to views that are obviously in need of some re-alignment. Things get easier from the second week of March onwards, when a more friendly and co-operative trend prevails. You can then count on others to pull their weight and give you the support you need.

MONEY

A casual conversation with a friend around mid March gives you a new slant on finance and motivates you to overhaul your existing portfolio. You may find a profitable sideline could be developed by joining forces with another person or with a small group of like-minded individuals. The co-operative atmosphere makes this a good month for support if you are raising funds for charitable projects. Career interests continue under an expansive trend, and luck attends your efforts if you're after promotion.

Lucky dates
4th, 8th, 17th, 26th

April

Aims and objectives that are central to your world are likely to run into difficulties around the 6th or 15th. The fiery planet Mars is at odds with unsympathetic planets, warning you not to push your luck or throw your weight around if you're to avoid antagonising loyal friends or colleagues. A situation will probably put your patience to the test, but problems won't be sorted any quicker by losing your cool. Basically, it's a time when you are obliged to take a more critical view of what you're aiming for and perhaps face the fact that some re-structuring may be necessary. By looking at a situation critically you will emerge stronger and more likely to succeed.

TRAVEL

Make the most of Mercury's enlivening energy in your own sign from the 9th onwards, especially if you need to arrange a meeting, attend an interview or embark on an important journey. It's a prime time for cultivating a wider circle of contacts and developing a creative dialogue with others if you need to clarify or pull your ideas into better shape.

Your increased clarity of mind helps you to come up with the right answers if any problems arise, and you'll have an uncanny knack of finding the right words if you're called upon to give an opinion or make an important on-the-spot decision.

LOVE

Venus continues retrograde until the third week, and maybe you need to accept the fact that what seemed like a promising start to a romance is simply going nowhere. A change of feelings is indicated, and maybe you are only now beginning to realise that your deeper emotional needs have changed and matured in recent months. Whatever happens, a certain element of bridge-burning may be needed if you are to make the best of future potentials. Trying to cling to an attachment that is obviously passed its sell-by date is only going to generate a whole load of negative emotions. This is the kind of thing by which you could easily sabotage your own happiness. It certainly looks good up ahead, so if things are currently at a low ebb don't despair. The Fates are moving in mysterious ways and time is of the essence. You just need to believe in yourself, that's all!

Increased clarity of mind will help you find the right answers

MONEY

If possible, aim to get any loose ends tied up and outstanding debts out of the way before the middle of the month. Something marked private and confidential needs careful and detailed attention in the first week of April.

If this worries you, don't hesitate to get the appropriate advice, especially if complicated forms need to be completed. From the 9th onwards a lively trend guarantees a productive phase of activity for the commercially minded, and if you have any new ideas about making the most of your skills or experience, earning more money and boosting your resources don't be afraid to translate theory into practice at this time. A touch of lateral thinking now might pay dividends down the line.

Lucky dates
4th, 12th, 17th, 22nd

May

There are two pivotal dates during this month, namely the 17th and 27th, when you can expect a fruition of efforts and a chance to widen your range of influence. The key to success at this time hinges on your ability to combine a highly structured approach with your broad imagination, especially in those areas that focus on long-range objectives. Perhaps one of your spare time interests or hobbies will begin to take up more of your time and attention, and maybe you'll be getting more serious about perfecting your creative abilities. All in all, this promises to be a month of far-reaching developments so seize the opportunities as soon as they arise.

LOVE

Your love life is about to go through some intriguing transformations in the coming weeks, and what finally pans out will probably be a complete contrast to what you expected.

Events taking shape behind the scenes are brewing up the kind of chemical reaction that is sure to make you fizz, but you need to realise that things are perhaps not as straightforward as you think, and any attempt to play the innocent victim will definitely not do you any good. At worst, you'll end up feeling exploited, deceived and used.

The forces of attraction are powerful but are liable to lead you into temptation, so be careful that you are not being drawn into secretive or even dangerous territory.

At best, this is a time when amorous experience will show you what a vast difference there can be between genuine love and pure lust.

MONEY

If possible try not to procrastinate if there are any problems that need to be dealt with in the first week. After the 7th it would be unwise to take too much for granted, particularly in regard to commercial and business transactions. Also, any attempt to cut corners or do things on the cheap is simply not going to work. If a fund-raising scheme is obviously not delivering the goods, your best policy would be to put it on hold for a few weeks, get back to the drawing board, and give it another try later on. And finally, be wary of one-off business deals and be sceptical of those who promise to make you a quick buck.

TRAVEL

If your work involves long range travel and dealings with overseas concerns, you have a highly successful month ahead. Events taking shape towards the end of May open up an entirely new horizon, which could mean that in the near future you'll be winging your way around the world. Closer to home, be prepared for minor disruptions if you have arranged a short trip or a special meeting, especially in the third week. You may find that your thoughts are out of key with other people's ideas, so be prepared to consider wider options rather than getting too fixated in your own opinions.

Lucky dates
1st, 10th, 21st, 31st

June

After the rather ambiguous experiences of the previous month, you can expect something of a complete contrast in June. In fact this is very much your month, and with no less than three planets moving through your sign there's bound to be something that makes you feel really great. For a start there is Mars, giving you an energy boost and making you more determined than ever to make your mark on the world. Mercury ensures you have the clarity of mind and the ability to make the right connections, while Venus enables you to indulge your pleasure loving instincts. Grab these opportunities and make the most of them.

LOVE

It almost goes without saying that this is going to be a charismatic month as far as romantic encounters are concerned. Whenever Venus and Mars come together in your sign the portents are extremely auspicious, promising instant attractions and blissful encounters.

In other words, love making is likely to become very intense at this time, and if you do fall in love it's more likely to be something special than a passing encounter. If there is a downside to this euphoric trend it is simply that passions are inclined to get just a bit too intense. Nothing wrong in this of course, but where it turns negative is when an element of possessiveness enters the frame. Your tendency to go off into an epic sulk if the other person does not wish to play your game is

the main bugbear. Much will depend on your level of self-awareness and degree of emotional maturity.

MONEY

This is where you'll get a second chance if a financial or business project failed to meet its targets the first time around. If mistakes were made in the past, it's likely you learned a valuable lesson and will now be feeling confident that you are getting it right.

The second half of June sees commercial activities gaining a productive and profitable momentum, so make your best efforts if you're aiming to diversify your outlets and broaden your base of useful contacts. At a day-to-day level, you're now in the mood for a touch of retail therapy and should have plenty of spare cash to indulge your tastes.

If you fall in love it's more likely to be something special

HOME

A powerful Solar trend coming into force during the third week of June shows a fortunate link between the advancement of your career, your finances and your domestic affairs.

The message is one of expansion and enrichment, and indeed there is every indication that the upgrading of your material fortunes enables you to cultivate a lifestyle that's more in accord with your needs and wishes.

Luck is on your side where major changes are going forward, especially if you are planning a change of residence or are setting up home for the first time. This could be the month to take the plunge on a new property. Altogether June offers a bright prospect, giving you cause for much optimism.

Lucky dates
9th, 19th, 21st, 28th

July

As the sign of Taurus belongs to what's called the "Fixed" quality, you are the kind of person who holds onto thoughts, ideals and beliefs that make you feel secure within yourself and your world. Stability is what you aim for at all levels – material, mental, emotional and spiritual. This is why other people find you very dependable and reliable, because you are not inclined to change with every passing breeze. However, in July you may begin to feel that certain ideas and beliefs are cramping your style. A phase of inner growth is moving forward, so try to cultivate a greater openness to experience in order to widen your already strong skill set.

MONEY

Matters of a practical nature take centre stage in your world this month. This puts you firmly in your natural element and gives you a chance to focus on reorganising your material interests and putting things on a more productive and efficient basis. Cash flow is likely to gather momentum, and later in the month you might find it hard to keep your act together.

Provided you don't give way to impulse and impatience, your fortunes will go from strength to strength. Be prepared to consider alternatives if not entirely satisfied with current financial arrangements.

LOVE

If a recent romantic development contains a strong element of rose-tinted spectacles, what happens in the early days of July will open your eyes to reality. Everyone knows how blissful, euphoric and slightly crazy being in love can be, but generally there comes a point when the relationship is put to the test. If it's found wanting, then you might find it hard to make the right emotional adjustments. If it's real, then a slight dissolving of the rosy mists reveals something that is more than just a passing show. What it all boils down to is a case of getting things in clearer perspective, and this means being completely honest about your real feelings and making sure you respect that your lover is a real person and not just a hook for your amorous fantasies. If your relationship is already well founded, the feeling of true togetherness will be greatly enhanced.

TRAVEL

Mercury's swift trajectory between the 3rd and 17th introduces an element of diversity into everyday affairs. The pace of life gathers momentum and your mind will be working overtime.

You're certainly on the right wavelength if you're seeking vital information and wish to make contact with like-minded individuals. Your clarity of mind enables you to come up with the right answers and take decisive action where it's most needed.

You'll be on the move, probably not going far from home, but nevertheless clocking up high mileage. You'll certainly have no cause for feeling bored!

Lucky dates
8th, 19th, 25th, 26th

August

Although you may want to continue with the way things are in regard to your current aims and ambitions, it seems that something or someone is about to challenge you and make you see that a slight re-structuring could bring you a more lasting benefit. You may experience conflict between what the world at large wants and expects of you, and what you would really like to do at a more creative level. Be ready to make a firm decision during the second week of August if you do in fact find yourself at a crossroads. Psychologically it's now time to reflect on what you really want as opposed to what you have been made to feel you're supposed to want!

LOVE

For romantically inclined Taureans magic moments are linked with a journey, especially around the 8th, 17th and 27th. The proverbial 'holiday romance' is a strong possibility, but there is also much to suggest that this kind of attachment has something more enduring than the usual run of the mill affair.

Even if you're not planning any far-flung excursions, the chances of meeting your affinity are greatly increased on these dates, but here too it's likely to be directly or indirectly connected with a journey. Equally, it could be a message that provides the key to your heart's desires, and maybe someone you encounter through various Internet communications grabs your attention.

Incidentally, if you're the kind of person who isn't afraid to use dating agencies, this could turn out to be just the right channel for you in the weeks ahead. Join up and prepare to meet the person you've been looking for.

MONEY

You'll need to keep tabs of your spending in the month ahead, because money is liable to run through your fingers at an alarming rate. It's unlikely you'll be short of cash, but expenses and outgoings may be heavier than expected, probably due to the car or other machinery needing urgent repairs. Business and commercial activity will keep you on your toes and at times you'll feel like you're running just to stay put. However, play your cards right, stay cool, and you'll be pleasantly surprised at how much ground you can cover during these weeks. It may be hard, but try to make haste slowly.

HOME

Events taking place in the affairs of relatives call for pleasant outings and get-togethers in the second and third weeks of August. If someone has been away from home, chances are that a family reunion is due for celebrations later in the month. Meanwhile, Taurean parents can expect a lively atmosphere within the family circle and plenty of time to enjoy the fun. Younger Taureans may wish to be out and about, but don't be tempted to get selfish around the 18th if you wish to keep on good terms with your parents or other members of your household. Finally, an exuberant party atmosphere will prevail later in the month, so let your hair down and have a good old boogie!

> A party atmosphere will prevail later in the month for Taureans

Lucky dates
8th, 13th, 17th, 22nd

September

Bearing in mind that the pace of life is about to increase for you, it would be in your best interests to have a well-organised schedule in September rather than leaving too much to chance. It's going to be a case of getting your priorities sorted out and making sure that you're not pulled off course by any trivial distractions or the unreasonable demands of other people. By taking a fairly firm line of approach and sticking to it you can expect to cover a lot of ground. The hectic pace is not likely to faze you either. On the contrary, you'll be at your best when there's a sense of challenge and a feeling that you are making a real impact on the world around you.

LOVE

Established couples rather than singles are more likely to feel the benefits of prevailing trends, though this is not to imply that new romance is totally off the agenda. Psychologically and emotionally you are feeling more relaxed within yourself and with your partner, which makes this a time when a deeper and more vital rapport can be established between you. It's an excellent month for making up for lost time if the events of life have had the effect of driving a wedge between the two of you recently.

Symbolically speaking, there are indications of a new chapter in your life, and this is good news for newly weds and those hoping to marry in the not too distant future. The prospect of setting up home is likely to appear less formidable and you'll feel that everything is moving in the right direction.

MONEY

The pressure is off and you can expect recent financial turmoil to settle into something more manageable. There's no need to get anxious if changes are impending at work or a major career decision is looming on the horizon. It's best to go with the flow during September rather than force issues, especially if this is likely to have an impact on your financial prospects. At the very end of the month information you receive clarifies issues and restores your confidence. After a rather wobbly phase, you'll quickly get a much firmer hold on your finances and be able more confidently to explore wider options.

HOME

The emotional climate within the family circle settles into a condition of fair weather throughout the coming month. Existing tensions fade into the background and a co-operative state of affairs prevails between Taurean parents and their offspring. From a practical point of view, the helpful influence of Venus (your ruling planet) motivates you to improve your living space and create a more congenial atmosphere.

The sooner you go ahead with this the better, because it looks like you'll be entertaining more visitors than usual or throwing a special party later in the month.

Lucky dates
7th, 9th, 16th, 26th

October

As Jupiter starts to pick up a more positive momentum from mid October onwards you can expect a more optimistic and expansive feel in regard to your main aims and ambitions. Events taking shape during the second week of the month could prove decisive and highly welcome if there's been a question mark over your status in recent month. The bottom line is that after a phase when the situation seemed to be in hanging in limbo, things begin to move forward for you. Before the end of the month you will begin to feel that a more successful path is opening and you are at last gaining recognition for your efforts and abilities – about time too!

LOVE

What was only a hint of a promise in the previous month is destined to blossom into something truly blissful in October. What takes shape in the first two weeks could make all the difference to those who have been feeling a bit neglected or rejected lately. A key date is the 7th, when there's an intimate link between love, luck and social life. Indeed, you're likely to be in popular demand as well as feeling more gregarious and fun loving than usual. However, it has to be said that prevailing trends are more favourable to single Taureans of more mature years; but if you do find yourself attracted to a person a bit older than yourself you can definitely take this as a good omen. Meanwhile, established relationships go from strength to strength, and towards the end of the month you may have cause for celebration over your partner's good fortune.

MONEY

This is one of the best months in 2009 for making efforts to improve your earning potential, either by seeking a better paid job or upgrading your skills. Whatever you are aiming to achieve, a more expansive prospect kicks in, and even without trying you're likely to find the right opportunities appear to land in your lap. Don't be afraid to stick your neck out if something interesting crops up around the middle of the month. You may be able to do a bit of strategic string-pulling and be in a position to call the shots. It's definitely not a time to underestimate your abilities or take a back seat. Take the bull by the horns and make things happen for you.

> **Make an effort to improve your earning potential**

HOME

The fiery planet Mars activates the home area of your solar chart from the middle of October onwards. Don't worry though, this is no cause for alarm, but you may find that visitors who arrive without invitation are inclined to test your patience – particularly on the 26th and 29th. Taking a more positive slant on this energising trend, you can expect to make great progress in everything to do with property transactions and home improvements.

The same applies if you're thinking of pulling up sticks and settling elsewhere. Take the initiative. The sooner you get the ball rolling the better, and if something interesting presents itself in the third week of the month, don't hang about. You may miss the chance of a lifetime!

Lucky dates
7th, 13th, 27th, 29th

November

Powerful Lunar influences coming through your own sign enhance your sensitivities and put you in a reflective frame of mind early in the month. As the outer planet Neptune is strongly activated, dreams and intuitions are likely to be highly significant and should definitely be taken seriously. If you're interested in mystical explorations, yoga and alternative therapies, important insights will be gained and your mental and spiritual horizons will be greatly enhanced during November. It will be a promising month for creative work and artistic endeavour and you'll find there's plenty of tasks about that will fire your imagination and widen your vision.

LOVE

Romance is likely to emerge in a highly glamorous guise in the coming weeks. In other words, you stand a good chance of meeting your dream lover, or at least someone who is destined to play a very special part in your life. The presence of Venus in your House of Partners intensifies the powers of attraction and makes you more than usually responsive to the prompting of Eros. Whatever happens, the events of November are almost certain to make a tremendous difference to your emotional equilibrium, and this will be a particularly welcome development if your love life has been disappointing in the past. It's certainly a highly auspicious month for Taureans who are taking the plunge into marriage or wish to put a relationship on a more secure basis. Altogether, it seems that intimate ties of affection are especially blessed at this time.

TRAVEL

Make the most of helpful trends in the first two weeks to carry through important negotiations, sign a contract or deal with matters of an official nature. Efforts to cultivate a wider circle of contacts prove inspiring and generates lively dialogue. If there's been a bone of contention between yourself and a colleague, now is your chance to lay your cards on the table. Swallow a bit of pride, and reach a more mature understanding. Finally, those engaged in educational pursuits or public relations will have reason to feel pleased before the month is over.

HOME

Mars continues to throw a sharper focus on domestic affairs and continues to do so into the coming year.

The winds of change are likely to be felt more strongly during this phase, and if an element of disruption does enter the frame you can be sure that this is all part of a beneficial transformation that's going forward from this month onwards. Indeed, this is an excellent time to take the initiative if you're hoping to find your ideal home in the year ahead. The changing pattern of events makes you more determined than ever to break free of restrictions and upgrade your lifestyle.

Lucky dates
2nd, 6th, 23rd, 26th

December

By now you're probably feeling slightly dazed at how swiftly this year has flown by. However, this is nothing to feel sad about. All it means is that you've packed an unusual amount of activity into the previous months and not had much time to sit back and think about what's going on. As the end of the year approaches you can expect the active and perhaps quite changeable pattern of experience to continue, but this is not something that is likely to worry you. Of great significance is an unexpected change of pace early in December that enables you to realise a cherished wish sooner than anticipated. Seize the opportunity and you'll benefit quicker than you thought.

LOVE

The forces of transformation are about to stir up intriguing developments in your love life this month. Single Taureans are likely to experience something that has a profound effect emotionally, the final result of which changes your attitude to love, making you more aware of your deeper needs and desires.

What seemed out of reach until fairly recently now moves into a closer orbit, and before you know it your cherished dreams are realised. This could in fact turn out to be a time when your emotional learning curve takes a sharp upswing. And the lesson will be that it's quality rather than quantity that counts.

If there is a problem, it will be of your own making. And what this means is that you have to be out with the old before the new can really begin to flourish. Coming down to earth, there's good news concerning the success of your partner later in the month so be sure to support them and prepare to celebrate.

MONEY

Both personal and joint financial interests take a smooth course as the festive season approaches. It's unlikely you'll be short of funds when it comes to splashing out on gifts and goodies. Indeed you are probably feeling easier about spending simply because your own and your partner's fortunes are going through a decidedly healthy phase. There's promise of better things to come in the weeks ahead. What puts you in an optimistic frame of mind is an added bonus or perhaps lucky windfall that arrives in the third week of December. Finally, you'll be amazed at the generosity of a friend later in the month.

Your fortune is going through a healthy phase this month

TRAVEL

There may be times when you're faced with a conflict of duties, so keep your travel and other arrangements as flexible as you possibly can. It's around the 25th that an element of confusion could enter the picture and what you had carefully planned could go pear-shaped. A likely scenario is that someone who promised to pay you a visit has to cancel at the last moment leaving you a little in the lurch. However, apart from an element of disruption it's unlikely to have any major impact on the seasonal merriment.

However, it might be an idea to keep things on quite a modest scale when it comes to the party spirit this month, otherwise you could risk the situation quickly descending into chaos!

Lucky dates
6th, 11th, 15th, 28th

For your fantastic weekly & monthly cash, career and romance and forecasts

Call 0905 515 003

Starlines are updated every Tuesday. BT calls cost 60p per minute and last abo 5 minutes. Cost from other networks may higher. SP: Eckoh Herts HP3 9HN

Gemini
may 21 to june 20

Zodiac fact file

Planetary Ruler: Mercury

Quality & Element: Mutable air

Colours: Yellow, black & white

Metal: Platinum, aluminium

Wood: Beech

Flower: Larkspur

Animal: Monkey

Gem: Tiger's eye

Fabric: Cotton

January

Taking a broad angle on the changing cosmic pattern for the year ahead for Geminis, there's much to suggest that an unusually fortunate trend in your affairs, and what takes shape during January will give you a hint of things to come. This optimistic picture is largely coloured by Jupiter throwing a powerful angle to your own sign, highlighting the urge to widen your horizons either through travel, educational activity or a spiritual quest. Whatever happens, you'll have reason to feel increasingly confident this month, as opportunities arise and you're inspired to enrich the quality of your life – you'll have a great start to 2009 if you take these chances.

TRAVEL

Bearing in mind what's just been said, this does not mean that you're about to be given any free tickets or that you can sit back on your laurels. The decisions facing you in this early part of the New Year call for a clear mind and a sense of realism. It's essential that you take a longer view, then you can be sure that the immediate results will take care of themselves. Don't take anything for granted after the 11th when your ruling planet Mercury shifts into reverse gear. Be prepared to ask awkward questions if you are unsure of the messages you're receiving from other people.

LOVE

Affairs of the heart are not exactly high profile in your scheme of things early in the year. This is unlikely to be causing you any angst, and in fact you are reluctant about intimate involvement at present. Perhaps your attitude to relationships is changing and past experience has taught you that love is not something that's suddenly going to come out of the blue and create instant happiness.

You're beginning to realise that the quality of your close personal attachments depends very much on the inner quality of your own personality.

In other words, you first need to develop the capacity to respond to love on a deeper level before you can expect to find something that truly answers to your heart's desires. However, it's a much simpler picture for those already married or in a relationship. What takes place at a practical level with your partner does much to generate a feel-good atmosphere between you.

Develop your capacity to respond to love this month

MONEY

Both personal and joint financial interests are under a progressive and forward-looking trend throughout this first month of 2009.

Although there may be a glitch somewhere around the 21st, this is unlikely to amount to a major setback. However, it's in your best interests to focus on soundly based and long term issues such as investments, insurance schemes and pensions.

Be prepared to cover the ground carefully and get a second opinion if you are considering any major financial commitments later in the month.

If in doubt, do some extra homework, get the facts straight, and don't hurry into making a rash decision that you might just regret down the line. Try to be cautious.

Lucky dates
5th, 7th, 16th, 24th

February

The month gets off to a positive start, and after a phase of indecision the pace quickens and the way ahead is made clear for you. Prevailing trends focus your mind very intensively on the need to make desirable changes and improve your credentials. Symbolically speaking, wider horizons beckon as much energy is being turned towards the quest for fresh experience and new territory to conquer. You'll find that whatever enables you to improve your mind and widen your range of significant contacts during February will bring you lasting benefits. If you wish to make life more interesting, now is your chance to make a real difference. Go for it!

LOVE

An unusual twist of events around the 6th may create disruption in a current romantic attachment, but strangely enough this is likely to be a blessing in disguise so don't jump to conclusions. Even if there's a complete parting of the ways, or a feeling that you're being 'dumped', this is no reason to think that it's the end of the world. The truth is that someone you've been on friendly terms with for several months moves into closer orbit and finally turns out to be a genuine soul mate. Whatever happens, don't despair if everything seems to go into meltdown early in the month.

The rescue remedy is already on its way to you and by the end of February your cherished hopes and wishes are transformed into reality. On the whole there seems to be a friendly aura around you at this time, so it's unlikely you'll be feeling left out in the cold.

TRAVEL

A tremendous accent on the travel area of your solar chart guarantees an exciting month and greater scope for varying your usual routines. Journeys are high profile on your agenda, and even if you have nothing planned for February it is likely that future trips are a central focus of your thoughts. It could mean that overseas contacts and communications play an important role. The pattern of events opens up marvellous scope for enriching your mind and realising all your dreams.

HOME

It's likely that you'll experience a shift in the pattern of domestic life while Saturn moves through the lower sector of your chart in 2009.

As this planet links with Uranus early in February you'll see more clearly the way in which the winds of change are blowing. Don't be alarmed. It looks as if you're making a conscious decision to alter your life at this level.

Family life over the past year motivates you to change your domestic situation. The outcome is sure to please, but there's no need to rush things.

Lucky dates
1st, 3rd, 12th, 24th

March

Recent events have made you realise that there's a whole new world out there to be explored, and that perhaps over the past few years your mind has become caught in a rather narrow circle of experience. If you've been feeling unaccountably restless lately it's because something deep within your soul is kicking and screaming to be let out. In view of the very positive astrological pattern gaining force since the start of the year, events taking shape should help to point you in the right direction and throw you a lifeline. There's no excuse, in other words, to complain that life has become dull! Excitement is there for the taking during March.

LOVE

There's an element of ambiguity in your love life during March. Something you believed would be instant bliss and the answer to your dreams may begin to lose some of its glamour in the cold light of day.

Psychologists often tell us that what we look for in a partner is what we actually lack in ourselves. The trouble is that this causes us to project all kinds of wishful fantasies onto a person we find highly attractive.

It's the old story of being in love with the idea of love and the tendency to over-idealise another person, which of course puts this other person in the impossible position of having to live up to our ideal. The final result is usually disillusion and, perhaps worst of all, you end up blaming the other person for betraying you.

This is a rough outline of the kind of script you're likely to be writing for yourself in the month ahead. So, try not to completely lose sight of the fact that it's a real person over there and not someone who's been sent to answer your ideals.

MONEY

Aim to tie up lose ends and deal with matters of an official and legal nature in the first half of the month. From the 15th a highly dynamic force kicks in and you're plunged into a phase of increased activity that's geared to improving your status and furthering your career.

Much depends on your own motivation and initiative if you wish to move forwards and get where you want to be. There'll be no lack of opportunity, especially for those aiming for promotion and a position of greater influence. It's a time of advancement and breakthrough, which thankfully is bound to impact favourably on your income.

Aim for a promotion or a position of greater responsibility

HOME

The atmosphere within the family circle becomes rather sensitive in the second week of March, so it's essential that you approach any problems with care and understanding.

Don't let work pressures or other demands cause you to get impatient if your partner or a younger member of the household needs some sympathy and support. Granted, this is going to be a busy month when you're likely to be absorbed in your work, but it would be unwise to lose a sense of balance and think that the world revolves only around you. If things are a bit sensitive at home it calls for an equally sensitive approach. It can be easy to lose sight of those things that are most important to us when we're busy.

Lucky dates
4th, 14th, 22nd, 25th

April

A progressive and fast-moving trend continues and it won't be until the final week of April that the pace finally begins to ease. In the meantime, however, you're very much in your element if it's your intention to further an ambition, raise your game and move into a position where you can call the shots. There are times when the competition could get rather tough, but this is unlikely to faze you. Indeed, whether it's your career, a campaign you wish to promote or a serious sporting interest or other hobby, the exhilarating sense of challenge is sure to bring out the best in you. Your motivation is high during April, so make sure you pull out all the stops and go for it!

LOVE

So far this year the path of true love has perhaps not been exactly smooth, and by now you're beginning to wonder if some cosmic joker is playing tricks with you. Don't despair, there's light at the end of this particular tunnel.

As Venus begins to pick up a more positive pace in the second half of April prospects brighten, and by the end of the month there's promise of something to warm your heart.

If past experience has made you a bit cautious about emotional commitments, events taking shape either now or in the very near future will do much to dispel your fears and renew your faith in the power of love. But give it time, there's no hurry. All you need to do is cultivate the gentle art of allowing things to emerge naturally, rather than trying to impose your own agenda.

HEALTH

As already suggested, it'll be a fairly high-octane month as far as your own expenditure of energy is concerned. Indeed, you do need to be on top form in order to make the best of the progressive trend, but this is no reason to lose sight of the fact that everything has a sane limit beyond which you're asking for trouble. Danger points occur on the 6th and 15th, when you're advised to ease the pace or take a break. Matters closer to home may need your attention at these times, so be prepared to make small sacrifices if someone needs your attention.

TRAVEL

Group activities, teamwork or a special club will give you the right platform on which to express your versatile mind and increase your popularity.

Your social life has a purposeful quality at this time and you're likely to gravitate into the company of people who are very much on your own mental wavelength. Travel continues to be a main theme, with highlights in the third week. Whether a journey is for business or fun (or a mixture of both), luck is in attendance.

Lucky dates
1st, 5th, 16th, 26th

May

Although you'll experience something of a slowdown during these weeks, this is nothing to get anxious about. It might not be so obvious immediately, but it seems that the pattern of events contrives to shift your destiny in a brand new direction. It's a time when past efforts will be brought to a focus and you feel much more secure within yourself. There are indications that a chapter in your life closes and a new door swings open. New objectives come into view and they will motivate you to diversify your experience and develop a wider field in which to express your real self. All in all, it's a month of many exciting possibilities despite its slower pace.

LOVE

Passions are liable to warm up considerably throughout the month, with dramatic encounters forecast on the 1st, 11th and 21st. Attractions are instantaneous and the feelings are mutual, so be prepared to be completely bowled over backwards at the emotional impact! OK, this might be overstating the case, but it is almost certain that romantic experience will take off like a rocket. With such powerful amorous energies in force you'll need to take care not to upset various third parties, especially friends.

An element of rivalry cannot be entirely ruled out, and there's a danger of flirtatious impulses sparking off bad vibes between you and an otherwise friendly person. All it means is that you need to keep your eyes open and your sensitivities sharpened just in case there are hidden complications written in the script.

> A romantic experience will take off like a rocket in May

TRAVEL

Just when everything seemed to be on target and going swimmingly, something unexpected throws a spanner in the works early in the second week of May. Your ruling planet, Mercury, abruptly slams into reverse gear, signalling a delay concerning a project you had hoped to bring to completion sooner.

You may have to go over ground already covered due to a previous oversight. This glitch could, however, give you much-needed breathing space and a chance to pull your ideas into better shape.

Travel is highlighted later in the month and contact with foreign lands proves inspiring and spiritually enlightening.

HOME

The presence of Saturn in the home area of your solar chart makes 2009 an important year for establishing a more secure background for yourself.

Property interests are therefore likely to be a major focus of your attention, and if you're planning a major move or seeking a place to put down some roots it could be said that the Fates are on your side at this time.

Events taking shape around the 17th of May could prove decisive for house-hunters that are looking for something that suits their needs without breaking the bank. Keep an eye out for a bargain!

Hang on in there as any obstacles you've been up against so far this year are about to fade into the background and your patient efforts will finally be rewarded.

Lucky dates
5th, 10th, 24th, 31st

June

The most important influences in your life in the coming weeks are coming from a place that is slightly out of your direct line of vision. Events taking place off stage have a subtle effect on the way your mind works. New ideas come to the surface and you may discover that one of your little-used talents can be put to good use. Psychologically speaking, it is as if you are beginning to tap into a deeper source of energy, and perhaps various ideas you've been mulling over in the back of your mind suddenly find a definite centre of gravity. These are interesting times to try something new. Your efforts should be rewarded and you may even end up surprising yourself.

TRAVEL

By nature you are a highly communicative person and never happier than when you are in touch with a wide circle of friends and acquaintances. How you interact with others at this time has a highly stimulating effect on your mind and gives you a chance to air your views.

All matters relating to education and learning are a source of satisfaction during the second half of the month. It's a prime time for cranking up your learning curve, taking a course, and focusing your mind on the need to improve your credentials and perfect your skills.

LOVE

If romantic developments have recently put you in a mood of euphoria and you feel that all your birthdays have come at once, the situation continues to look good. The difference is that there'll be a calmer feel to the situation enabling you to appreciate your good fortune.

For those still hoping to find their affinity, it might not seem that much is happening, but there is a lot to suggest that the Fates are moving in mysterious ways, weaving you into a web of events that ultimately fulfils your heartfelt desires. Something you hear through the grapevine around the 21st makes you realise that someone admires you greatly, so be prepared to feel highly flattered. If you have an established relationship, take care not to put the situation under stress by indulging in extra-curricular flirtations. Temptation could get the better of you, so be warned!

MONEY

Your desire for a more secure lifestyle is reflected in your attitude to money. It's unlikely that people will accuse you of being a skinflint, but it seems that you are determined to get more organised and far-seeing in regard to financial issues.

It probably won't be until after the lunation on June 22nd that a hold up passes, but from then on it's progress all the way, particularly if you are planning to make an investment or launch a business. It's a great month for casting your net wider.

Lucky dates
1st, 7th, 11th, 21st

July

Your ruling planet, Mercury, covers a lot of cosmic ground throughout July, signalling a state of affairs that is sure to put you firmly in your element. Experience offers you the kind of variation and diversity that enables you to make optimum use of your special abilities and puts you in touch with the types of people who satisfy your mind. The pace quickens considerably in the second half of the month. This is when your uncanny ability to juggle with several activities simultaneously stands you in good stead and gives you the reputation of a genuine whizz kid! Your multi-tasking skills will work in your favour throughout July.

LOVE

The presence of both Venus and Mars in your own sign in the second half of July enhances your personal magnetism and ensures that you're not short of admirers. In other words, it's something of a star month for romantically inclined Geminis.

If it's going to happen it'll happen quickly, and if you are sceptical about the notion of love at first sight what you experience at this time is likely to change your mind! However, it would be unrealistic to say that there are no potential pitfalls in this delightful scenario. Adverse trends early in the month suggest that you could sabotage a promising encounter through clinging onto an existing romantic attachment that is really going nowhere. It may sound rather brutal, but you would be doing yourself a huge favour by burning certain bridges and facing squarely the fact that it's time to cut old ties and move on.

MONEY

Now that you are relatively free of recent financial complications, your motivation to put things on a more productive basis is thrown into higher gear.

For commercially minded Geminis, a lively, fast-moving state of affairs gives you an ideal platform on which to try out new ideas, widen your network of helpful contacts, and put things on a more streamlined basis. A key date is the 16th July, when an unexpected turn of events or an unusual offer will enable you to add a lucrative string to your bow. This is a time to aim for diversity rather than put all your eggs in one basket.

Balance your risks and with a bit of planning you should come out on top.

Aim for diversity and don't put all your eggs in one basket

TRAVEL

The general drift of events throughout 2009 can be described in terms of a widening horizon.

This is likely to take a very obvious turn in July, with an important and long-range excursion likely to be high on your agenda. The old saying that travel broadens the mind could never be truer for Geminis than at this time.

Your spectrum of experience and knowledge can be greatly enriched through contact with other countries or with people from different cultural backgrounds. Seize any travel opportunities offered and use them to advance your understanding.

Likewise it's an inspiring month for those in search of spiritual insight and explorations of the higher reaches of the mind.

Lucky dates
2nd, 12th, 19th, 28th

August

With the energising planet Mars beating a path through your sign you may be feeling restless, but at the same time your motivation to push ahead with what's important reaches a new level of dynamism. The pattern of events presents you with a fresh sense of challenge as happenings demand a greater energy input. Whether it's a business venture, a journey of discovery, or a major sporting event that focuses your attention, your success is guaranteed. All the signs during August are positive, it seems your confidence level is at an all-time high and you'll certainly not be content to take a back seat. Basically, if you want it, now is your chance to get it!

LOVE

The powerful influence of Mars is likely to impact in a dramatic way in the sphere of amorous experience. Although this is something of a two-edged sword, there's no doubt that this is going to be an unusually eventful month for romantically inclined Geminis.

Stirring developments are forecast during the second week, when someone you chance to meet while travelling proves instantaneously appealing. There's a potentially life-changing ingredient written into this scenario, and even if a romantic affair is not destined to last, it'll certainly change your perspective on what it is you're really seeking. You may suddenly realise why previous attachments seem to have got caught in a downward spiral of negative feedback. From now on things can only get better, so don't fret if an August romance is over before it's begun.

MONEY

By all counts it seems that you have a firmer handle on financial affairs and will be feeling easier about splashing out on the things that make life worthwhile. For instance if you're taking a much-needed vacation, this is unlikely to plunge you dangerously into the red, though you may need to curb the urge to spend later in the month. There are hints of an added bonus or a gift heading your way in the third week, and cash flow is taking a smoother course at this time. Efforts to improve your earning potential will meet with success.

TRAVEL

Whether you're dealing with more serious issues like property transactions and home improvements, or aiming to chill out at home, there's something to satisfy all tastes during August.

The most propitious dates for pushing ahead with practical affairs are the 13th and 18th, when you'll be able to speed things up and get a positive response from others. If you wish to invite friends around, throw a house party, and aim to spend more time with your immediate family.

Lucky dates

2nd, 13th, 16th, 22nd

September

September

There appears to be something of a seismic shift in your destiny going forward during September. This is unlikely to amount to any major trauma, but you may be forced to realise that you have reached a turning point and a break with the past is now required. The underlying theme revolves around a conflict between the old and the new, with the new exerting a very powerful pull on your deeper instincts at present. From a psychological angle, there seems to be a radical shift in your attitude and a more focused approach to life. At a practical level, an old routine becomes less restrictive. This is a time to reflect on past actions and bring them into the present.

MONEY

There's an enterprising atmosphere which will motivate you to take fresh initiatives and put financial affairs on a more progressive and profitable basis. You may now find that your goals can be raised a peg or two, particularly if you are feeling more confident about your financial credentials and are not afraid to act boldly.

Provided you are coming from a pretty secure base, the sky's the limit for you at this time. Bear in mind though that Mars is the prime mover and therefore mistakes could be made through reckless and premature action. You're in the driving seat, but watch your speed!

LOVE

The changing pattern of your life introduces you to a broader social scene and puts you in touch with people on your own wavelength. Links of a more sympathetic nature are being woven, and if it's a more meaningful and intimate relationship you're after, then you won't have far to look.

Don't turn down any invitations, even if they are not immediately appealing. It's the last-minute changes of plan, short journeys and chance meetings that will provide an essential key to your heart's desires in the coming weeks.

An alternative take on the current situation could mean that a relative or close friend announces an engagement, wedding, or something similar that calls for impromptu celebrations in the second half of the month. Whatever finally pans out, there's bound to be something to warm your heart and stir your passions during September.

TRAVEL

Keep your wits about you while your ruling planet is in retreat from the second week of September onwards.

Special arrangements are likely to be disrupted, and you may have to do some quick re-checking if you're hoping to succeed in an educational venture or take part in some high-level discussions. Also, insist that others make themselves absolutely clear in conversations because this is a time when it will be easy to get at cross-purposes and end up having a lot of explaining to do. Towards the end of the month, a message you receive gives you the green light for a project you were obliged to shelve a couple of months back. This will give you a new impetus to succeed and a chance to pick up on previous ambitions. You'll discover that you can see things with new eyes after a short break.

> There will be celebrations in the second half of the month

Lucky dates
1st, 11th, 12th, 29th

October

A promising month lies ahead for you, with a much more settled trend and a feeling that things are definitely falling into place. If you've had to steer your way through a difficult watershed recently, you'll feel you are now beginning to see the light and, before October is out, a more definite sense of direction comes into view. Whenever a new chapter opens it naturally brings an element of disruption with it, but now that you are getting your bearings you'll find that in some mysterious way luck attends your major decisions. In short, the winds of change may have caused some turbulence in recent times, but at last you're sailing out upon calmer waters.

LOVE

As far as your love life is concerned there is much to suggest that everything is going from strength to strength. In fact it's the special person in your life, as well as friends, who will give you emotional support.

However, if you're without a soul mate at present, this is no reason to get despondent. With Venus activating a highly romantic area of your solar horoscope in the second half of the month it's as if you're being singled out for special treatment. The chances of meeting your affinity are greatly increased, and it'll be those odd twists and turns of events that work the magic. Key dates for love and lovers are the 16th, 27th and 29th, when you can also expect to be in high demand socially.

MONEY

In the first half of the month don't take too much for granted if business negotiations are under consideration. Attempting to rush things or cut corners could land you with extra expense, so don't overlook the finer points and be ready to alter your strategy if you see an obstacle. Once Mars takes leave of the money sector of your chart midmonth you'll be able to breathe more easily.

The bottom line seems to be that a phase of heavy expenditure is coming to an end, giving you greater scope for re-structuring your finances and putting things on a more secure base.

TRAVEL

There's a pleasing accent on leisurely activities in the month ahead. Not only will you be involved with a wider social network, but it seems that you'll find a more productive outlet for creative interests.

Travel contains an element of luck, and a turn of events around the 20th could open a whole new window on the world. Those involved in education and intent on developing their skills can expect to make progress. And if you have children, you'll have reason to feel pleased with how they're growing.

Lucky dates
4th, 7th, 16th, 24th

November

The pace of life is programmed to reach a hectic level during these late weeks of the year. Being the kind of person who thrives on movement and variety, this state of affairs is unlikely to throw you out of key, and in fact it will probably bring out the very best in you. However, there are times when your ability to juggle with several activities can be stretched to the limit. During the second week of November try not to leave things to chance and certainly don't let the demands of other people put you under stress. If you allow this to happen you'll begin to feel like a hamster running like crazy around its little wheel and going absolutely nowhere!

LOVE

As you've probably realised by now, love is not something that you can take for granted, and it isn't something that works like a magic pill.

There's a fine line between happiness and illusion, and if you have been seeing someone through rose-tinted spectacles the ideal may begin to show a few fissures in the coming weeks. Basically, you need to be honest about what you really feel, instead of making a desperate attempt to paper over the cracks. The person you believed to be your one and only may actually just be playing you along. If you know this in your heart of hearts, maybe you should listen to the inner signals before you make a total a fool of yourself.

The ultimatum date is the 19th, when a hint from a friend is likely to open your eyes and

put you wise. But take heart as from late month onwards the prospect brightens.

TRAVEL

As already suggested, it's going to be a hyper-active month when you'll be run off your feet. To avoid ending up in a state of chaos or physical and mental collapse, it would be in your best interests to get your priorities sorted out early in the month and have a fairly clear idea of what's on the month's agenda. It'll be only too easy to get distracted by trivia and end up kicking yourself for wasting time.

Packing a lot of activity into a day is actually something you relish, and there'll certainly be plenty to keep you occupied, but remind yourself that there are only twenty-four hours in a day. Don't put yourself in danger of burnout as you'll achieve much more by taking it steady.

Get your priorities sorted early on in the month

MONEY

Occupational and vocational interests will have a high profile during November, which could turn out to be a crucial month if you're aiming for a promotion or wish to land yourself with the kind of job that offers you greater freedom and better pay.

What happens around the new moon in the middle of the month could give you the break you've been looking for. Something unexpected is likely to turn up, so be prepared to act quickly if you don't want to miss the boat.

Particularly favoured will be those aiming to work on a more freelance basis or develop a profitable sideline.

You will discover some opportunities that allow you to expand your horizons without jeopardising your existing income so take advantage.

Lucky dates
6th, 7th, 17th, 26th

December

After the breakneck speed of the previous month, December offers you something of a contrast. This is not to imply that your life is about to become predictable and boring, but rather that you'll find you have more time to catch up on the things you have perhaps neglected or overlooked in recent months. Relationships on all levels are sure to benefit and you'll find more time for enjoyable leisurely and convivial encounters. Above all, you'll be in the right frame of mind to make the most of late month revels and what promises to be a highly memorable occasion. Bear in mind though that there's no need to force the pace this month – you'll get there anyway.

LOVE

Established relationships come under the harmonising sway of Venus throughout the month. Now that the pressure of work and other commitments is easing, you'll have greater scope for creating more quality time.

This is probably just what's needed right now, especially if recent events have tended to compartmentalise your life and caused you to neglect your loved one. So, make the most of prevailing trends to get

re-acquainted! Any romance that emerged over the previous couple of months is by now beginning to feel right, and perhaps your thoughts are turning towards the prospect of a wedding in the New Year. Amorous ties are being woven more closely at this time, and at last you are beginning to feel that the Fates are on your side. For single Geminis the prospect is equally sweet.

MONEY

The efforts you made to improve your earning potential in previous months are about to start paying dividends. Welcome news is winging its way to you during the second week. It looks as if your budget for the month ahead is put in a much healthier state due to an added bonus, rebate or windfall, and this may

call for some pre-festive celebrations. At all events it's unlikely you'll be short of funds when it comes to splashing out on gifts and goodies – though it would pay you to be more thoughtful about what you buy. Don't let good fortune go to your head!

TRAVEL

Throughout 2009 your desire to widen your horizons has had a fortunate effect on your soul. This trend continues, with a promise of exciting developments connected with travel in the near future.

A surprise message is likely to arrive around the 7th. It's likely to be a blast from the past, and someone you've not seen for years could suddenly renew contact. Whatever happens, it's bound to be a nostalgic delight, with plenty of news to catch up on.

Lucky dates
2nd, 8th 18th, 30th

For your fantastic weekly & monthly cash, career and romance and forecasts

Call 0905 515 0040

Starlines are updated every Tuesday. BT calls cost 60p per minute and last about 5 minutes. Cost from other networks may be higher. SP: Eckoh Herts HP3 9HN

Zodiac fact file

Planetary Ruler: The Moon

Quality & Element: Cardinal Water

Colours: Silver, pastels

Metal: Silver

Wood: Birch

Flower: Convolvulus

Animal: Crab

Gem: Moonstone

Fabric: Voile

Cancer

june 21 to july 20

January

Having just about every planet in the opposite sector of your solar horoscope might make you feel at the mercy of forces beyond your control, but really it means that certain developments will act as a guide and show you the best strategy to adopt in pursuing your main aims. Not only can you now count on other people to pull their weight and give you all the support you need; you won't feel guilty about taking more of a back seat and cultivating a certain detachment from the hurly-burly of life as the New Year begins. Besides which, you'll only end up frustrated by trying to force the pace at this point so just let it dictate itself.

LOVE

Close ties of love and affection, as well as special friendships, are greatly strengthened under prevailing positive trends. It's through interaction with other people that you are able to express yourself more fully at this time. Whether this is a lover, marriage partner, or someone who is otherwise important in your scheme of things, the indications are that your life is tremendously enriched through a vital exchange of energies.

Single Cancerians hoping to find a kindred spirit are heading for unexpected delights

towards the end of the month, so don't get too despondent if nothing much seems to have been happening in your love life recently. A fairly lengthy journey or a long distance contact could provide you with the key to your heart's desire, and if romance does suddenly materialise it's bound to embody your ideals.

MONEY

It's going to be an important year ahead when you can expect welcome transformations in both personal and joint financial interests. Jupiter, planet of expansion and good fortune, begins to activate a significant area of your chart, signalling a phase of steady progress and tremendous determination on your part to overcome obstacles and put material affairs on a secure basis. The main accent falls on long-range interests,

making January a prime time to overhaul your investments, optimise your current resources and strengthen your position on a very practical level. Start the year on a financial high!

TRAVEL

It's a promising and potentially delightful month for longer excursions or for taking a break from the old routines. If this is not on the immediate agenda, then you're likely to be dwelling a great deal on an exotic holiday or cruise that you would like to take later in the year.

As for communications, it's a good policy to get all loose ends tied up before the 11th, after which you're likely to meet with awkward delays and glitches due to your own or others' absent-mindedness. Take special care in dealing with official matters around the 18th – the details may be misleading.

Lucky dates
3rd, 10th, 19th, 29th

February

If the pattern of events has seemed to be pushing you around recently, or you've felt a little bit out on a limb, this at least has given you a chance to stand back and get things in clearer perspective. The pattern changes from early February onwards, and before the month is out you'll begin to feel that you're firmly back in the driving seat. This doesn't mean that you can simply ignore limitations and roar ahead regardless of consequences though. It's important to remember that before you can change gear you have to go through neutral, so take a natural break before hitting the gas. Once you get this straight in your mind, you'll motor on!

LOVE

An intensification of passion is indicated and new romantic encounters are likely to disturb your usual emotional equilibrium. At best, the final outcome of February's stirring events will be a dream come true, and what you have long been seeking will be brought within your reach.

However, as always when feelings are strongly stirred, it can often be something of a double-edged sword. This is an apt metaphor now that the fiery planet Mars is the moving force. To put it in plain words, you're rather susceptible to falling headlong into one of those mad infatuations that come on like with a bang and disappear as quickly with a whimper.

A kind of love-hate relationship is liable to develop in February, leaving you emotionally exhausted in the end. So, if it all gets a bit too much for you and starts taking on the feel of a soap opera, don't say you haven't been warned! You should take the time to consider your options.

MONEY

The trend continues favourably and you have it in your power to manoeuvre your financial affairs into a stronger position. There's much to suggest some extra funds coming from a direction other than your main source of income. It could be an unexpected bonus, a rebate or even a small legacy. As jointly held resources are especially highlighted it also looks as if your partner's fortunes are due for a boost too. Whatever finally transpires, it is almost certain that you'll be laughing (well, at least grinning) all the way to the bank later in the month.

HEALTH

The sign of Cancer belongs to the element of Water, and therefore you are essentially a deeply emotional creature. Often you experience a rather unsettling swing between a high and a low mood – a kind of mild manic depressive pattern. Generally speaking you take this in your stride, but during February you may be inclined to get a bit too intense and preoccupied with your own feelings. However, the strange thing is that this represents a beneficial transformation taking shape deep within your psyche, so be prepared to go with it and try to listen to what the inner voice is telling you. It may seem a little disrupting now but the conclusions you reach after some deep thinking will put you in a stronger position to successfully forge ahead in the coming months.

> You'll be grinning all the way to the bank this February

Lucky dates

7th, 13th, 16th, 24th

March

The unusually lengthy sojourn of Venus in the top sector of your solar chart from February to early June suggests an easing of work pressures and an important opportunity for you to create a more satisfying work/life balance. You'll be more inclined to reflect on what it is you actually wish to achieve and come to a decision whether to stick with the status quo or start looking around for something that's more in line with your changing needs. Don't worry if everything appears to go into a state of limbo during this month; you'll see that in fact it's all part of a bigger picture that ultimately shows you the right direction to take.

LOVE

Venus is of course the planet of love and in the coming weeks throws an important light on established and on-going romantic attachments. A more relaxed state of affairs allows you to create a closer rapport with the special person in your life. If you experienced a noticeable cooling in your love life recently this will turn out to be a blip. But it will make you realise just how easy it is for a relationship to languish if your attention slips and take things too much for granted. As in most things that have to do with happiness, it's a question of achieving the right balance; so if you've been getting too preoccupied with your career or an obsessive interest, there may be a valuable lesson to be learned. Meanwhile, single Cancerians may find that romance is a scarce resource, but don't fret – your good angel has not forgotten you.

TRAVEL

Whether you're travelling far and wide, pursuing special studies, or engaged in high level discussions, Mercury's stimulating vibes ensure that everything meets your expectations. Mentally you're on top form and will benefit greatly through exchange of ideas and by broadening your range of contacts. In one way or another it seems that this is a time when you can enrich your personality through learning, so make the most of this positive trend for cultivating a constructive dialogue with those who are on your own wavelength.

MONEY

Astrologically you are in a privileged position, and what happens in March brings a realisation that you are in the clear to make a major decision concerning the future.

The trend is decidedly progressive, particularly in regard to jointly held resources and business partnerships. You'll realise that some things that seemed like an obstacle can be turned into a bridge, and perhaps the only reason it was an obstacle is only because you've been looking at it in the wrong way.

A touch of lateral thinking will make all the difference, so don't let your cautious instinct block your path.

Lucky dates
7th, 14th, 22nd, 26th

April

Your level of motivation is moving into a higher gear and your determination to push ahead with plans and projects now becomes unstoppable. Looking at the broader cosmic picture, everything points to speedy progress due to your own tenacity and sense of purpose. However there is a note of caution when Mars is in adverse aspect around the 6th and again in the middle of the month. You are warned not to push beyond certain limits so that you end up bulldozing through other people's sensitivities. Impatience and the temptation to barge ahead with blinkers on could land you in trouble, so take time to stop and think.

LOVE

The situation is looking much brighter for those who have been through the mill emotionally in the previous month or two.

With Venus regaining a more positive momentum from the 17th, you can expect the distance between dream and reality to be reduced as something more promising appears on your horizon.

There's a window of opportunity between this date and the 24th, and what happens then could set your inner emotional compass pointing towards a new wave of magnetic attraction. However, don't get too excited, otherwise you'll end up rushing in where angels usually fear to tread.

If true love is destined to enter your orbit it'll do so in its own good time. Someone may say something highly flattering that sets your heart all aflutter, but this is no reason to act as if you're totally desperate! Play it cool and you'll discover time is on your side.

TRAVEL

Two dates to be avoided if travel is on the agenda are the 6th and 15th. The trends are decidedly stressful, and in fact these are among the year's astrological danger zones. OK, it's highly unlikely you'll be involved in some kind of international disaster, but it'll probably be something very disruptive like the car breaking down in the middle of nowhere, or being left stranded at the airport due to some emergency. If possible, therefore, leave important travel arrangements till later in the month, and in the meantime make sure your car is well serviced and all schedules are in place.

Leave any new travel arrangements until later in the month

MONEY

After a relatively uneventful phase, career-minded Cancerians can expect the pace to pick up a more satisfying momentum from late June onwards.

If everything seems to be at a standstill, this doesn't mean that you need to be totally inactive or resigned to your plight. The unexpected lull in activity this month will give you an excellent opportunity to do some extra homework, gather information and put out a few feelers, especially if you're seeking ways and means to improve your earning potential. Play your cards right and what takes place in the final days of this month could turn out to be an opportunity well worth preparing for. Your fortunes are changing so take full advantage.

Lucky dates
2nd, 9th, 17th, 25th.

May

The forces of transformation are once again gathering momentum and pointing towards the direction of a new beginning. Throughout the year the pattern of events seems geared towards a freeing up of energies that have perhaps been confined to a relatively small circle in recent years. Certain limitations are easing and, either this month or in the near future, you'll experience a break with the past. This is certainly nothing to get alarmed about, though it could indeed entail a slight element of disruption. The good news is that there's a feeling of renewal and the opening of an exciting new chapter in your life.

LOVE

There's a danger that practical demands interfere with the smooth course of love in the coming weeks. Once again, it might be hard to get the balance right, but provided you don't totally neglect personal and intimate affairs by becoming too wrapped up in your own ego then problems can be avoided.

For singles, it's not until the third week that the love light begins to shine, but from then on any doubts about your feelings for another person will be blown to the winds. There are indications that you'll find yourself strongly attracted to someone who has an authoritative aura or great kudos. It might not mean that you're about to run off with a pop star or football celebrity, but there does appear to be an element of glamour woven into the situation. Altogether these are interesting times, and the best is yet to come!

TRAVEL

Something marked private and confidential may need your close attention during the first week. If something is puzzling or worrying you, don't hesitate to seek specialist advice. From the middle of the month onwards you may find that certain lines of communication suffer an element of disruption due to the unreliability of friends and other associates. Keep arrangements flexible, especially if you are involved in group activities or trying to organise an event.

If it all goes pear-shaped, be prepared to put things on hold until the end of May, after which speedier progress can be expected.

MONEY

Financial affairs, especially those that have to do with longer-term and soundly based interests, continue to be a focus for you. The combination of Jupiter and Neptune later in the month suggests a dissolving of restrictions and greater scope for improving your fortunes.

The portents are favourable, but make sure you don't get carried away by the misplaced optimism of someone close to you, or commit yourself to a financial loan that stretches you to the limit and beyond.

Lucky dates
9th, 11th, 24th, 26th

June

This promises to be a month when most things meet your hopes and expectations. This is particularly so at a very practical level, where you'll find much ground can be covered by teamwork rather than going it alone. A project that you were obliged to abandon several months back will come back for reconsideration and this time around you can count on others for the necessary support. The enthusiasm and positive influence of certain friends is bound to have a creative and inspiring impact on the way you approach life at this time. What's more, the increased activity adds a brand new dimension to your social life.

LOVE

Whenever Venus joins forces with Mars the potential for amorous encounters is greatly enhanced. This applies especially to Cancerians in June, because these planets are directly linked with your cherished hopes and wishes. All of which adds up to a star-spangled month for the romantically inclined.

With your social life also gathering a pleasant momentum and new friends gravitating into your orbit, it's unlikely you'll be languishing in the lonely heart's club! Although you are the kind of person who tends to hide yourself away at times, especially if your experience has been emotionally fraught, what transpires throughout the coming weeks will draw you out of your shell and restore your faith in the power of love and friendship.

By late month you'll probably kick yourself for not realising sooner that someone you care about really does think you're wonderful.

MONEY

What takes place out of your line of immediate vision will nevertheless have a helpful influence on financial and business affairs in the long run. There's an undercurrent of good fortune backing you up, so don't be afraid to stick your neck out if a money-making opportunity presents itself, especially in the third week. The only proviso is that Jupiter now begins a retrograde cycle, advising greater caution in regard to loans, investments and the urge to change.

By focusing on consolidating current assets you can't go wrong, so don't be led astray by those who try to persuade you otherwise.

June will be a star-spangled month for the romantically inclined

TRAVEL

Interaction with friends and kindred spirits stimulates and enriches your mind in the first half of the month.

Two (or more) heads are better than one if you are trying to come up with new ideas or crack a thorny problem that stands in the way of current objectives.

A chance conversation with a stranger could prove enlightening early in the month, so do try to be open to all suggestions rather than allowing your prejudices to restrict your view.

Prevailing trends later in the month will work to favour those interested in psychic, mystical and occult studies. Perhaps something you read in *Prediction* magazine will bring you fresh inspiration! Whatever it is, listen to others to get the most out of it.

Lucky dates
6th, 9th, 19th, 23rd

July

The lunar and solar eclipses on the 7th and 22nd will have a direct impact on your own sign and therefore you can expect a month of far-reaching developments. It's a time when your attitudes are changing, and what you previously considered important may begin to appear less so. An element of restlessness or dissatisfaction enters the frame, but this is unlikely to have a negative effect. On the contrary, it is more likely that you are determined to get rid of excess emotional baggage and break the habit of a lifetime. At this time of revolution, a bunch of new interests beckon and life becomes more engaging.

TRAVEL

With Mercury zipping through your sign between the 3rd and 17th, it seems you're on the move, both physically and mentally. It's travel and the people you meet that provide you with food for thought.

If you've been dabbling with new areas of knowledge, this is where it begins to absorb more of your attention and creative energy. This is a time when you can do much to change and enrich your life by cultivating a wider network of contacts, exploring new terrain, and doing something to loosen the bonds of old and habit-bound routines.

LOVE

Your emotional reference points are liable to undergo a shift in light of what takes shape in July. This is not to imply that a trauma is about to descend and disturb your equilibrium, though you are strongly advised against getting drawn into an eternal triangle affair. There are indications that strong passions will tempt you onto potentially dangerous ground, which could seriously jeopardise an existing relationship. If you find yourself pulled between two powerful attractions, perhaps it would be better if you just let the whole thing ride a while. This may be hard, but by not trying to force any issues you'll find that the solution to your dilemma will arrive on your doorstep as if by magic.

If it's a case of having to break with an old romantic attachment, an unexpected twist of events does the job for you late month.

MONEY

You may be faced with some difficult decisions during these weeks, but provided you don't get careless it's unlikely you'll experience any setbacks.

The main thing to bear in mind is that first impressions will prove deceptive, so exercise caution if you're considering any new financial manoeuvres. Commercial interests gather a quicker momentum later in the month, but you're advised to test the ground before going ahead. Finally, keep your wits about you as there's a danger of falling foul of slick sales patter.

Lucky dates
2nd, 12th, 21st, 28th

August

If the emotional waters have suffered some turbulence in recent weeks you probably won't be completely free of the unpredictable currents until the second week of August. By now it has probably dawned on you that only very rarely do people fit your high expectations and that it's a mistake to believe they will change overnight. If you have experienced disappointment or had your eyes opened to something you'd completely missed recently, this is no bad thing if it's made you wiser and more realistic. From now on it's unlikely you'll be let down by mistaken judgements concerning who is and who is not on your wavelength.

LOVE

The presence of Venus in your sign guarantees your love life is about to enter a more satisfying and harmonious phase. If your experience has been a bit rocky in recent months, at least you are not likely to make the same mistakes again. You may be more cautious in making any fresh commitments emotionally, but at least this enables you to sift the gold from the dross.

The good news is that the events of August put the sparkle back in your eye, and it could be that you meet your affinity while travelling on unfamiliar ground in the latter half of the month.

Travel will have therapeutic value at this time, giving you much-needed breathing space to get your deeper feelings sorted out.

Even if you don't happen to meet the love of your life right now, at least you are clearer about what you do and don't want in a partner. You can now trust that things will finally flow your way.

MONEY

It would be unrealistic to say that this is going to be an entirely problem free month, but the underlying trend is helpful and you'll only have yourself to blame if you're faced with added expenses.

The best advice is to proceed with your usual caution in the second week. A new job offer or a chance to boost your earnings may look good at first glance, but it would be worth doing a bit of private investigation if you are not to be left carrying the can. It's best to stick with familiar territory at present rather than attempting to go for the big time. Wait until late month if you're thinking of purchasing luxury goods.

HEALTH

If you're taking a holiday and flying off to far horizons, don't get careless about the dangers to your health, like sitting out for too long and damaging yourself in the Sun. Also, go easy on exotic culinary delights and remember that being a Cancerian you do have a rather sensitive stomach. If in doubt leave it alone and don't be afraid to say no, even if others may taunt you for being a spoilsport. One false move on your part could ruin an otherwise great time. Apart from holidays, if you feel that your energy level is below par, don't let this worry you, but also don't attempt to remain in high gear if your body is signalling its time to ease off. Have a bit of down time to recharge yourself for the months ahead.

The events of August put the sparkle back in your eye

Lucky dates
6th, 8th, 17th, 25th

September

Although you might be obliged to catch up on various neglected matters this month, there's every indication of a highly progressive trend in the weeks ahead. The dynamic influence of Mars in your sign galvanises you into action and enables you to get where you want to be. What you achieve depends on your own energy and initiative, so if you're eager to push ahead with important aims and objectives now is the time to get where the action is and adopt a more assertive approach to life. Altogether it seems that you are now firmly in the driving seat and are able to make a positive impact on the world around you.

LOVE

As Mars has the highest profile in your solar chart in September, how you experience amorous encounters is likely to reflect the nature of this fiery planet.

What this means, quite simply, is that a new romance is liable to come on like the proverbial hurricane. It's a month when passions are stirred and attractions are irresistible, but always with the potential for throwing you off centre emotionally. Nothing is inevitable, but with Mars it's often a case of short and sweet.

In other words a new love affair may seem to answer all your deepest desires at first, but in the end it turns out to be just one of those mad infatuations that are not destined to last much further than the end of the month. Nevertheless, it'll be bliss while it lasts and there can be little doubt that this is a great month for lovemaking.

MONEY

Now that you've gained the upper hand in regard to financial affairs, you won't need to feel guilty about spending money on what can best be described as pure self-indulgence.

Provided you don't become a total shopaholic, Septermber is a good month for splashing out on luxury items and the things that give a more comfortable ambience to your lifestyle.

If you are, like many Cancerians, a keen collector of curios and objets d'art you'll certainly have a nose for a bargain and may come across something valuable quite by chance – and at a very good price too.

HOME

Domestic affairs have perhaps not had a very high profile in your world up to now, but from this month onwards the pattern will change.

For various reasons events focus your attention on matters closer to home, and this could mean that you have more than your usual quota of visitors, especially in the first half of the month. Between the 7th and 18th, however, keep your arrangements flexible as it looks as if people will be in the habit of arriving at your door at very short notice – or none at all. If you're a parent, keep a wary eye on the antics of youngsters.

Lucky dates
4th, 16th, 22nd, 29th

October

The pattern of events continues to demand a high energy input from you, but it's unlikely you'll be daunted if faced with a fresh challenge. Make your best efforts in the first half of October if you wish for speedy progress and an enthusiastic response from others. From the 16th onwards the pace will begin to ease, giving you greater scope for leisure and relaxation. However, until then it will be in your best interests to stay at the cutting edge of things, especially if you are aiming to raise your status and keep your ambitions on track. October is definitely not a month in which to underestimate your abilities or take a back seat!

LOVE

There seems to be a subtle shift in your attitude to intimate relationships under the changing cosmic influence. The experience of what may have been a rather brief but passionate affair recently has caused you to reflect more deeply on what exactly it is you're looking for in a partner.

You're a psychologically complex person, inclined to be a prey to unaccountable changes of mood, which means that someone who gets emotionally attached to you can easily get perplexed. One minute you're up and the next it's as if you're all boxed up inside and hard to reach. However, now that you appear to be reaching a new level of maturity and integrity, a new romantic attachment established now or in the very near future is certain to answer to your deepest needs. On the other hand, if you're happy with an existing relationship the situation can only get better!

HOME

You're the kind of person who instinctively seeks security, so you'll be pleased to know that the changing cosmic picture throws an increasingly helpful light on all things domestic during October.

Traditionally your sign has a deep affinity with home and family, and it seems that developments taking shape in the month ahead (and, in fact, for some time to come) make you feel far more settled. Property interests are brought into focus, with every indication that important transactions produce satisfying results.

On a lighter note, with the festive season still two months away, this is a splendid month for convivial get togethers in the comfort of your own home.

> **This is a splendid month for get togethers in your own home**

MONEY

After a fairly lengthy phase of hard work, you are about to reap the rewards for your efforts and dedication.

What happens on or soon after the 13th gives you a clearer sense of direction where career and employment are concerned. If therefore you are seeking a change of job and want something that allows you better scope for expressing your real potential, luck is on your side.

Experience gained over the past year or two will stand you in good stead and will give you a sense of increased empowerment. Altogether, you can expect a fortunate trend in all matters of practical importance so this could be the time to make that investment you've been considering or to review your monthly outgoings.

Lucky dates
2nd, 7th, 18th, 27th

November

If you get the feeling that the forces of destiny are taking a stronger hand in your affairs than usual, you won't be far off the mark. An unusual combination of influences gathering force around the new moon on the 16th suggests that you are breaking free of your old restrictions and are opening a new window on the world. It might only be a small beginning, but a seed is definitely being sown around this time that will eventually blossom into something highly satisfying. If you're seeking ways and means to improve your creative skills and widen your field of self-expression, the gods are with you all the way during November.

LOVE

The breathtaking events of recent weeks show no sign of abating, and if you're still unsure about a romantic affair it's unlikely you'll be in a state of limbo for long.

In some ways this could be described as a highpoint of the year for amorous encounters. It could be that a liaison begun several months back that's blown hot and cold finally settles into something much more fulfilling. For those still hoping to find a soul mate, the prospects brighten considerably. Under the gentle sway of Venus you won't be short of opportunity to make acquaintance with someone who appeals to you.

You are not inclined to hide yourself in the shadows during these weeks, and as your social life seems to be gaining added sparkle the chances of meeting someone highly attractive are greatly increased. Altogether luck and love are intertwined.

MONEY

Now that you are in the driving seat financially, it's unlikely you'll be wasting time when it comes to making good use of your resources. With Mars dominating the money sector of your chart you can expect a progressive and fast-moving state of affairs, with plenty of incentive to push full speed ahead with projects. You are not spendthrift by nature, so the usual warning about impulsiveness and extravagance are perhaps out of place. However, be prepared to meet with increased pressure on your bank balance later in the month, and think twice before forking out on new equipment.

TRAVEL

Creative energies are stirring within you and this is greatly helped by the people you mix with in the month ahead. As already mentioned you can expect a more varied social life, giving you plenty of scope for exchanging ideas and making new contacts.

Travel contains an element of unexpected luck, and here too it could be a chance encounter that brings fresh inspiration and enables you to see things through a wider lens. If you're into crafts or blogging, there's plenty of grist to your mill these weeks!

Lucky dates

2nd, 8th, 16th, 23rd

December

Uranus, planet of the unexpected, signals an unusual twist of events early in the month. This may entail disruption to your well-laid plans, but it could well be an opportunity that shouldn't be missed. Information that comes to light will rouse your curiosity and motivate you to revive an old interest. If you're in search of a guru, and you take a serious interest in the spiritual dimension, it's likely that the people you encounter during December will prove highly inspiring. Any line of knowledge that is somehow off the beaten track becomes a source of deep personal enrichment and works to give you a whole new slant on life.

LOVE

The keynote for relationships this month can be summed up in the word 'stability'. Being the kind of person who instinctively seeks a secure base in life this is music to your ears. It's certainly good news for all married Cancerians and those with an established partner.

From a practical point of view it seems that you're feeling more settled and inclined to give serious consideration to home and family interests.

Meanwhile, if you're single and hoping to find your affinity there's more than just a hint that an encounter over the festive season will answer your heart's desire.

Generally speaking there's an easier feeling surrounding amorous attachments, so if things have been a bit wobbly in recent months you can now look forward to something more in line with your wishes.

Meeting up with an old flame late in the month could prove promising!

HOME

People born under your sign are described as home birds, and in view of prevailing trends it seems that the events of December answer to your deepest needs. Although it might not be in the forefront of your thoughts with the festivities approaching, there's an unusually favourable accent on property interests and the things that are geared to making you feel more rooted. For those considering starting a family or moving to a more spacious residence, the outlook for the year ahead is highly encouraging. What takes shape in the coming weeks puts you in an optimistic mood on this score.

TRAVEL

The influence of other people is a key factor in your scheme of things as the winter solstice approaches. Whether you're involved in high level business negotiations, academic discussions, or just plain chit-chat, contact and dialogue with various people is sure to make life interesting.

Early in December there may be a sudden change of plan and an impromptu journey. What emerges from this could throw a totally new light on what you had in mind for later in the month. However, if you're not too tied down with your responsibilities, it would be in your best interests to go off at a slight tangent and trust your instincts. Be brave this month and you will be rewarded in due time for all your efforts.

> Go off at a slight tangent this month and trust your instincts

Lucky dates

3rd, 5th, 16th, 21st

For your fantastic weekly & monthly cash, career and romance and forecasts

Call 0905 515 004

Starlines are updated every Tuesday. BT calls cost 60p per minute and last about 5 minutes. Cost from other networks may be higher. SP: Eckoh Herts HP3 9HN

Leo
july 21 to august 21

Zodiac fact file

Planetary Ruler: Sun

Quality & Element: Fixed Fire

Colours: Orange, gold

Metal: Gold

Wood: Walnut

Flower: Marigold

Animal: Lion

Gem: Citrine

Fabric: Brocade

January

You may feel like you're swimming against the current in the early stages of the New Year and therefore it might be a good policy for you to ease the pace and take things one day at a time. There's absolutely no need to feel that you must always be making things happen, especially in January when you're liable to turn too many corners and end up right back at square one. It's better to stand back and see what happens, then you'll be able to gage what's really important and what can be safely thrown overboard. By conserving your energies early in the year you'll be ready to meet new challenges later on in the right way.

LOVE

The most interesting cosmic event in 2009 is the transit of Jupiter into your opposite sign. This favourable trend kicks in as early as the first week of January and signals a highly fortunate year ahead for married Leos and those who are planning to take the plunge in the coming months.

This is an exceptionally good omen if you're currently single and hoping to find a new partner that you can relate to on more than just a superficial level.

If you've previously shied away from the thought of a long term commitment, preferring instead a more freewheeling approach to your love life, this pattern is due to change and you're likely to find yourself getting more serious about personal relationships throughout January. Jupiter's favourable influence points to an enrichment of your life and personality via intimate partnerships. In other words, luck favours lovers in the coming year.

MONEY

It's not only the demands of work that keep you on your toes through January, but it also looks likely you'll have to cope with a load of extraneous duties, especially in the final week of the month. You're not likely to experience any major financial dramas, and indeed there's promise of welcome extra cash coming your way via a bonus or rebate around the 23rd.

The main danger is that you end up feeling resentful because life seems to be all work and very little play. If you feel that other people are taking advantage of your generous nature, it's better for you to confront the issue straight away than simply putting up with it.

TRAVEL

You're advised to tie up loose ends and get any minor tasks completed before the 11th.

This applies especially to business communications, and anything of a legal and official nature.

Other people may be unreliable in the second half of the month, and at times you'll feel that there's a conspiracy afoot to deliberately irritate you. You should be prepared to keep your own counsel rather than asking favours from others or taking at face value any promises that are made. To minimise hassles, make sure you double-check travel plans and don't ignore the fine print if you're signing any agreements. Check small details now to make sure plans run smoothly in the long run.

> Keep your own counsel rather than asking favours from others

Lucky dates
9th, 16th, 21st, 24th

February

An unusually powerful accent on your opposite sign signals a challenging month ahead but this is unlikely to prove daunting. It's the people you meet and talk to that bring out the best in you and enable you to establish potentially helpful alliances for the future. Taking a broad view, it seems that your attention focuses on the lives and interests of other people at this time. The influence of certain persons, either those you are currently in dialogue with or maybe someone you have read about, has a profound effect on your attitude and perhaps sets you in quest of new realms of knowledge. Enjoy the challenge.

LOVE

With such an intensity of planetary energies activating your House of Partners, this is sure to be an eventful month for the romantically inclined. The underlying trend favours your cherished hopes and wishes, but at the same time the situation is rather changeable.

The main problem comes from the fact that you are beginning to feel dissatisfied with an existing romantic attachment but are unable to get your feelings in order. The fact is that you've probably outgrown what has, up until this point, been a relatively steady relationship, and sooner or later the crunch is bound to come.

The real complications come later in the month when a newcomer turns out to have a deep affinity with you. Perhaps you'll realise the truth that you have to be off with the old love before the new can emerge. Trust your deeper feelings, even though they are changing.

MONEY

In a month when the winds of change are blowing strongly, it's likely you'll be faced with a major decision that has a bearing on your finances. Early in the month a direct link between Saturn and Uranus suggests that you need to resolve a dilemma. What it means is that circumstances necessitate a break with an old order in order to optimise future developments. If it's a career choice or a new job offer that's on the cards, being cautious is likely to be a form of self sabotage.

You're in a position of strength, so don't be afraid to stick your neck out.

HEALTH

It's likely that you've been living life in the fast lane for the past few months and are now beginning to long for a bit of breathing space.

Although the demands of other people appear to be rather heavy in February, the fact that Venus traverses a favourable sector of your solar chart gives you something of a lifeline if you're losing momentum. You should definitely not ignore warning signals if suddenly your vitality plunges to a low ebb.

It's an excellent month for leisurely travel, so you'd be doing yourself a favour by taking a break from usual routines.

Lucky dates
8th, 12th, 17th, 28th

March

A pattern of events that's been taking shape since the start of the year comes to a sharp focus during March. New horizons beckon for those feeling adventurous and in need of a change. A shift in your lifestyle is under way and this is largely due to certain connections and relationships that have been established in recent months. In short, it seems that the Fates are somehow shifting the goalposts and pulling you towards a new centre of gravity. It doesn't mean that your current lifestyle is about to evaporate as if by magic, but rather your need for wider experience is felt more intensely. It's time to spread your wings.

LOVE

The general pattern of relationships in your life continues to go through a phase of transformation and re-structuring. In fact these two words give you a major clue to the course of your destiny in 2009.

You are beginning to see that people who previously have been important in your scheme of things fade into the background, while newcomers - in the shape of friends or lovers - become a force for significant change. Even if your love life goes through some rather dramatic ups and downs, the underlying trend is nevertheless in your favour.

What takes place throughout March helps you get your thoughts, feelings and dreams into a much clearer perspective.

Your vision of the ideal lover takes on a slightly different colouring, and an encounter with someone you find attractive later in the month makes you realise that maybe you've been looking in the wrong direction.

MONEY

Avoid being pushed into making any new financial commitments in the first half of the month. The misplaced enthusiasm of other people might be infectious, especially when it comes to get-rich-quick schemes. But be warned that a hasty move now could land you in debt.

From mid month onwards you're in the clear as a highly progressive trend comes into force and enables you to put both personal and joint financial resources on a more profitable basis. Keep your wits about you around the 22nd if you are seeking a bargain, but be sure to steer well clear of gambling and games of chance.

TRAVEL

Be prepared to re-schedule any travel arrangements

you've made for March. Events beyond your immediate control are liable to disrupt a journey and force you to postpone a visit you've been looking forward to. The situation might prove inconvenient at first sight, but it could turn out to be a blessing in disguise.

From a different angle, prevailing cosmic influences favour those involved in research and who take a serious interest in psychology, spirituality and the healing arts. Whatever occupies the central focus of your mind, this is definitely a time when fresh insights dawn and important discoveries are made. If you have a brainwave, stick with it.

Be sure to steer clear of gambling and games of chance

Lucky dates
4th, 9th, 17th, 26th

April

This is a month of abrupt endings and new beginnings. Well, perhaps that's a slight exaggeration. As they say, when the going gets tough the tough get going. What this essentially means is that although certain obstacles are likely to be thrown across your path you'll be more determined than ever to get the better of them - or even turn them to your advantage. Being a Leo, you have tremendous willpower and are able to plug into a deep source of creative energy whenever you feel you need to take firm action. April might not be a totally problem-free month, but you're definitely the one at the controls so enjoy it.

LOVE

If a relatively new romantic attachment seems to be causing you some angst in April, this is no reason to immediately lose heart and call the whole thing off.

If your partner is going through an emotionally wobbly phase, this probably won't be a reflection on you. Just try to be understanding and don't always turn the whole thing into a drama in which you cast yourself as the tragic hero. There's a very simple and ordinary answer to the problem, and all you need do is be there to give support or a shoulder to cry on. By late month such negative features should quickly fade into the background and it'll be as if a new light is beginning to dawn. With Venus voyaging into a more resonant area of your solar chart you can be certain that the coming attractions will warm your heart.

MONEY

If the going does get a bit tough as already hinted, it's in the area of immediate financial interests that you are likely to experience some tense moments. Provided you keep a very firm handle on your existing resources and are not tempted (or panicked) into making any hasty moves, by late month you'll be back on track. It would be in your best interests to devote careful thought to how you organise your personal economy, especially if this involves a business or marriage partner. You may now find that a bit of well-timed strategic cost-cutting gives you a position of greater strength and peace of mind.

TRAVEL

Important messages and journeys put the focus on career and business interests most of the month. There might be some pressure on you to come to a decision around the 25th, but this is unlikely to be a problem if you are well aware of longer-term consequences and how this might affect others.

If you're seeking something more leisurely and fun-loving via travel, prevailing trends coming into force in the final week of April put you in the right frame of mind. Alternatively, someone who promised to pay you a visit several months back (but had to postpone) arrives and quickly puts you in the party mood.

Lucky dates
1st, 5th, 14th, 24th

May

An exciting month lies ahead for you, particularly if you're on the move and are seeking a broader range of experience and self-expression. Psychologically there's an easy flow of energy between yourself and the world, and it seems that what you are aiming at is a creative balance between being a nomad and a sedentary citizen. In other words, if you're feeling a bit cooped up and suffocated by an all-too predictable routine, you now have opportunity, as well as the incentive, to break the habit. You should now consider exploring new horizons in order to do full justice to your natural creative vitality.

LOVE

Vibrant lunar influences in your sign put you in your element as the month begins. Your social life gains added sparkle and draws you into the kind of situation that allows you to really shine.

As both Mars and Venus are woven into the picture, your magnetic appeal is greatly enhanced and guarantees that you'll not be lacking in admirers during May. Amorous attractions are likely to be powerful and instantaneous and this is sure to restore your natural confidence after what has perhaps been a rather difficult emotional transition in recent months.

A chance encounter early on in the month has all the makings of the ideal romance, especially if you are travelling or visiting a foreign country.

Don't worry, however, if everything appears to go quiet after all this romantic excitement. It's just a lull in events! The whole situation suddenly gathers momentum around the 21st and a happy ending is in sight.

TRAVEL

Experience is bound to please and inspire you if a far-flung trip is on the agenda for the coming month. Even if you can manage to get away for just a couple of days, it'll be excellent therapy.

A change of scenery at this time helps you to clarify your mind and renew contact with your inner self. Not only this, but it seems that significant new friends will be made via travel. Don't be surprised if a journey turns out to be an appointment with destiny. Either you'll fall in love with a place you visit, or do the same with someone you chance to meet on your wanderings (as already hinted).

> A change of scenery will help you clarify your mind

MONEY

Difficulties you had to contend with in recent months are now coming full circle, and by the latter half of the month you'll begin to feel that you're getting back on the right track.

Saturn swings into a more positive mode and motivates you to be very organised in dealing with immediate and long-term financial interests. Matters focusing on the need for material stability now occupy your attention and you can expect to see a steady improvement in your income and status from this month onwards. Exercise patience if you are awaiting news concerning a job interview or business venture. This could also be a good time to concentrate on your future financial commitments and make sure all paperwork is up to date.

Lucky dates
1st, 5th, 11th, 27th

June

There might be times during these coming weeks when you feel a sharp clash between the ongoing demands of your work and your need to enjoy the lighter side of life. The fact is that this is going to be a crucial month in regard to your main aims and ambitions, so you'll have to accept that the balance is weighted on the side of work rather than play. There's a dynamic aura around you throughout the month, and with Mars riding high in your solar chart you'll be empowered to get where you want to be - and you'll get there fast! You're under a progressive and successful trend so don't be afraid to go the extra mile in June.

MONEY

Starting with a steady improvement over the past month or two, you can expect the situation to gain a more positive momentum in the coming weeks. You'll now be in a stronger position to structure your finances. Your desire to improve your status, boost your income and be on top of your game will get the right results. Your ability to win friends and influence people works like magic at this time, enabling you to get the recognition that justifies your current level of achievement.

LOVE

Fast-forwarding to late June sees you in a state of euphoria as far as your love life is concerned. Developments over the past month or so come to fruition, and if you're contemplating the possibilities of marriage, the pattern of events favours your hopes and wishes.

There'll be new friends, too, gravitating into your orbit, and in one way or another it seems that the changing pattern of significant relationships will be highly satisfying and personally enriching. Symbolically speaking, the prevailing cosmic pattern suggests that you're on top of the world and riding the crest of a wave right now. The main ingredient in this vibrant state of affairs has a strong flavour of Eros. So altogether it seems you are now in a win-win situation as far as affairs of your heart are concerned. For married Leos it's likely to be a truly memorable month.

TRAVEL

Your mental energies are strongly focused on matters of a very practical nature in the first half of the month. Journeys are likely to be for business rather than pleasure, and it seems there's a rather intense discussion going forward during the second week of June.

A more relaxed state of affairs prevails from the middle of the month onwards, when certain activities that involve you in teamwork and close co-operation with others draw you into the spotlight.

Interests geared to wider social issues and world affairs are under positive trends, making this a prime time for drumming up support if you're campaigning for a cause or involved with a charity.

Lucky dates
7th, 17th, 18th, 28th

July

I t's important to the Leo sense of self-esteem to be able to stand out in some way, or to be original. Where it sometimes all goes wrong is when you try too hard to be original. All you end up with then is an attempt to copy someone else's idea of what originality is supposed to be. In short, what it comes down to in the end is the importance of simply being yourself. You can't get more original than that! This is important now, because in the coming weeks you can expect to be attracting new friends into your orbit, and if such friendships are to be valuable, lasting and genuine any pretence on your part will get you absolutely nowhere.

LOVE

The importance of being yourself rather than an imitation of some media image is of the essence where intimate attachments come into the picture.

In view of the changing cosmic influence there is much to suggest that your most heartfelt hopes and desires are heading for fulfilment. Someone you've been acquainted with on and off for several months is beginning to appear in a more attractive light, and what takes shape in the second half of July transforms a friendly attachment into something much more passionate.

Established ties of love and affection come under an equally promising trend during July. If an important relationship has suffered neglect recently and seems to have lost a vital spark, now is your chance to set the balance straight and do something to show your loved one you really do care. Choose the 19th and 28th for arranging something extra special.

HEALTH

Although you're not likely to experience any drastic blips in your current level of well being, it would be in your interests to go easy around the 7th and 22nd. The lunar and solar eclipses have a direct bearing on matters of health, and if you have been driving yourself hard recently this is where your body is liable to send out warning signals. No worries, of course, if you've arranged to take a leisurely break or vacation at these times; but a continuing attempt to live your life in the fast lane is inviting trouble. Take a break, chill out. You owe it to yourself.

TRAVEL

Not only will you be doing yourself a favour by escaping from usual routines and getting away from it all, but a change of scenery will work wonders for your personal morale. There's a powerful accent on friendship throughout the month, and if you've arranged to take a special journey with a group of friends you can guarantee a great time will be had by all.

If, however, you are seeking a temporary retreat and wish to re-connect with your inner self, the prevailing trend during the third week of the month is decidedly calming and therapeutic. Later in July certain people you meet socially add variety to your life. New friendships will flourish and there's a special emphasis on contacts made in entertainment or sports venues.

> Take a break and chill out. You owe it to yourself

Lucky dates

2nd, 14th, 23rd, 28th

August

A lunar eclipse on the 6th suggests that your feelings towards certain people are beginning to change. It's worth remembering too that perhaps their feelings are changing towards you. There seems to be a lot of two-way traffic going on here, and what it means is that you should be totally honest about certain relationships. This probably won't have a significant bearing on intimate ties, but it could mean that some friends or people you've worked with become less significant in your current scheme of things. If you feel that certain associations are cramping your style, perhaps it's time to address the issue.

LOVE

Romance takes on a rather secretive aura throughout August and what takes shape behind the scenes is destined to put a sparkle in your eye.

But this is not a time to plunge into an amorous affair on the strength of a flirtatious impulse. There's a danger that you'll invite the kind of person who is out to take advantage of your warm-hearted nature into your life. It's a case of not allowing your susceptibility to flattery to get the better of you, as this could turn you into your own worst enemy. Also, steer well clear of the kind of emotional involvement that you know contains all kinds of potential complications and rivalries. Basically you can afford to play it cool, because it seems that when the time is ripe the Fates will present you with someone whose presence feels right. As Venus moves into your sign late month, you won't have long to wait.

MONEY

Financial considerations are high on the agenda most of the month and you can expect to make speedy progress in all areas that call for quick decision and business acumen. Best dates for dealing with commerce and fundraising are the 11th, 13th and 18th, but don't push your luck if an element of risk enters the frame. If you're celebrating your birthday, prepare for unexpected gifts (one of which might be from a secret admirer).

On a more serious level, in the third week of August, timely advice from an older person gives you the solution to a long-standing problem.

TRAVEL

In many ways it's an ideal month for holidaymakers and globetrotters, but if you're hoping for a wild time in exotic places you're likely to end up feeling badly let down. Most favoured are those who seek something slightly off the beaten track and away from bustling crowds. The prevailing cosmic influence inclines you to take a more reflective attitude to life, and attempting to go against this grain is liable to be emotionally exhausting. It's an excellent month for mystically inclined Leos interested in meditation and spiritual growth.

Lucky dates
2nd, 13th, 20th, 27th

September

Don't be made to feel guilty if you're not always going forward and breaking new ground. There are times when it is necessary to go back in order for you to move ahead successfully. It sounds contradictory, but all it means is that perhaps you've left something of yourself behind in the rush to keep ahead of the game. Now that Saturn and Uranus are challenging each other, it seems that there's a need to renew contact with the past in some way in order to keep a sense of inner balance. By easing the pace and taking a more reflective stance, you'll end up making the future a better place. Take a step back and enjoy the view.

LOVE

Venus in your sign ensures harmony and understanding between you and the special person in your life. If there are any negative undercurrents, a little gentle persuasion enables you to clear the air and remove obstacles to your heart's desire.

The best dates to talk over matters that have caused disagreements recently are the 11th and 15th. The message here is that it's best to put the past behind you and stop over-dramatising something that's no longer an issue.

The influence of Venus in September sends out a good vibe to those hoping to meet a kindred spirit. You're very much in the spotlight and socially popular during these weeks. Add to this the magnetic aura radiating from your personality and you simply cannot fail to attract admirers and potential lovers into your orbit.

What's most appealing to you is that romance comes with a touch of glamour. Get ready to be spoiled!

MONEY

You might be faced with an important decision around the middle of the month when a conflict of options forces you to alter your perspectives. If something new is creating tensions because it appears to undermine past endeavours, perhaps it's time to do some serious re-thinking, especially if this ties in with a job offer or a potential career change. If in doubt, take your time and seek professional guidance. It's a case of carefully weighing the evidence and taking a conscientious approach. Once Mercury turns around later in the month, the light dawns and new events point you in the right direction.

TRAVEL

Be prepared to meet with an element of unpredictability in your daily routines from the second week of September

Romance comes with a touch of glamour this month

onwards. In the meantime, be sure to double check things like travel schedules, meetings and special appointments. Also, if you're charged with handling sensitive information, try not to let your attention slip. A small mistake could lead to a major embarrassment and could undo a lot of your careful planning.

You'll need to be patient with relatives and youngsters around this time who are liable to make inconvenient demands just at the wrong moment. Remember to stay flexible and maintain your ability to react in an appropriate manner, otherwise you'll end up a complete nervous wreck! A contact made on a previous trip could help you see the future in a new light.

Lucky dates
7th, 16th, 18th, 24th

October

Events taking shape around mid October give you the feeling that the tide of fortune is flowing more strongly in your direction. After a lull in the action and a feeling that everything had come to a standstill, the pace begins to gather momentum and circumstances give you more room to manoeuvre. Other people play an important part in your life at this time, and a chance meeting could inspire you to change your outlook on life. It's as if someone is building a bridge for you and introducing you to a whole new world of possibilities. All in all, an exciting prospect comes into view so welcome each new challenge as it appears.

MONEY

The message is pretty straightforward as far as your material fortunes are concerned. If a lack of funds has cramped your style over the past year or so, you'll be pleased to know that from now on a steady improvement is forecast.

Saturn, planet of limitation, finally takes leave of the money area of your solar chart towards the end of the month. No doubt you've learned some valuable lessons under this planet and experience has taught you how easy it is to get caught up in a repeating cycle of false expectations. What happens earlier in the month gives you a hint of better things to come.

LOVE

Your experience of romance in recent months has perhaps left you feeling a bit perplexed. Passions were stirred and for a moment you believed that this was the real thing, but then quite unaccountably the flame went dim and all you were left with was a dull routine. Don't despair. The end of this particular tunnel is in sight.

Once Mars pushes into your sign around mid month the flame of love begins to burn more brightly and more steadily. It might not seem so at first, but someone you meet around this time could be destined to change your life and make you realise what real love is all about. Perhaps you've been taking too narrow a view of love, and maybe the influence of media hype has skewed your vision and put you out of touch with your real needs. If a new affair seems slightly off the conventional track, take it as a good omen.

HEALTH

Since late August you probably experienced a fall off in your usual energy and vitality. Maybe you've been working too hard or putting yourself under too much pressure to prove yourself and make your mark on the world.

You would be doing yourself a disservice to attempt to keep up a high level of activity when really an inner voice is telling you to relax and enjoy life.

With Mars coming to the fore around mid month you'll be back on form and you'll be able to cover much ground without danger of burnout. If sport is your passion, you'll now feel confident of scoring a triumph.

Lucky dates
10th, 16th, 20th, 29th

November

The energising planet Mars begins an unusually lengthy transit of your own sign during November, signalling the start of an exciting progressive and forward-looking trend in your affairs. This fiery planet is very much at home in the sign of Leo and therefore you can expect to feel extremely vibrant and positive, both now and for several months to come. What you experience in the coming weeks gives you great self-confidence and empowers you to change your life for the better. It's a time when your actions and initiatives have a powerful impact . You should take care to make sure this doesn't turn into an ego-trip!

LOVE

As Mars is the dominant force, it's likely that romantic experience will become intensely passionate - for better or worse.

Attractions are likely to be powerful, instantaneous and irresistible, and perhaps your friends will think you have gone slightly off the rails. Amorous experience could indeed take you to ecstatic heights, but as Mars wields something of a double-edged sword you might find that the whole thing quickly burns out, leaving you feeling rather bruised emotionally.

It's no good advising that you take a cool and cautious approach to romance in November, because this is definitely not where it's at. The heart may have it's own kind of reasons that the head knows nothing about, and at best a new attachment formed this month could turn out to be more than a passing infatuation. How it finally pans out only time will tell.

One thing's for sure, you'll be feeling confident that this relationship is for keeps. However, beware your heart doesn't run away with itself.

HOME

Matters closer to home suddenly take a higher profile in your general scheme of things. Not only will you be more inclined to focus on domestic and family interests, but this is an excellent month for taking a critical view of your immediate surroundings and seeing where improvements can be made.

The influence of Venus enhances your good taste and gives you an eye for what will and will not look good. So, if you feel that things could do with a makeover, now is the time to go ahead and create the kind of ambience that suits your changing style and will also impress your friends.

TRAVEL

You probably won't be planning to venture far from home in the first half of the month. In fact if travel does enter the frame it's more likely to be other people coming to visit you rather than the other way round.

Any significant journeys you do take are likely to have a strong element of duty rather than pleasure. An older relative, for instance, might need your assistance and you may be obliged to play the role of the Good Samaritan.

Lively trends in the second half of November throw a positive light on educational interests, recreational pursuits and spare-time activities, while a chance conversation late in the month proves lucky for courageous Leos.

> A chance conversation proves lucky for courageous Leos

Lucky dates
4th, 10th, 15th, 26th

December

A pleasant and lively aura surrounds you as the festive season approaches, with new friends gravitating into your orbit and plenty of scope for manoeuvring yourself into the centre of things. It's as if you're tuning into a deeper source of creative energy at this time and will find that whatever you turn your hand or mind to brings successful results. A combination of imagination and enthusiasm enables you to exert a powerful influence in whatever field of endeavour you're currently engaged in. Best of all, Leos interested in the arts, entertainment or sport can expect to hog the limelight throughout the month.

LOVE

There's a feeling of euphoria surrounding your love life as the year draws to a close, with more than just a hint that you're well on your way to realising a dream. What began as a rather stormy romance recently reaches a natural watershed at this time.

If the relationship stays intact beyond mid December you can be almost certain it'll go from strength to strength. However, don't think it's the end of the world if it takes a crash landing and leaves you feeling slightly dizzy. Just put it down to being part of life's rich tapestry, and if you feel you made an idiot of yourself at least you're not likely to do so again.

By late month your self esteem will be intact. Someone you meet during the last ten days of the month gives you the feeling that all is right with the world.

MONEY

Matters of employment are highlighted during the second and third weeks, with every indication of increased job satisfaction and a pay increase. This is an excellent month for younger Leos who are seeking the kind of work that does justice to their skill and potential. If you now feel that you could go one better by improving your credentials you'd be doing yourself a great favour. In the coming months there are indications of new opportunities heading in your direction, so if you wish to boost your chances, prepare the ground now.

TRAVEL

If you planned to break the old routine and do something completely different over the festive week, you're unlikely to be disappointed. Make sure you announce your intentions well in advance if other people are not to feel miffed.

Venus throws a favourable aspect to your sign throughout the month and inclines you to feel more self-indulgent than usual. There should certainly be plenty of scope for expressing your pleasure-loving instincts, and if other people do feel that you're being selfish, well, perhaps that's their problem. It's an enjoyable end to the year.

Lucky dates
3rd, 11th, 15th, 16th

For your fantastic weekly & monthly cash, career and romance and forecasts

Call 0905 515 0042

Starlines are updated every Tuesday. BT calls cost 60p per minute and last about 5 minutes. Cost from other networks may be higher. SP: Eckoh Herts HP3 9HN

Zodiac fact file

Planetary Ruler: Mercury

Quality & Element: Mutable Earth

Colours: Browns, greens

Metal: Platinum

Wood: Ash

Flower: Clover

Animal: Magpie

Gem: Agate

Fabric: Linen

Virgo

august 22 to september 22

January

You might sometimes be described as a stickler for detail and routine, but as 2009 arrives it seems you'll be in a highly enterprising frame of mind and determined to express yourself more fully. Embrace departing from the norm. The changing pattern of planets suggests that you're more determined than ever to get your act together and make efficient use of your creative energies. As Jupiter changes signs early in the month it sets the scene for what could turn out to be a phase of opportunity and expansion, particularly in areas that have a strong practical focus and allow you to make optimum use of your expertise.

LOVE

Prevailing cosmic influences couldn't be much more favourable, both for new romantic encounters and established ties of love and friendship. If you've not had a great deal of luck in love recently you might be pleasantly surprised just how quickly the situation can turn around.

Mars puts a very positive spin on intimate affairs and lovemaking throughout the month, and with Venus holding sway in your House of Partners the chances of meeting a soul mate are on the rise.

You may not be aware of it as yet but sympathetic links are being forged in the early stages of the New Year that could end in marriage. Perhaps it won't all fall into place in the twinkling of an eye, but an unexpected twist of events around the 23rd promises to put you in touch with someone who could be destined to fulfil your desires and change your life.

MONEY

You're in a confident frame of mind and highly motivated to improve your earning powers in the year ahead.

With Jupiter beginning to activate a very practical area of your solar chart, luck and opportunity focus on matters of employment. It promises to be a successful year ahead for seeking the kind of work that allows you to express your best potential and gives plenty of scope for

promotion. What happens in January demands an enterprising spirit, so don't be over-modest about your capabilities. If you see a chance to do a bit of string-pulling to advance yourself, take it!

HEALTH

Jupiter is a key factor in enabling you to reach the peak of well being during 2009, and if you're intent on getting yourself into optimum shape both physically and psychologically, you can be sure of a satisfying result.

Be prepared to take extra care of your health later in the month, when a solar eclipse signals a drop in your vitality and greater vulnerability to seasonal ailments. It might be an excellent month for pushing ahead with practical tasks and furthering your career, but it doesn't mean that you're obliged to work 24/7. Therefore don't tempt fate!

Lucky dates
5th, 7th, 16th, 24th

February

For many born under the sign of Virgo, 2009 could turn out to be a year of destiny in more ways than one. The presence of Saturn in your own sign inclines you to take more seriously the need to find a definite sense of direction. This planet represents the urge to get your act together by taking a realistic view of what is and is not in the realm of possibility, and at best endows you with tremendous patience and staying power. All of this makes February an excellent time for developing and perfecting your skills and gaining greater control over how you organise your life generally. It's time to plan now for a smooth 2009.

LOVE

Recent experience has perhaps caused a change of heart and made you see clearly that feelings can be fickle and the loving touch can become rather claustrophobic.

With Venus eyeballing Pluto early in the month it could mean an ultimatum and a clean break with the past. The sense of freedom regained (or a narrow escape) may surprise you, but there's no need to feel guilty about it.

Amorous passions do have a habit of crashing in on one's life and often leaving just as abruptly. This is no disaster but rather see it as a learning curve. Your attitude to love is undergoing a deep transformation, which means that when you meet the right person (which may be sooner than you think) you'll know instinctively that this is on a different plane completely and puts an end to all doubts.

With this in mind, don't cling on to something you know has gone way beyond its best-by date or you'll miss the chance to meet someone new.

MONEY

Employment and professional activity seem to be the absolute centre of gravity in your scheme of things in February. An expansive and forward-looking trend comes into force, guaranteeing a phase of productivity and progress. Much depends on your energy and initiative at this time, particularly if you aim to manoeuvre yourself professionally into a position of greater influence.

It's a month when your naturally conscientious approach and sense of order stand you in good stead, and ensure that your abilities will certainly not go unrecognised. If a new job offer comes up, waste no time deliberating - go for it!

If you're considering moving, or the end of your fixed mortgage term is looming, now is the time to give it some serious thought.

Manoeuvre yourself professionally into a position of influence

HEALTH

An invigorating trend prevails throughout the month and it's unlikely you'll suffer any ill effects from what could be a high-energy state of affairs.

The only proviso is that around the lunar eclipse on the 9th something might throw you into a rather negative mood. You're advised to steer clear of people who tend to wind you up or bring you down. Don't be insensitive if you feel that someone is genuinely in need of a bit of sympathy. If you're interested in the healing arts and want to improve your expertise and qualification, success will attend your efforts.

Lucky dates
1st, 4th, 12th, 21st

March

The story line this month concerns the way you relate to other people at all levels. You're encouraged to widen your circle of significant contacts and get involved in a more purposeful dialogue with people on your own wavelength. It's a time to sit up and take more notice of what comes up in conversation, what you read in the papers or come across while Googling (has such a word made it into the English dictionary?). Whatever happens, it's a time when your desire to get in touch with the world around you and find out what's really going on enriches your personality, brings fresh inspiration and makes life more interesting.

If you already feel good about a current romantic attachment, there's no problem, but where everything seems to be a state of limbo it's no good attempting to force issues.

Venus, the planet of love, is doing one of those strange orbital reversals. It's a phase of transition that gives you the feeling that your emotional life is at a standstill. It doesn't mean that you have to resign yourself to the lonely hearts club, but maybe you should simply get on with your life and cultivate the gentle art of allowing things to emerge. You don't need to be anxious about making things happen - even if this is the message you're constantly bombarded with via the media.

How about simply seeing what happens? It's a matter of giving yourself some space and letting time take care of itself.

TRAVEL

The influence of other people brings tremendous mental stimulation and helps you to hammer out new ideas and clarify your thoughts.

Discussion, either with another person or within a group, gives you scope for expressing yourself and making good use of your fine critical abilities. If you're involved in education or any kind of intensive learning you're likely to be taking a quantum leap forward during these weeks. Make the best of helpful trends for gathering information, seeking advice and establishing contact with people who share your interests and aims.

At a day-to-day level you'll experience no major problems financially, but when it comes to serious and long-term interests you're advised not to take things for granted.

If you are not entirely in agreement with your partner, it's essential that you spend some time discussing the issues and coming to some form of compromise. It would certainly be worth the time and effort needed to sort out matters such as investments, insurance schemes, pensions, and in fact anything that relates to the need for future stability.

The good news for you is that an added bonus may be on its way later in the month.

Lucky dates
2nd, 5th, 11th, 22nd

April

You'll be wasting your time and energy by trying to push ahead too quickly during April. There will be times when you need to adopt a careful strategy in order to not antagonise others and sabotage your own interests in the process. Even with the best of intentions you're liable to be misunderstood, so if possible aim to keep a fairly low profile and steer clear of any controversial issues. The potentially stressful trend begins to ease after the middle of the month, but in the meantime if the whole world seems to be against you, try not to make matters worse by insisting on your rights while forgetting about your responsibilities.

LOVE

In some ways this is going to be a testing month for relationships, and you'll need to be very honest and self-critical about your own feelings if the situation is to be kept afloat.

Underlying tensions are likely to surface quite suddenly, especially around the middle of the month when there's a danger of minor disagreements turning into an full-blown epic drama.

It's a time when what is true in a relationship will be sifted from what is false, so if a romantic attachment is actually a product of your wishful thinking, don't be surprised if the whole thing promptly dissolves like the morning mists.

It's not exactly an easy prospect, but taking a wider view of the situation, what now seems like a crisis could turn out to be a blessing in disguise. It's as if your inner psyche is sending out signals to break free of the kind of emotional entanglement that's going precisely nowhere.

TRAVEL

The presence of Mars in your opposite sign warns you that it's easy to antagonise other people by letting your critical tongue run away with you.

You are a born analyst and are acutely aware of the foibles of other people, but watch out that this doesn't turn into petty fault picking. This is bound to get you into trouble in the first half of the month, and it'll be no good trying to play the innocent. If you don't entirely agree with someone's opinions or behaviour (or even the way they dress), keep it to yourself.

A word out of place could lead to a total communication breakdown, so be warned!

MONEY

It might not be the easiest of months for dealing with people, but as far as material

things are concerned it's an entirely different picture. Make the most of helpful trends in the first two weeks of April for dealing with matters of a legal or official nature - particularly if you're making a claim and feel you have a good case.

Towards the end of the month you get the go-ahead for a project that had to be abandoned earlier due to lack of funds or poor support. Some serious thinking you've been devoting to a business venture over the past couple of months at last begins to pay dividends. It's now time for you to put the effort in because if you get it right at this point, the future will take care of itself.

What seems a crisis now could be a blessing in disguise

Lucky dates
9th, 16th, 26th, 30th

May

Although you might find it necessary to go over the same ground twice, or you may have to rearrange your ideas if a new project is in view, this is unlikely to undermine your determination to transform your life and achieve your aims and ambitions. With Saturn taking a more positive turn in your sign from the middle of the month onwards it seems that a phase of preparation is coming full circle, and from now on you feel more confident that you're heading in the right direction. Usually routine is not something you kick against, but perhaps you are beginning to realise that it can cramp your style. The door stands open!

LOVE

Both symbolically and psychologically speaking there's been a kind of death and rebirth situation taking shape in recent months, and it's only now that you are beginning to see light at the end of the tunnel. What this means in plain terms is that perhaps you found that you had outgrown a relationship.

For a while all the usual reference points seemed to dissolve and maybe it was a case of being cruel to be kind. Maybe the divorce rate has been rather high among Virgos recently! The good news is that this transition now gives way to something much more positive. Emotionally and spiritually you are reaching a new level of inner maturity, and this is sure to be reflected in your love life from mid May onwards. There's no need to get impatient - just let the dream unfold.

MONEY

Restrictions are easing and a major obstacle is finally overcome. In other words, you can expect both personal and joint financial affairs to take an upswing in the coming weeks. It's an excellent month for overhauling your current economic status and seeing where you can make better use of current assets. Although you might be faced with added expenses in the third week, this is unlikely to make any great dents in your bank balance.

Not only could a welcome pay rise be on the cards, but you stand to gain via an added bonus, rebate, or perhaps a lucky windfall too.

TRAVEL

If possible, make sure that important travel arrangements are made early in the month. At a more immediate level be prepared to make a last minute journey around the 9th, when a relative or friend may need your help.

You'll need to keep a clear mind in the second half of May if you're dealing with matters of an official nature. You are not the type to overlook details, but other people are not so meticulous and are could cause delays. Insist that others say what they mean and mean what they say.

Lucky dates
4th, 15th, 17th, 31st

June

You'll have a distinct impression of sailing out onto calmer waters as the summer solstice approaches. This could work out quite literally in the shape of a pleasant journey at some time in the coming weeks. More importantly, it's the psychological and spiritual dimension of the situation that receives the beneficial influence of prevailing cosmic vibes. Another way of putting it would be to say that a new window on the world is about to swing open for you in June, giving you a view over a much wider horizon. In short, it promises to be a month when your experience of life will be greatly enriched so make the most of it.

LOVE

The popular media version of love seems always to suggest either an ongoing trauma or something like a magic pill that guarantees instant ecstasy.

Thankfully when it comes to real life the situation is never quite as black and white! If it were, then love would be a strange mixture of soap opera and Disney cartoon. This is not to imply that your own love life has run along these lines in the past, but perhaps you are now reaching a level of self-awareness and wisdom that reveals to you how different genuine love is from fantasy and wishful thinking.

If you happen to meet someone attractive in the coming month, chances are that you're on your way to a completely new experience, perhaps something you have at best only dreamt about up to now. What takes place around the 21st June might just hold the key that transforms all your dreams into the real thing.

HOME

Lunar trends throw a powerful spotlight on all things domestic around the 7th. At worst, this could mean that the emotional atmosphere within the family circle is rather sensitive and you'll therefore need to tread tactfully.

If you're a parent and feeling a bit anxious about the behaviour or moods of a youngster, don't jump to hasty conclusions or attempt any direct tactics. A sensitive and sympathetic approach is more likely to have the right effect and reveal to you that really there's nothing to worry about.

At best, you can expect a very welcome visit from an old friend or work colleague that you may have lost regular contact with.

Take the chance to escape from familiar surroundings

TRAVEL

With Venus throwing a pleasant light on travel, it's the distant horizon that exerts a strong magnetic attraction throughout June.

If a business trip is on the agenda, it's the first half of the month that favours your interests. From the middle of June onwards a journey taken purely for the fun of it is sure to satisfy. Even if you had not planned to take a break or a vacation, it could be that an unexpected message from a friend overseas gives you a chance to escape from familiar surroundings for a few days.

Whatever happens, a journey is sure to have an uplifting effect on your spirits.

This could also be a good time to plan a trip for later in the year. Your enthusiasm for discovering pastures new is at an all-time high.

Lucky dates
1st, 9th, 21st, 28th

July

Your ruling planet covers a wide arc of cosmic space during these weeks, and this is reflected in the themes and variations of your own life. More than ever you're motivated to loosen the limitations of familiar routine and cultivate greater diversity in your interests and your social life. Friends, both old and new, are a significant focus of attention and can be relied upon to support your own ideas and objectives at this point. In the latter half of the month your pace of life gathers momentum and there's a heavier demand on your energies. If you're seeking a fresh sense of challenge, then this is definitely your month!

LOVE

Don't expect new romance to arrive in the shape you expect during these weeks. There could be an element of surprise woven into an amorous encounter, and this is bound to be pleasant.

If you find yourself attracted to someone of an ambitious nature or who has an aura of power and authority, take this as a good omen. Your friends might think you're going slightly off your head or being a bit snobbish in your tastes, but the fact is that your instincts are leading you in the right direction. It might not be exactly that you fall in love with your boss, but it could be something similar.

Whatever finally transpires, the month ahead holds some intriguing possibilities for the romantically inclined. For married Virgos, there may be cause for celebration as your partner brings welcome news of promotion and success.

MONEY

Now that you're gaining confidence and have built up a solid foundation of experience, there is no reason why you shouldn't take a more ambitious approach to your career. Getting stuck in familiar routines is a common experience with those born under the sign of Virgo, but for a while now you have probably been feeling restricted. Maybe you're also feeling resentful that other people seem to be getting all the breaks. With Mars pushing into the topmost sector of your solar chart in mid July, initiatives aimed at boosting your status are unlikely to misfire. If you want it, you can get it!

TRAVEL

A journey or message you receive early in the month has a fortunate link with your current aims and ambitions.

There's a friendly aura around you, which guarantees success in any activity that calls for co-operation and teamwork. If you're into local politics, green issues and alternative lifestyles, now is the time to broaden your network of contacts and exchange ideas.

Someone you meet quite by accident around the 16th could end up not only changing the way you think about life, but will also become a very good friend. Altogether, it's an exciting month for making connections.

Lucky dates
8th, 12th, 16th, 25th

Virgo ♍

August

The month gets off to a lively start and continues on this theme throughout the following weeks. It doesn't mean you're about to be plunged into an endless round of frivolous social life - though there will be plenty of scope for having fun and doing your own thing. Between the 11th and 18th you may be obliged to take on extra chores and responsibilities, so be prepared to put your own immediate interests on hold for the time being. As you have a dutiful character by nature, this won't amount to any big deal. On a positive note, it will make you feel highly virtuous and will work wonders for your self-esteem!

LOVE

Meeting the kind of person you can relate to on more than just a superficial level can be quite a tall order in your case. This is because you are by nature a perfectionist and therefore rather particular when it comes to choosing friends and lovers.

This is not usually a problem, and you're rarely in a hurry to commit yourself to an intimate relationship.

The good news for single Virgos is that someone you chance to meet during this month fits your ideal image and answers all your cherished hopes and wishes.

Intriguing developments are forecast, and for those seeking a true soul mate what takes place around the 8th or 17th August makes you realise that sometimes it really is worth waiting for the right person.

Provided your idea of the perfect partner is not totally in the realms of cloud cuckoo land, you can expect to find something very close to your heart's desire over the next few weeks.

TRAVEL

The month ahead offers you tremendous scope for varying your activities and breaking free of usual routines. Your ruling planet Mercury whizzes through your sign and inclines you to be on the move, dabbling with new interests and establishing a wider network of friendly or useful contacts. Travel is likely to be high on the agenda, with an exciting month promised for those in globe trotting mood and those winging away to far horizons. Journeys provide an unusually enriching experience, bringing new friends into your orbit and offering the kind of experience that opens at least one new window on the world.

MONEY

Your confidence is high as career interests continue under a progressive trend and you now feel that things are moving in the right direction.

A major decision seems to be looming during the second week of August, but provided you don't attempt to go beyond your real level of competence a successful outcome is assured. The main thing is to think carefully if a new job offer comes up. In theory it may sound wonderful, but in practice it'll be a different story. If at all in doubt, stick with what you're familiar with rather than jumping in at the deep end for the sake of a few extra quid and a great deal more stress! Instead, invest your confidence in a current project to ensure you're making the most of it.

Think carefully if you receive a new job offer

Lucky dates
5th, 13th, 18th, 29th

www.predictionmagazine.co.uk • *horoscopes 2009* **91**

September

Without wishing to sound over dramatic, there is much to suggest that your life is about to turn an important corner during September. Everything comes to a focus when Saturn makes an exact link with Uranus on the 15th. Symbolically, this represents a tension between the old and the new. Put more bluntly it evokes the image of a demolition job! However, this is no cause for alarm, because when the old building is cleared a new one soon rises. In other words, what takes shape in the coming weeks marks the start of a new chapter in your life, allowing you to break down and break through your old restrictions.

LOVE

It would be a mistake to jump to conclusions or get anxious if a promising new romantic development appears to lose momentum. Emotionally and psychologically it seems that there are subtle readjustments taking shape in the background.

Try to realise that tender plants cannot be forced and the best relationships don't usually follow a pattern of instant coffee and microwave meals. One of the main lessons of wise old Saturn in your own sign is to know the value of time and of the need to build a solid foundation. To expect everything to fall into place in a moment simply leads to frustration and resentment. Once Venus moves into your own sign on the 20th it'll be a different picture as the seeds of doubt are blown to the winds and the flickering flame of love begins to burn with a steady glow.

MONEY

Exercise care and patience if a financial or business venture runs into difficulties in the first half of the month.

Be prepared to hold your horses and do a bit of re-thinking before going ahead with anything too adventurous. The urge to branch out, experiment and diversify your money-making activities will be strong at this time, but it'll be only too easy to misjudge the situation and end up having to back-pedal very quickly. Even Virgos can sometimes overlook essential details, and it is indeed the seemingly insignificant things that could trip you up. If in doubt, try again late month.

HEALTH

People born under the sign of Virgo are naturally attuned to health interests, and this is why the healing arts often have a strong appeal. Under the prevailing astrological influence such interests are likely to gain a more intense focus, and maybe you'll discover within yourself a genuine healing ability.

As regard to your own well being, it's essential that you cultivate a relaxed frame of mind, particularly if the events of September amount to a fairly crucial point in your destiny.

You can rest assured that things fall into place and prove to you that your worries are totally misplaced.

Lucky dates
1st, 11th, 18th, 29th

October

Virgo

What takes place around the middle of October is likely to take the pressure off and give you a wider margin of freedom. After a fairly lengthy phase of hard work and a full agenda, you'll have more space in which to cultivate necessary breathing space, to stand back and congratulate yourself on what you've achieved over the past couple of years. With Saturn now coming to the end of a lengthy sojourn in your sign you can expect to start reaping the benefits from past efforts and find a work/life balance that allows you to be more spontaneous and stylish in the way your express yourself. Enjoy the rewards!

LOVE

The presence of Venus in your sign guarantees harmony and a closer rapport with your loved one. Established romantic attachments reach a more satisfying level and you'll begin to take more seriously the possibilities of a wedding in the not too distant future.

You are now moving away from a phase of being unsure of your feelings, which is something that has perhaps played havoc with your love life until fairly recently. If you feel that you took a wrong turning in the past and ended up in a cul-de-sac, it's unlikely the same thing will happen again. This is where the positive energy of Saturn comes to your rescue. This planet can be a hard taskmaster, and when it comes to personal relationships there may be a few lessons to be learned. But the end result is increased self-awareness and integrity. From now on it's plain sailing all the way.

The presence of Venus in your sign guarantees harmony

MONEY

Any delays and setbacks you experienced in the past month are unlikely to get in the way of progress in the coming weeks. Now that you've got everything sorted out and firmly in place the way ahead is relatively free of obstacles, and therefore you can expect to cover a lot of ground before the month is out. Commercial and business interests are particularly favoured, and your ability to quickly assess a situation, plus your shrewd approach to wheeling and dealing, is sure to pay some real dividends.

Having extra cash in your hand gives you an easy conscience if you feel like a bit indulgent retail therapy.

TRAVEL

Matters of a very practical nature are likely to be the main centre of gravity throughout the month. Prevailing trends give you tremendous motivation to upgrade your knowledge and expertise, and you're guaranteed a successful result if you're taking a test or sitting an exam at this time.

If you believe a lack of qualifications has been the main obstacle to your advancement over the past year or so, you'll now find yourself in a better position to do something positive about it.

With Jupiter gathering an expansive momentum, you'd be doing yourself a great favour by embarking on a course of further study or special training. All the signs suggest you'll meet the new challenge head on.

Lucky dates
4th, 7th, 18th, 20th

www.predictionmagazine.co.uk • *horoscopes 2009* **93**

November

There's something very pleasing about the heavy hand of Saturn having finally lifted from your sign. Although this planet is not completely unfriendly to Virgos, it's likely that over the past couple of years there have been times when you felt that you were carrying a rather heavy load. At best Saturn indicates a constructive trend, making you very determined to get your act together and gain useful experience. Now that new doors are about to open, the efforts you've made in the past stand you in good stead and enable you to make the best of a timely opportunity. The lid is off and you're on your way to achieving your aims.

LOVE

If amorous experience has been something of a shifting sand or a desert over the past year or so, you're now heading for an oasis that will definitely not turn out to be a mirage.

Again, it's the exit of Saturn from your sign that gives a warmer emotional breeze and makes for a more relaxed approach to personal relationships. Married Virgos who have been struggling to stay afloat at a basic material level can expect a marked change for the better from November onwards.

There's especially good news heading your way around the middle of the month, which puts an end to any worries about very mundane (but important) things like housing or your children's welfare. Single Virgos are equally favoured later in the month, when an unexpected invitation or change of routine throws you together with someone who instantly appeals.

MONEY

Your attitude to material affairs takes a very structured direction from this month onwards. Although there's pressure on you to overhaul a current investment or business venture, this is unlikely to prove daunting. It probably won't be a case of downsizing or being forced to adopt a lower-maintenance lifestyle. What it does mean is that you're becoming acutely aware of what is and is not useful in your current scheme of things. It's simply a case of getting rid of excess baggage and knowing what you do and do not really need. Remind yourself that a rich life is not a cluttered life.

HOME

Relatives (and perhaps in-laws) are likely to be a significant focus of attention at various times during the coming month.

You may occasionally be at a loss as to what they want from you, but perhaps this is where your notable organising skills could save the day. Later in the month it looks as if something delightful is taking place close to home. A relative or member of your household announces something that calls for impromptu celebrations, and perhaps an unexpected visitor gives you a chance to catch up on the news and fill in the gaps since last you met.

Lucky dates
2nd, 7th, 17th, 28th

December

You're in a position to take a more easy-going attitude to life, but whether or not you'll be content to go with the flow is something only you can decide. What it means really is that there's no need to get anxious or neurotic simply because the world keeps telling you to be always busy-busy and going forward! There comes a time when the positive needs a bit of the negative in order to maintain a healthy current and avoid blowing a fuse. If you insist on keeping up a frenetic pace, you'll be your own worst enemy. What's more, you'll undermine your ability to relax and have fun later in the month. Take your foot off the pedal.

LOVE

Following a rather busy few months, you now have an excellent opportunity to spend time and establish a deeper emotional rapport with the one you love as the year draws to a close.

As the pressures of work ease and the demands of other people become less onerous, you'll be able to make up for lost time and cultivate a wider margin of quality time devoted to the things closest to your heart.

For married Virgos and those hoping for a wedding in the New Year, prospects suddenly brighten and enable you to see your way to the realisation of your hopes and wishes in the coming year.

From both a material and an emotional point of view, it seems you're heading for a phase of increasing contentment. And it's an equally bright prospect for single Virgos who hope to find a kindred spirit. Events taking shape later month indicate that the Fates are moving in mysterious ways!

HOME

Domestic and family interests benefit under the harmonious vibes of Venus as the festive season approaches. If there's a choice between staying put or spending the latter days of the month away from familiar surroundings, it might be better to go for the former option. The fact is other people will be counting on you to be there to work your usual miracle of organisation. It looks like you'll have a pretty crowded house and be entertaining friend you've not seen for ages. It might be a good idea, therefore, to devote time and attention to giving your immediate surroundings a bit of face lift!

You will now have time to spend with the one you love

MONEY

Prevailing astrological trends suggest a healthy financial base and plenty of available cash to splash out on gifts, goodies or a lavish party.

It's likely that over the past couple of months you've been absolutely determined to build up a reserve fund in order to give the old year a great send off. Whatever the case, it seems that you're feeling more secure in regard to present and future material interests, and can therefore give yourself and everyone else the kind of treat they deserve - without having to face the music (the dance of debt) later on!

A steady rise in your fortunes awaits you in the New Year so enjoy an indulgent December and make the most of the extra cash you've built up over the past couple of months.

Lucky dates
2nd, 8th, 18th, 25th

For your fantastic weekly & monthly cash, career and romance and forecasts

Call 0905 515 0043

Starlines are updated every Tuesday. BT calls cost 60p per minute and last about 5 minutes. Cost from other networks may be higher. SP: Eckoh Herts HP3 9HN

Libra
september 23 to october 22

Zodiac fact file

Planetary Ruler: Venus

Quality & Element: Cardinal Air

Colours: Pale green, pink, blue

Metal: Copper

Wood: Sycamore

Flower: Orchid

Animal: Dove

Gem: Opal

Fabric: Silk

January

There's a feeling of growing optimism for Librans in 2009 and in some ways it could be said that you are astrologically privileged. Jupiter, the planet of luck and opportunity, activates an area of your solar horoscope focusing on creative interests, leisurely activity – and, most exciting of all, luck. It promises to be a year when your desire to develop your best potential and express yourself more fully is no longer felt as an uphill struggle. Of course, much depends on the efforts made on your part and the experience gained in the past, but if you now feel eager to take the world by storm, the Fates will be with you all the way.

LOVE

Of tremendous significance is the fact that Jupiter highlights romantic attachments and guarantees something good is heading in your direction.

Over the past year or two there were probably times when you felt marginalised. What seemed a highly promising relationship simply faded out, and perhaps still you're scratching your head about what happened. By now it seems you have regained your inner equilibrium and are feeling a great deal stronger, both emotionally and psychologically, which is all to the good in view of what's promised. Even better, this could come much sooner than you expected.

Towards the end of January you may decide to make a clean break with what's gone before and do something to pull yourself out of what may have become something of an emotional backwater recently. From now on it really can only get better.

HOME

There's more than just a hint of important transformations taking shape on the domestic scene as the New Year gets into full swing. Quite recently the mysterious planet Pluto has shifted into the 'home sector' of your solar chat, and with Mars in attendance throughout January it looks like the winds of change are now beginning to gather force.

If an element of upheaval enters the frame, there's probably good reason for this so it's not something that will be out of your control. On a positive note, it's likely you'll make a firm decision to push ahead with desirable change now that you are free of any past restrictions.

> *Matters relating to learning are under a fortunate star*

TRAVEL

Many Librans will be increasingly motivated to push the boat out and do something towards improving their knowledge and skills in the year ahead.

All matters relating to education and learning are under a fortunate star throughout the year, and the earlier you get the ball rolling the better it will be.

Those involved in teaching, publishing, creative interests and sports can expect a successful trend, with increasing scope for widening your sphere of influence and making your presence felt.

If a journey, whether local or further afield, is planned, be prepared to make last minute re-adjustments during the third week of the month. You should have plenty of notice so there's not much upheaval.

Lucky dates
5th, 8th, 16th, 30th

February

If you're a sports fanatic, either as spectator or competitor, there's no holds barred in the month ahead! Whatever your special field of interest, there's bound to be something that fires your enthusiasm and puts you in a cheerful frame of mind. All Librans will feel the effects of an unusually invigorating cosmic configuration, so no matter what turns you on it looks like you'll have reason to congratulate yourself. Generally speaking, there's a very positive feeling that the tide of events is carrying you forward and life is sending out all the right signals. It's a positive time so be prepared to pull out the stops and express yourself.

LOVE

In view of the high impact astrological trend, it promises to be a month of intriguing developments for the romantically inclined.

The atmosphere becomes electrical in the second week, and even more so towards the end of the month, when attractions are likely to be irresistible. There is increased potential for turbulence under such powerful and passionate influences. You are usually a cool and well-balanced person when it comes to emotional attachments, but there are times when even you can go over the top. Amorous attachments are liable to burn brightly and quickly burn out, so maybe you shouldn't set your hopes too high at present.

On the other hand, established ties of love and affection go from strength to strength, and for many Librans thoughts of marriage zoom into a brighter focus.

TRAVEL

There's much to suggest that familiar routines are beginning to loosen their hold, giving you increased scope to do your own thing. Your social life gathers a pleasing momentum and the people you strike up conversations with give you much food for thought and encouragement to revive an old interest.

Journeys are highlighted in the second half of February, and whether you're off abroad or simply travelling locally, an element of luck enters the picture. If you're into the arts and entertainment, you can expect to get the right breaks, but keep your wits about you.

MONEY

You're in an enterprising frame of mind early in the month and you get the go ahead for a project that you were obliged to shelve a few months back.

Efforts to improve your financial base and add a lucrative string to your bow are now more likely to meet with success. Although you're advised to avoid taking major risks, it would do no harm to stick your neck out and take a more experimental approach.

Lucky dates
5th, 12th, 17th, 24th

March

The month gets off to a lively start bringing you plenty of scope for fresh initiatives and activities that engage your creative and intellectual energies. A forward-looking frame of mind is sparked off either by information you come across yourself or through the influence of other people on your own wavelength. This gives you a tremendous incentive to widen your field of influence and self-expression. It's as if there's a fresh breeze starting to blow through the windows of your mind, inspiring you to make more valuable use of your spare time and get more purposefully involved in various social affairs and media issues.

LOVE

Your ruling planet, Venus, is now doing an apparent orbital back-step throughout the month, which could make this an emotionally uncertain phase for your love life.

The worst that could happen is that either you or your partner has a complete change of heart with regards the relationship, and you finally agree to call the whole thing off. If something like this does occur, the strange thing is that it'll be completely amicable. You won't be heartbroken.

There will be no hard feelings, and in fact you'll probably remain genuinely good friends. Also, it's unlikely that you will be in any desperate hurry to establish another amorous connection.

This kind of laid-back philosophy is, in fact, a notable quality with Librans, particularly when it's a question of finding the right partner. You know instinctively how to exercise the gentle art of allowing things to happen – and in most cases your instincts lead you to your heart's desire.

MONEY

Occupational and professional interests come under the enlivening influence of Mercury in the second and third weeks, promising a phase of increased productivity and job satisfaction. If however you're not entirely happy with your current set-up, this is an excellent time for looking around for something that would be more in line with your ever-developing potentials. With Mars entering the frame in the middle of March a situation may arise that demands quick action and an energetic approach. This is definitely not the time to let your usual Libran deliberation and indecision sabotage your best interests.

HEALTH

For no apparent reason you may find that your vitality takes a plunge during the second week. Don't attempt to keep up the usual pace if you're obviously feeling below par and your body is sending up an SOS. This is in fact an ideal time to arrange to take a short break, or at least adopt a more leisurely and relaxing schedule.

You don't need to keep pressing on, and indeed at a practical level the situation has a momentum of its own. Although your sense of duty may be particularly strong at this time, there's absolutely no reason to let this work you into a state of mental and physical exhaustion. Take a step back and give yourself a bit of an easier time. You'll benefit from this approach later on in the year.

> Don't try to keep up your usual pace if you're below par

Lucky dates
4th, 13th, 17th, 26th

April

Venus continues retrograde until late in the month, signalling an element of ambiguity in your attitude to certain people. You are perhaps realising that attitudes and feelings change and what once seemed so important to you fades into the background as fresh experience gives you a new centre of gravity. What it all boils down to is that in the coming weeks you're likely to see an unusual number of arrivals and departures. How this works out in real time remains to be seen. But before the month is out it's almost certain that you'll be viewing the world through a different window, and it's one that opens on a brighter view.

LOVE

Although it might be something of a waiting game for those hoping to find their affinity, there's no reason to fall into a state of gloom. You're going through a time of transition and it'll be no good attempting to force issues, even if you are aware of a potential new romance on the horizon.

Time is on your side, so don't think that you've been left out in the cold just because everything seems to have gone quiet. In any case, you probably need breathing space after what was perhaps a rather stressful affair a few months back.

For those planning to take the plunge into matrimony in the coming month, this is not the time to make any hasty moves. If there seems to be an obstacle holding up the process, don't worry. An interesting turn of events late month throws an new light on the situation.

MONEY

Constructive trends in force from the second week onwards give you the incentive to overhaul joint financial interests and bring yourself up to date in areas such as investment, insurance, and credit. If you now feel that you're not making best use of existing resources, waste no time in seeking advice and exploring ways and means to improve your assets. By focusing on details and doing some extra homework, you'll be surprised at the savings that can be made. Whatever happens, don't get into the situation where you allow things simply to drift.

HEALTH

At the risk of seeming to harp on about health, it has to be said that there are a couple of dates when you need to be extremely careful, particularly if you work with machinery or are involved in activities that are physically demanding. If possible, steer well clear of these things on the 6th and 15th, when there's increased danger of sudden accidents due to carelessness.

It seems that Librans are becoming increasingly health conscious and more organised in matters of diet. Your desire to get in better shape is not likely to be just a passing fad.

Lucky dates
4th, 9th, 18th, 25th

May

This could turn out to be one of the most eventful months of the year for Librans! A pivotal date is the 17th when Saturn beings to move towards your own sign. There might not be much evidence of new developments, but nevertheless the forces of Destiny are turning in your direction. From small beginnings something far-reaching is likely to emerge and give a new sense of purpose to your life. Moving from one cycle of life to something new often takes place in darkness, so don't worry if things appear to be in a state of suspense, because what happens late month throws an optimistic light on to your future.

LOVE

The presence of both Mars and Venus in your House of Partners promises to make this a time of stirring encounters. What you experience is likely to present a complete contrast to a previous romantic attachment that finally fizzled out a couple of months back.

Just when you are starting to resign yourself to a sojourn in the lonely hearts club, a chance encounter around the 21st opens your eyes and warms your heart. If there is a downside to these two planets, it is that they often indicate intense and passionate affairs that are, alas, not destined to last. The experience is usually blissful and gives you the feeling that nothing else matters.

Your friends might shake their heads and think you've completely flipped, and in retrospect you will end up agreeing with them. Equally this could mean that you meet the love of your life. Really it's a fifty-fifty sort of thing!

> *A chance encounter opens your eyes and warms your heart*

TRAVEL

If a lengthy journey, either for business of pleasure, is on the agenda be prepared to have your plans thrown out of gear during the second week. People you had arranged to meet are liable to leave you in the lurch and you'll be obliged to improvise in order to keep things from descending into chaos.

Take a sceptical attitude to any high-sounding promises or propositions that are made to you, otherwise you risk ending up carrying the can.

It's better to stick with tried and trusted friends or people you know who are not out to exploit your amenable good nature than to hook up with new contacts at this point.

MONEY

Don't get impatient when dealing with legal or official matters in the second half of the month. It'll be very easy to overlook important details and make hasty decisions simply because it all begins to look impossibly complicated.

If in doubt, make sure you get a second opinion; or better still put the whole thing on the back-burner and let it ride a while. Even if it means foregoing a potentially profitable deal, in the long run you'll be quids in.

Joint financial interests are in focus and you might find yourself in disagreement with your partner, maybe over a potential investment. Don't be hasty and force the issue, it's not worth it. The whole situation falls into place soon after the 31st and you'll be back on harmonious terms.

Lucky dates
1st, 10th, 18th, 24th

June

There's a decidedly lucky feel in the early days of June, so don't be surprised to find that certain aims and objectives take a quantum leap forward at this time. It's a month of opportunity for those who are feeling adventurous and in need of fresh experiences. Deep creative energies are stirred into action, and perhaps something you've been working on for several months suddenly takes on a very satisfying momentum of its own. An expansive vibe ensures that you get the right breaks and your instincts lead you in the right direction. Don't be afraid to back your hunches and aim high as this month you've every chance of success.

LOVE

If a recent romantic attachment survives intact to June, then you can be almost certain that it is destined to be something special. The underlying trend suggests that your emotional learning curve is taking an upturn and that subtle transformations deep within your psyche are changing your attitude to intimate relationships.

Put simply, it means that you are unlikely to plunge into an unsuitable love affair on the strength of a frivolous flirtation.

For married Librans and those hoping to tie the knot, prevailing cosmic vibes give you good support. Any obstacles that have previously stood in the way are due to fade into the background. If money, housing or a previous relationship has been a problem, then it's not likely to be so for much longer. A very happy ending seems to be in sight!

MONEY

As just hinted, any difficulties you may have experienced recently give way to a more encouraging prospect. This is particularly so in regard to jointly held resources and anything that focuses on soundly based and long-term financial interests. The fortunes of someone closely associated with you are on the upgrade, which is something that might call for celebration.

It's an excellent month to get more serious about money, especially if you're aiming to make an investment or improve your domestic lifestyle.

TRAVEL

Communications go with a swing and far-flung travel broadens your horizons in more than the most obvious sense.

The second half of June provides something of a highlight for those taking a vacation. There's a decidedly inspiring dimension woven into your experience, perhaps also a strange feeling of déjà vu.

Journeys are also attended by an element of luck, and perhaps a change of scenery could end up changing your life! If you're travelling for business purposes, success attends your efforts and powerful deals are clinched.

Lucky dates
3rd, 11th, 18th, 30th

July

Libra ♎

The solar and lunar eclipses in July show that the winds of change are on the increase and bring an element of restlessness into the picture. This is not necessarily bad news, though it could mean the introduction of some disruption in your usual routines for a short while. Basically, you're moving into a phase of transition that gives you a feeling that something important is held in the balance. This is where your instinctive good judgement and ability to see both sides of a question stand you in good stead. There's no need for you to panic or force any issues – the answer emerges in its own good time so just be patient.

LOVE

Apart from the first week, when married Librans might not quite see eye to eye with their partner, the month ahead promises some unexpected delights for those hoping to meet their affinity.

Rushing headlong into a love affair is not something you're noted for, mainly because you always unconsciously seek an ideal. It's important that you are able to test the ground before making any deeper emotional commitment, but once you feel easy with another person the whole thing will fall into place.

Be careful in July that you don't spend too long thinking about it, otherwise the other person may feel that you're not really interested. There's more than one way of showing you care, and tokens of affection don't always have to come in the shape of grand displays of emotion or expensive gifts. Just keep it on a friendly basis and don't feel you have to put on an act.

TRAVEL

You couldn't have chosen a more promising time if a far-flung vacation is on the agenda for the weeks ahead. The second half of the month contains exciting potential for those who feel adventurous and are not afraid to wander off the beaten track. It's better still, if a holiday is combined with a sporting interest, like sailing, surfing, or anything that gets your adrenaline flowing. Travel also connects with friendship and social life later in the month, and if you're learning a language or getting more familiar with a different culture, this is a time when experience is sure to enrich your mind and soul.

> It's a promising time for adventures in far-flung places

HOME

There's a slight re-shuffling process going on close to home and perhaps your thoughts are turning towards changing the backdrop.

As already mentioned, the eclipses give a hint of the change to come, and this is most likely to be felt in the sphere of domestic affairs.

If you're a parent with grown up children, chances are that one of them is soon to make a bid of greater independence. Alternatively, you'll become more firmly committed to the idea of pulling up sticks and moving elsewhere.

A new addition to the family could prompt you to relocate nearer to your offspring in order to provide support. Whatever happens, there is more than just a hint that a new chapter of your life is about to begin.

Lucky dates
8th, 16th, 19th, 28th

August

The highs and lows are pretty evenly balanced during these coming weeks, but if you wish to minimise the lows it's essential that you have a fairly well organised agenda and avoid any distractions as much as possible. OK, this may sound a bit unrealistic, especially as you're the kind of person who likes to keep everyone happy all the time. Saying no doesn't necessarily mean that other people are going to think any the worse of you. In fact, by insisting on doing your own thing you'll be even more highly respected. It's time for you to make up your mind about what's important to you. This will help prevent you from feeling used.

LOVE

A conflict of loyalties could generate spikey vibes between you and your partner during the second week and again at the end of the month.

If you're away from familiar surroundings, what you consider to be fun might not suit everyone's tastes, so be prepared to do a bit of tactful negotiation if disagreements are to be avoided. Or maybe you're heavily involved in work projects and preoccupied with external demands and commitments.

This is where your ability to do a balancing act will be put to the test. If you end up being accused of neglect, you'll only have yourself to blame.

For single Librans the prospect of meeting a soul mate is perhaps not the brightest, but be sensitive to what happens around the 8th when a chance encounter could contain hidden formula for romance.

MONEY

With your ruling planet (Venus) riding high in your solar chart the way to success takes a smoother course and opportunities for advancement appear as if from nowhere. It all depends on your own readiness, so keep your ear to the ground if you're currently seeking ways of improving your career and fortunes.

Dates of significance are the 13th and 16th, when you're more likely to get the kind of lucky break that justifies your past efforts. For those involved in the arts and the glamour professions, a quantum leap forwards is forecast.

TRAVEL

Mars continues to throw a positive and energetic light on far-flung excursions, which guarantees a good time will be had by all.

Once again, it's the element of challenge in connection with travel that inspires and brings you satisfaction at this time. Maybe a holiday will turn into something of a spiritual journey and you meet up with someone who makes you see life from a richer and more creative angle.

Doing a mystical take on this situation, it seems that travel holds a key to your destiny.

Lucky dates
8th, 17th, 24th, 27th

September

Whatever you're aiming to achieve, the ball is in your own court if you wish to make best progress between September and the end of the year. The current pattern of events has an energising influence and provides you with fresh motivation, so it's unlikely you'll be doing your usual indecisive act if a new door opens for you. Although there might be a few tricky decisions facing you in the coming month, this is unlikely to be a major stumbling block. Lateral thinking and your ability to approach things from alternative angles finally gets you well ahead of the competition. You're on course to finish the year on a high.

LOVE

In previous months amorous experience has perhaps been something of a non-starter, and by now you are beginning to wonder what exactly it is you're getting wrong. The answer is probably staring you in the face, and by a slight readjustment of perspective you may suddenly realise that a kindred spirit has been circling in your orbit since the start of the year.

Cherished hopes and wishes are likely to materialise in unexpected and mysterious ways, and you'll end up kicking yourself for not seeing sooner that the person you've been looking for is perhaps someone you meet nearly every day.

Alternatively, it could be a friend who quite unknowingly provides the connecting link that leads you to your heart's desire. Established ties of love and friendship come under the harmonising influence of Venus, so now is your chance to make up for lost time. If you've lost contact with someone recently, now is the time to get back in touch.

TRAVEL

You'll need to act quickly if you're hoping to settle an agreement or finalise important negotiations. With Mercury turning retrograde in your own sign on the 7th, procrastination is sure to create endless delays and complications – which is precisely what you don't need at this time.

If you feel that someone is deliberately holding things up, don't be afraid to confront the issue and insist that what you want is action now rather than vague promises. Later in the month be prepared to seek confidential advice if you're unsure of your rights regarding claims and benefits.

MONEY

Your motivation to push ahead with important aims reaches a new level of intensity in the coming weeks, enabling you to break new ground and make a positive impact on the world.

Efforts to improve your status and boost your earning powers meet with success, so don't be afraid to act boldly if your career or a business venture is reaching a crucial stage. The main thing is to keep an open mind, rather than allowing old ideas to restrict your vision.

The fact is that some lucky opportunities are likely to present themselves soon in an unexpected and rather unconventional manner, so make sure you keep your wits about you!

An outstanding loan you made some time ago may be repaid to you, replenishing your funds for future investment.

> Efforts to improve your earnings and status meet with success

Lucky dates
1st, 7th, 16th, 26th

October

I t'll be only to easy to get distracted, waste your time and end up precisely nowhere, so be sure to keep your mind on what's most important to you during the coming month. A progressive energy comes into force empowering you to translate ideas into action and realise your aims and objectives. Your attitude to life takes on a more serious tone during October as Saturn shifts into your sign, which means wasting precious time and energy in the pursuit of frivolities is off your agenda. This doesn't mean that all the fun is about to disappear from your life, but rather that you are getting more fussy about the company you keep.

LOVE

If your love life has recently been surrounded by uncertain feelings, everything is about to come into clearer focus. In fact this is a time of seemingly miraculous transformations, and by late month you'll hardly believe your luck!

Once Venus enters your own sign on the 14th you'll begin to feel that all your birthdays have come at once, though it would be unwise to jump to conclusions on the strength of a chance encounter.

The real beauty of this situation is that you don't need to get anxious about making the right impression. There'll be a natural magnetic aura around you, which guarantees you'll not be short of admirers. When Venus links up with Jupiter at the end of the month you'll begin to realise that the past is now behind and it's plain sailing from now on.

TRAVEL

All activities that involve you in team work gather a progressive momentum. Not only do these activities enable you to find a wider field of self-expression, but more importantly you'll have the ability to win friends and influence people in ways that cannot fail to bring success. The urge to get out of a rut and explore a range of interests has an unexpected spin-off in terms of a renewed sense of purpose. Socially you're more popular, and psychologically you'll be more confident.

MONEY

What takes shape early in the month helps you get a clearer take on a fairly long-standing financial blip. You'll get the distinct impression that your luck is changing and you are able to steer things in the right direction without a juggling act to keep your head above water.

With Jupiter switching to a more positive key on the 13th you can expect all financial and business interests to gather a more expansive momentum from then onwards.

Luck and opportunity are likely to be more in evidence, giving you the feeling that at last you're getting it right.

Lucky dates
7th, 13th, 16th, 29th

November

Now that Saturn is firmly placed in your own sign your sense of direction and purpose becomes far clearer and your determination to establish your credentials takes on a more serious tone. Although this planet has a rather sombre reputation in astrology, this is mainly because it signifies a time when you need to get your act together. What this means is that experience obliges you to get real and to keep your feet firmly on the ground. Saturn is well placed in the sign of Libra, and the next year or two mark a phase of personal growth and material attainment. Knuckle down and focus on what it is you want to achieve.

LOVE

Over the past two or three months you probably noticed that amorous experience took a turn for the better. Whereas previously you had begun to think that your good angel had deserted you, you now realise that there's some truth in the saying that the darkest hour is before dawn.

If you're still hopefully seeking your affinity, then it doesn't look as if you'll have much longer to wait. What takes shape in the first week of November contains all the makings of a fairytale romance.

There's a touch of glamour surrounding a romantic encounter as Venus links with mysterious Neptune. It might seem quite unreal at first and give you the impression that you're being written into a dream sequence. Are you simply seeing everything through rose-tinted spectacles? Well, maybe. However, in the final count it seems that your dreams are about to materialise!

MONEY

A helpful trend ensures that cash flow takes a smooth course and there'll be plenty left over for a bit of self-indulgence. Your fortunes are on the upgrade and this is helped greatly by an added bonus, a lucky windfall, or maybe a very generous gift. For commercially-minded Librans it's a good month for cultivating useful contacts and taking a more diverse approach.

If you simply want a good price for something you wish to sell or trade in, now is the time to take action. If you're a keen collector of objets d'art your efforts are likely to unearth genuine treasures at the right price. Attending an auction or fair will prove fruitful.

> There's a touch of glamour surrounding a romance

HOME

The changing pattern of events during the second half of 2009 indicates that you are now feeling a great deal more confident about going ahead with major changes in your life.

This is especially important in regard to improving your domestic background, and now that Saturn is the dominant feature you can expect to make good progress in all to do with property and housing.

If your current home life is cramping your style, now is the time to do something about it. If you're house hunting this month, a property that you may have previously discounted, perhaps on price, could come back into contention.

Whatever you decide to do, a combination of luck and determination enables you to get the result you're looking for so go for it!

Lucky dates
3rd, 6th, 18th, 26th

December

Changes taking shape over the past few months reach a more definite watershed as the year comes to a close. Not only will this bring a more relaxed feeling to Librans, but it also seems that you are moving into what could be an unusually creative chapter of your life. Psychologically you are now reaching a new level of inner integrity and maturity and this will be particularly evident in the way you approach your main aims and objectives in the year ahead. The bottom line here combines a clearer vision of what you really want, the determination to achieve it, plus an element of luck to help you on your way!

LOVE

It promises to be a lucky month for the romantically inclined. A twist of fate throws you together with someone whom you feel an immediate rapport.

Dramatic encounters are forecast over the festive season, when it looks as if you'll be in great demand socially as friends both old and new gravitate into your orbit. Don't be surprised if someone you've known on a friendly basis for several months turns out to be a passionate admirer. What seemed rather nebulous suddenly comes into clear focus, so be prepared for some flattering revelations before the month is out.

The cosmic energies radiate with warmth on ties of love and affection, ensuring that an optimistic aura surrounds you as the New Year approaches.

HOME

A lively accent on domestic and family affairs suggests a whole spate of visitors coming and going, especially in the first half of the month. You'll need to keep your arrangements flexible in order to minimise any inconvenience and potential aggro.

Relatives could prove demanding and there'll be times when you feel that others are taking you too much for granted. Although the situation calms down from mid month onwards, don't leave anything to chance if you're hoping to get through the festivities without your nerves unravelling. Above all, beware of gatecrashers on the 28th!

MONEY

A powerful element of luck enters the frame in December. A project you've been working on for several months is brought to fruition and you're likely to find yourself in a position to do a bit of strategic restructuring in regard to financial and business interests.

Certain limitations that you've been battling against loosen their hold, leaving you free to update your objectives. Now that you can see your way ahead clearly you'll be in an optimistic frame of mind, and your generous mood won't be out of place later in the month!

Lucky dates
2nd, 6th, 11th, 22nd

For your fantastic weekly & monthly cash, career and romance and forecasts **Call 0905 515 0044**

Starlines are updated every Tuesday. BT calls cost 60p per minute and last about 5 minutes. Cost from other networks may be higher. SP: Eckoh Herts HP3 9HN

Scorpio

october 23 to november 21

Zodiac fact file

Planetary Ruler: Pluto

Quality & Element: Fixed Water

Colours: Dark red, brown, black

Metal: Iron, steel

Wood: Redwood

Flower: Anemone

Animal: Scorpio

Gem: Jasper

Fabric: Tweed

January

2009 promises to be a year of significant change and new beginnings for Scorpio! A phase of uncertainty and transition comes full circle, giving clearer focus to your aims and interests. Although you might not see much evidence of major change early in the year, everything seems poised to steer you in a new direction and give you the opportunity and incentive to enhance your lifestyle, broaden your outlook and enrich your personality. Things might seem to be in limbo throughout January, like you're simply treading water, but the Fates do sometimes move in mysterious ways so don't be disappointed at a lack of action.

LOVE

Love and luck are closely intertwined as the New Year gathers momentum. Your social life continues to figure prominently in your scheme of things, and no doubt this will give you greater scope for making friends and perhaps meeting someone who really turns you on.

A twist of events and a chance encounter could prove an eye-opener later in the month; and if you are sceptical about love at first sight, this is where you might have to adjust your views!

An unusual pattern of astrological trends gives a magic touch to amorous experience during these early weeks of the year, so if your love life has been in the doldrums recently this is where it does a turnaround. The only proviso is that if you cling to the past it'll be like standing in your own shadow where you are unable to see a new light dawning.

HOME

The transit of Jupiter through the 'home area' of your solar chart, beginning early in January and lasting most of the year, signals a phase of expansion and enrichment in domestic and family interests. Prospects are favourable if you're thinking of a change of residence in the year ahead. The expansive nature of Jupiter could mean that you begin to feel restless as domestic arrangements are cramping your style.

The good news is that your fortunes are on the up and your motivation to improve and enhance your living space is given a kick start.

TRAVEL

Journeys and meetings go swimmingly until the 11th, but from this date onwards be prepared to accommodate the unreliability of other people and be sure to have a suitable plan B ready and waiting.

In the final ten days of the month, journeys may have to be cancelled or postponed due to circumstances beyond your control. There's no need for you to be dashing around all over the place. Take it easy, give yourself breathing space and get life in perspective. Try to enjoy any lengthy journeys - they can be very relaxing!

Lucky dates
5th, 13th, 19th, 23rd

February

What makes 2009 particularly interesting for Scorpios is that the subtle energies of transformations are gathering force. The pattern of events will somehow manoeuvre you into a situation where a break with the past becomes your best option. However, there's no need to be alarmed at the prospect. The fact is that you are feeling increasingly motivated to make changes and are not afraid to create a certain element of disruption if the end result is geared towards a more satisfying and creative lifestyle. It could be said that you are being offered a chance to get out of a rut and break the habit of a lifetime.

LOVE

Recent developments have probably given you a completely different take on romantic needs and desires.

Someone you met recently has made you realise that perhaps you have been undervaluing yourself in the past. Now you're faced with the inevitable result that your love life has been caught in a cycle of disappointment.

The underlying pattern of change coming into force suggests an upswing of your emotional learning curve and a feeling of being more secure within yourself. All of which adds up to a brighter prospect as far as amorous experience is concerned.

What happens in February enables you to get in touch with your deeper feelings and find someone who answers to your real needs.

Existing relationships now put down deeper roots, so if you're planning a wedding now is the time to take the plunge and name the day. Don't just say you really care - show it!

MONEY

The theme of new beginnings puts an interesting light on financial affairs and especially on the way you make money.

Prevailing trends are particularly favourable if you work for yourself or are aiming to take a more independent line in pursuing your career. The early months of 2009 show an unusually fortunate and expansive trend for those who work from home or who wish to be more home-based in their work-style.

Financial affairs are now closely woven with long-term and soundly based interests, with property likely to be riding high on your list of priorities from this month onwards.

HOME

Having just about every major planet in the lower sector of your solar chart, it seems that matters closer to home become an intense focus of attention at this time.

At an everyday level you can expect a great deal of activity within the home and family circle. You'll certainly have more than your usual quota of visitors - some welcome, some perhaps not so welcome.

Be prepared for minor emergencies around the middle of the month when electrical gadgets are liable to go on the blink. Make sure you have contact numbers of plumbers, computer technicians and other services on hand! This is also a good time to check your insurance and warranties are up to date.

Property is riding high on your list of priorities

Lucky dates
2nd, 12th, 16th, 25th

March

Although there's no such thing as a magic wand to wave away all your problems in an instant, it certainly seems that you are finally breaking through the shell of a situation that has put you under some restriction in recent months. Whether this has to do with finances, your career, domestic affairs or health, you can expect to experience a freeing up of blocked energy systems as the Spring Equinox approaches. You mustn't worry if certain interests need to be laid aside for a while. Much now depends on sorting out your priorities, cutting back on any inessentials and cultivating a necessary breathing space for yourself.

LOVE

If your love life has been languishing in the shadows, don't despair! From mid month onwards you're heading for something that stirs passions and makes up for lost time.

If it's going to happen it'll happen quickly, so be prepared for dramatic developments. It's the invigorating influence of Mars that provides the key to amorous experience, and at best you can expect to meet someone who gets through to your soul and makes you feel one hundred percent. The only proviso is that with Mars there is an increased potential for going completely overboard emotionally and simply frightening the other person away by your overwhelming intensity. It's hard to say just how this will eventually pan out, but there is much to suggest that a new romance will finally settle down on the positive side of the equation.

MONEY

Your attitude to finance takes a rather serious turn during March and you'll be more determined than ever to put your assets on a more secure and productive foundation. A steady improvement in your fortunes is indicated which gives you greater confidence in regard to any new enterprises that you have in mind. Make your best efforts in the second half of the month if you're embarking on a project that carries an element of risk, but don't be afraid to stick your neck out if you are presented with new opportunities. Be patient, however, if you're considering a new job or career change.

HEALTH

There might be times during the first half of March when your energy level is inclined to dip and you find it hard to keep up with the pace of life. Don't let this worry you, but take it as a sign that perhaps you've been driving yourself too hard lately and are in need to some time out. Quite simply it's a matter of getting the work-life balance sorted out.

It's time to stop and reflect on the fact that it is possible to become a slave to your own activity and forget that there's more to life than the eternal grind of getting and spending. Yoga or meditation could work wonders at this time!

Lucky dates
4th, 13th, 24th, 26th

April

Although you might be impatient to get a new project up and running, be prepared to hold your horses and do a bit of lateral thinking in the first half of the month if you are to avoid future obstacles. A conflict between the old and the new seems to be putting a block on your creative energies, but from the middle of the month onwards it looks as if the situation takes a sudden leap forward. The urge to develop and express your special abilities intensifies, and if you're aiming to make your mark in areas such as sport, athletics or entertainment, it's your own initiative and will power that will carry you through.

LOVE

Amorous affairs continue to gather momentum under the passionate influence of Mars. In some ways this could be a testing time for existing romantic attachments, but if the relationship can get through to the end of the month you can be pretty sure that love is on the right track.

If tensions are bubbling over, watch out for possible confrontation around the 6th and 15th. If it all seems to be about to go pear-shaped it would be a mistake to jump to conclusions or let your suspicious nature get the better of you.

By checking out your own motives and being completely honest about your feelings, problems can be resolved. It might be that your emotionally demanding and possessive tendencies are generating hidden frictions, so try to head this off before the situation goes into a chain reaction of negative meltdown! Just remind yourself that love isn't a package deal.

TRAVEL

The presence of Mercury in your opposite sign from the 9th onwards helps you to establish contact with people on your mental wavelength. A lively exchange of ideas during the third week helps you to clarify your thoughts and stimulate your imagination. It's an exciting month for those engaged in educational activity, business negotiations and public relations. The influence of other people proves highly inspiring, so it'll be in your interests to cultivate mental flexibility and an open mind if you are to benefit from the current trend. Don't be put on the defensive if your views are criticised.

MONEY

Occupational and career interests appear to be in a state of limbo until late April, but don't let this cause you to lose any sleep.

The whole thing is likely to resolve itself quite naturally and in its own good time, so it'll be a waste of nervous energy trying to force issues. There are times when it's better to ease off and see what emerges, rather than be too proactive. You'll be doing yourself a great favour by taking this apparent lull in proceedings as an opportunity to get things in clearer perspective.

A welcome message you receive later on in the month has a positive and perhaps quite unexpected impact on your finances. Enjoy the windfall!

> **Don't be defensive this month if your views are criticised**

Lucky dates

2nd, 12th, 17th, 29th.

May

Matters of a practical nature occupy the greater part of your time and attention during these weeks. An important project you've been working on since the start of the year reaches a crucial turning point during May, and what takes shape around the middle of the month enables you to restructure your main aims and objectives. Not only will experience you've gained in the past provide you with a tremendous advantage, but you'll also have plenty of support from people who are in a position to further your interests. A person of mature years is likely to be important in your scheme of things later on in the month.

LOVE

At first glance the astrological trends appear to push romantic interests completely off stage. Maybe it's because you're so obsessively involved in work or other practical interests that affairs of the heart are not in the forefront of your mind.

If love does enter the frame, it'll almost take you by surprise and appear in circumstances where you least expect it to happen. A likely scenario is that a newcomer at your place of work holds the key to your heart's desire. Although you may be too busy to notice at first, it seems that the scales will suddenly fall from your eyes around the 21st. You may think that the kind of thing you read about in novels can never happen in real life, but experience is about to prove to you that fiction is never entirely divorced from fact. It's a month when romance blossoms in what is usually considered an unromantic setting!

MONEY

Do your best to settle outstanding debts and finalise business agreements in the first week. Attempting to cut corners, do things on the cheap or procrastinate over minor problems is definitely to be avoided if you're not to be lumbered with added expenses later on. Be especially conscientious in regard to joint financial resources during the second week, and don't be naïve when it comes to verbal promises and agreements.

Make sure you get things in writing, or seek professional guidance if you are considering changes to your finances or a new business venture.

HOME

Matters closer to home continue to flourish under the beneficent influence of Jupiter. There's much to suggest that domestic affairs are the major focus of satisfaction during most of 2009, and what happens later in May is likely to confirm this prognosis.

Restrictions are dissolving and your improving fortunes are giving you a more positive feeling about upgrading your living space or going for something that gives you more room. If it's a case of getting a foothold on the property ladder, luck is on your side!

Lucky dates

9th, 11th, 19th, 29th

June

Don't get too hung up if you are obliged to take a back seat in the month ahead. Being a Scorpio, you are inclined to get envious and resentful if others seem to be stealing all the limelight or if you feel neglected and unappreciated. All it needs is a bit of clear thinking to make you realise that the world is not in conspiracy against you or that other people are deliberately trying to get one over on you. Take it easy, try to be more centred within yourself, because this is where your real strength comes from. If you stop worrying and concentrate on getting on with your own life, things will eventually fall into place.

LOVE

The presence of both Venus and Mars in your House of Partners makes this a star month for intimate relationships! It would probably be unrealistic to say that everything is coming up roses, but you can certainly expect something out of the ordinary that appeals to your intensely passionate nature.

The potential for mad infatuation may be high, but equally you could meet a genuine soul mate; someone you can relate to on more than just a superficial level. Scorpios are not the easiest of people to please when it comes to amorous attachments, and this is because it's hard to find someone who can understand and respond to your deeper feelings and emotions. Often you end up feeling misunderstood and become cynical about finding happiness in love. However, in view of prevailing trends, the chances of finding the right partner are looking good.

The chances of finding the right partner are good

MONEY

Both personal and joint financial interests are due to gather a satisfying momentum from the second week of June onwards. A fairly longstanding problem is finally resolved and perhaps an old debt cleared. Whatever happens, you'll have more leeway for spending on the things you like.

Powerful solar forces in the third week of the month signal a feeling of optimism and a more relaxed approach to longer-term money matters. If you're married or are working alongside a partner, what takes place at this time is sure to have a positive impact on your fortunes. By late month you should be feeling decidedly solvent!

HOME

A feeling of increasing contentment surrounds home and family affairs throughout the month. Now that your fortunes are on the upgrade, you'll have more incentive to make the kind of changes that up to now have seemed like distant dream.

An unusually powerful accent on domestic and property interests makes this an ideal time for taking decisive action if you're looking for a more spacious abode or wish to give your home a complete makeover.

It's time for a spring clean and perhaps to turn your attentions to redecorating.

It's in this area that your creative energy and imagination can be used to best effect, so time to stop thinking about it and realise your dreams!

Lucky dates
6th, 9th, 21st, 28th

July

As a Scorpio, admitting defeat does not exist in your universe, and whenever you are faced with a problem or a challenge it brings out the best in you. You certainly have an uncanny ability to draw upon a deep source of strength and energy when the occasion demands, so it's unlikely that even the most difficult encounters will prove daunting. Fact is, certain obstacles or opposition may test your strength and endurance in the first half of July, but a calm and rational approach enables you to pull a potentially difficult situation back into line. Reacting defensively is not where it's at, so don't rise to the bait!

LOVE

It's a month of surprising developments for romantically inclined Scorpios. What begins as a light-hearted flirtation might quickly develop into a fiery passion that stirs you to the depths. Well, perhaps that's overstating the case.

With both Mars and Venus coming together in a decidedly erotic zone of your solar horoscope, it's certainly a prime time for intense lovemaking! Now, without wishing to throw cold water on this scenario, it has to be said that the emotional temperature may be a rather unstable equilibrium. This means that although the situation makes you feel higher than high, the whole thing is likely to burn out quickly and leave you with a feeling of vertigo. If you already have an established partner things can only get better. A break from usual routines brings you closer together.

MONEY

By joining forces with another person and pooling ideas you may find that you come up with an interesting formula for increasing your earning potential. Keep your ear to the ground for new ideas and be prepared to take seriously something suggested to you by a friend or colleague. You could be heading for a genuine breakthrough if seeking a more independent way of making money, for instance by giving a more productive slant to your creative abilities.

The pattern of events has the effect of rousing your enthusiasm and making you more determined than ever.

TRAVEL

This is one of the best and most fortunate months in the year for long-range journeys, either for business or simply for the fun of it (in fact you might be able to mix the two).

The old saying that travel broadens the mind couldn't be more apt at this time. Visiting unfamiliar territory and being in contact with alternative cultures can greatly enrich your experience and bring tremendous inspiration.

Travel is closely woven with destiny this month, so don't be surprised if a journey has the effect of changing your life.

Lucky dates
3rd, 10th, 16th, 30th

August

The pattern of eclipses during the previous month and into August signals an important turning point in your life. It's as if several threads are being drawn together enabling you to bring a project to completion sooner than you anticipated. New interests are likely to grab your attention, thanks to the influence and encouragement of friends or information that you discover quite by chance. A conscious effort to transform yourself and your circumstances may have surprising and very positive results. In fact, you might discover hidden talents within yourself. Altogether it's an exciting month of intriguing possibilities.

LOVE

Romance beckons on a far horizon in the coming weeks, so if you're taking a vacation in a far-flung and exotic corner of the world there's every chance that you'll meet the love of your life.

In the meantime, if a recent amorous attachment left you feeling rather bewildered, you'll be pleased to know that a much more harmonious and satisfying prospect now comes into view.

This isn't to suggest that a relationship that emerged in the previous month or two has been a total write-off. If you're still on good terms, there's a much better chance that it'll go from strength to strength. Otherwise, it would be a kind of self-sabotage to cling onto an affair that is obviously past its sell by date.

Don't despair if you suddenly find yourself in the lonely hearts club - it'll probably only be a temporary stay. The suggestion is that at some point in August a journey presents you with the key to love.

TRAVEL

You're guaranteed a delightful month ahead if you arranged to get away from familiar territory. Even if a journey is something of an impromptu event, it has all the makings of a truly memorable experience.

As already suggested, the romantic potential is high; but equally it could be that you fall deeply in love with a town or country you happen to visit. There's something connected with travel that makes a deep impression on you at this time and may inspire you to embark on a deeper spiritual quest. However, if you're simply seeking fun, a good time will be had by all!

MONEY

Make the most of progressive trends if you are aiming to upgrade your investments, embark on a joint business venture or go ahead with a major property deal.

Provided you spend time organising priorities and laying a solid foundation, this is an excellent month for strengthening your economic base and making better use of your resources.

A fortunate combination of shrewdness and luck enables you to realise your objectives, but you should be especially wary of anyone who approaches you with too good to be true promises and get-rich-quick schemes. It's very unlikely that they will succeed. A sense of realism is what gets you results at this time, so keep things true and get wise!

> A journey in August presents you with the key to love

Lucky dates
4th, 8th, 13th, 24th

September

Yo'll be in an adventurous and forward-looking frame of mind throughout the coming month and perhaps inclined to get impatient with anything or anyone who stands in your way. Your urge to broaden your horizons is stronger than ever, and whether you're aiming to upgrade your technical skills, improve your image, further your career or take an important journey, you'll not be short on energy and inspiration. Whatever occupies the central focus of your mind and aspirations, you'll have a clear vision of the direction you wish to take and the motivation to carry you forward. It's a positive time for making solid plans.

LOVE

Established ties of love and friendship come under favourable trends most of the month, but if you're single and hoping to meet your affinity you'll need to be patient.

A brighter prospect opens for those considering a wedding in the near future. Now that certain material obstacles are becoming less daunting you'll feel more confident about making big decisions and long-term commitments. Perhaps you've been through a phase of doubt and uncertainty in recent months and maybe a little despondent about what you want from life.

This rather negative trend changes quite radically from September onwards and you'll be pleasantly amazed how quickly a situation can turn around. Scorpios often finds it hard to trust life, but the events are about to lift your spirits, boost your confidence and renew your faith in the power of love.

TRAVEL

Whether it's for a holiday or other reasons, far-flung travel is a vital ingredient in your destiny in the weeks ahead. Even if there's no immediate prospect of a journey, the situation can change quite abruptly, so don't be surprised if you find yourself zooming off to far horizons before the month is out. Your longing for freedom and fresh experience is high at this time, making this an excellent month for taking a break and doing something completely different. Physically, mentally and spiritually, a change of scenery is the best therapy if you've been feeling a bit jaded and uninspired lately.

MONEY

Career interests and professional aims are unlikely to present you with any major obstacles. The way ahead takes a smooth course and you'll be in a better position to call the shots and do a bit of strategic manoeuvring.

Persons of influence are well disposed towards you and your efforts have not gone unnoticed. If it's a promotion or a pay increase that you have in mind, don't be afraid to ask. Being a Scorpio, your gut feelings are usually a safe guide, so trust your instincts.

Lucky dates
4th, 13th, 22nd, 29th

October

Your motivation to do your own thing and develop a wider margin of freedom and independence is very much in evidence at present. Provided this does not cause you to act recklessly and impulsively you can do much to bring about positive change. It's a question of weighing things up carefully and not losing sight of what is and is not a realistic option. With Jupiter gathering a more positive momentum from this month onwards the winds of change are gathering force, and there is more than a hint that a new chapter is about to open. Try not to get impatient - time is now on your side so use it to develop new ideas fully.

LOVE

There are times when the main obstacle standing in the way of your amorous hopes and wishes is yourself! Being an emotionally complex character you are rather hard to please, which is why your experience in love often ends up as a battle of wills.

Recent experience has perhaps made you a little more aware of the ways in which you tend to sabotage your own interests and end up in a downward spiral of emotion. What takes place during October will make you realise that someone out there really does hold you in high esteem and loves you deeply.

It's time to stop getting so wound up in your own unfounded imaginings, doubts, fears and suspicions, and to get real. The realisation of a dream is probably staring you in the face, and all you've got to do is open your heart and let it be - no strings are attached and there is no hidden agenda!

Someone out there holds you in high esteem

TRAVEL

After several small but irritating delays you'll get the go-ahead for a project that's been on the launch pad for several weeks.

If you've been doing battle with legal red tape, you'll finally be in the clear from the 10th October onwards, but in the meantime be careful not to overlook details. Matters of a private and confidential nature need careful handling around the middle of the month. If in doubt there's no need to waste time and money on professional advice. A sympathetic friend is likely to be much more helpful and enlightening. A change of routine late in the month adds sparkle and throws you into congenial company.

HEALTH

Lunar trends early on in October incline you to be hyper-sensitive to surrounding influences. It's essential that you steer clear of people who are liable to irritate you or make you angry.

There's also a danger that your health may suffer due to the heavy pressures of work that you've had to cope with recently. If at all possible, try and take a short break from your usual routines and simply chill out.

A more invigorating energy kicks in from the middle of the month onwards and you'll be feeling much stronger and ready to meet any fresh challenge that life decides to throw in your direction.

Use the down time to plan ahead for the festive season as much as possible as by late October you'll be really fizzing!

Lucky dates
5th, 12th, 21st, 28th

November

Life presents you with a kaleidoscopic pattern of experience in the coming weeks and there will be times when the pace of change could leave you feeling quite dazed. Birthday celebrations will be something special, and it's likely you'll be meeting up with friends from the dim and distant past. The prevailing cosmic picture presents a good omen for the whole of the following twelve months, and once again there's the underlying theme of an exciting new chapter about to open for you. Events taking shape from this month onwards enable you to put the past behind you and raise your expectations into 2010.

LOVE

One thing's for certain, it's going to be an unusually eventful month for romantically inclined Scorpios. If mistakes have been made in the past and your hopes have come to nothing, a welcome change for the better puts you on a completely different track.

What takes shape soon after the 8th could be quite overwhelming emotionally and you probably won't believe your luck. It could be that someone you've admired from a distance for several months suddenly comes into a much closer orbit, and it won't take long for you to get acquainted. What's most gratifying and surprising is that you discover the attraction has been mutual and that at last you begin to feel that you've met a genuine soul mate.

Psychologically it seems that a phase of personal growth comes to fruition and is reflected in the quality of relationships from now on.

TRAVEL

You'll be on good form mentally most of the month, so make the best of stimulating trends if you have something to discuss or a message you wish to get across. If you're looking for a new interest to add an extra dimension to your life, now is the time to make inquiries, follow up information and get in touch with the kind of people who can put you on the right track. It's an excellent month for all educational pursuits, so if you've been limited by a lack of qualifications or skills, don't waste any more time telling yourself how wonderful life could be. Go for it!

MONEY

This has all the makings of an unusually progressive month, especially for putting business and commercial interests on a more streamlined footing.

A combination of imagination and innovation provides the key to success, so don't be afraid to experiment and try out new ideas. With Mars riding high in your solar chart it's your own energy and initiative that gets the kind of results you're aiming for - and fast!

An exchange of ideas and information late in November enables you to boost your assets, and if you're shopping around for a bargain, a friend puts you onto something good.

Lucky dates
4th, 15th, 16th, 26th

December

Scorpio | ♏

An element of the unexpected enters the frame early in December and suddenly you'll find yourself moving in different social circles. A chance encounter has an inspiring influence and you're encouraged to revive one of your much-neglected talents. It's as if you're plugging into a deeper source of creative energy that brings a new sense of purpose. You might have noticed in the past couple of months that certain limitations have eased, enabling you to realign your aims, hopes and objectives. A new dimension of experience opens up and brings an exciting prospect for the coming year. What a great way to end 2009!

LOVE

Everything seems hunky dory for you as far as amorous experience is concerned. Compared with how you felt at the start of the year, the situation you now find yourself in seems a world away.

Emotionally and psychologically you are reaching a new level of inner wholeness and integrity, though perhaps you feel you had to go through the mill in order to attain it.

The old astrologers used to describe the sign of Scorpio as the 'battleground of life', and this is perhaps because you can sometimes be extra sensitive to deep currents of feeling and emotion.

It usually takes you ages to find the kind of partner who is able to respond to you in a way that makes you feel completely secure within yourself. Eventually, and after much trial and error, you generally land on your feet.

This is perhaps the story of your love life during 2009 - and it may come complete with a happy ending.

MONEY

With the festive season approaching there's usually trepidation about how to keep afloat financially. In view of prevailing trends the demands on your bank balance are not likely to amount to any major traumas. In fact, it looks as if you'll have plenty of spare money to give yourself and everyone else a real treat.

Cash flow looks decidedly buoyant throughout the month and this is helped greatly via a special bonus, pay increase or lucky windfall heading your way around mid month. What's more, it seems that your partner or a member of your own family circle is also feeling very flush at present!

HOME

With Jupiter and Neptune in cahoots later in the month, the festive week holds in store

some unusual surprises for Scorpios. A likely scenario is the arrival of an unexpected and highly welcome visitor. Whether he or she comes dressed as Santa Claus is beside the point; but it'll certainly be something of a blast from the past!

Someone who did a sudden disappearing act several years back is likely to renew contact with you at the last moment, and a happy reunion adds greatly to the festive atmosphere of merriment. Looking further ahead to 2010, it's good news as these powerful planets promise increasing good fortune and much contentment for the coming year.

> Cash flow looks buoyant throughout the month for Scorpios

Lucky dates
1st, 7th, 11th, 30th

Sagittarius
november 22 to december 21

For your fantastic weekly & monthly cash, career and romance and forecasts

Call 0905 515 004

Starlines are updated every Tuesday. BT calls cost 60p per minute and last abo 5 minutes. Cost from other networks may higher. SP: Eckoh Herts HP3 9HN

Zodiac fact file

Planetary Ruler: Jupiter

Quality & Element: Mutable Fire

Colours: Purple, Autumnal tints

Metal: Tin

Wood: Oak

Flower: Hydrangea

Animal: Horse

Gem: Amethyst

Fabric: Velvet

January

Sagittarius ♐

Temperamentally Sagittarians are the kind of people who prefer a fairly open-ended approach to life. In other words, you don't like to feel too confined by circumstances or to be caught up in a narrow routine. Although you will be obliged to narrow your focus and deal with things at a very practical level early in the New Year, it doesn't mean that you're about to be bored to distraction. Patience will be needed and you might feel a bit miffed at not being able to get ahead with something more interesting. By accepting certain limitations at present you'll have far more freedom to manoeuvre later on.

LOVE

The situation for single Sagittarians may seem rather flat and uneventful early in the New Year, and it'll be no use attempting to breathe new life into a romantic affair that's going precisely nowhere.

Prevailing astrological trends suggest that you are going through a transitional phase when everything appears to be in a state of limbo. It could be that you are generating a lot of unnecessary angst by languishing over past experience, but really you'd be doing yourself a great favour by getting rid of excess emotional baggage. Simply listen to your deeper instincts, which always urge you to break free of old ties and give yourself a clean slate.

As Venus joins up with Uranus later in the month you'll suddenly realise that it's time to put the past behind you and move on. A radical decision you make will work like magic.

A radical decision you make will work like magic

MONEY

You'll be in a businesslike frame of mind when it comes to dealing with financial and practical affairs throughout January. Demands on your resources are heavier than usual and you'll need to keep major priorities in focus if you are to avoid making mistakes. Don't be afraid to push ahead this month with new projects and take fresh initiatives if you're intent on boosting your earning potential.

The only proviso is to avoid extravagance and not to let yourself be conned into spending a large amount of money on impressive equipment you don't really need. Don't fork out more than you need to just to impress your friends either!

HOME

Domestic and family affairs run smoothly under the gentle sway of Venus throughout January. Well, that's the theory anyway. If in reality you find there are underlying tensions within the home you'll find it quite easy to restore harmony and create a more co-operative atmosphere.

If you're a parent, now is your chance to bridge the generation gap and cultivate a closer rapport with your offspring. A family outing will work wonders for bonding.

Later in the month there's a chance that relatives or neighbours will threaten to disturb your equilibrium, but you need to keep calm, stay detached and refuse to get drawn into arguments that are really not your concern.

Adopt a low profile and reserve your strengths.

Lucky dates
3rd, 7th, 16th, 24th

February

After a fairly quiet start the pace of life gathers momentum during February. In fact there'll be times when you'll find it hard to keep your act together, and maybe you'll wish that you could be in two places at once! Forewarned is forearmed, so make it a firm policy to stick to what's most important and try to avoid unnecessary distractions. It'll be only too easy to lose the thread of your main purposes, so be prepared to take a firm line with people who are inclined to make inconvenient demands or who seem to think that you're some kind of miracle worker. Make time for yourself even when catering to the needs of others.

LOVE

After a fairly lengthy phase of wandering in the wilderness, you'll begin to see signs of an improving climate from this month onwards. This applies not only to amorous encounters but also to social life and friendships.

Lively trends put you in a gregarious mood and more inclined to get out and about. There'll be greater scope for enriching your circle of contacts, and through someone you meet during the third week romance begins to beckon. Perhaps a friend will introduce you to someone whose immediate appeal sets your heartstrings twanging. However, don't expect love to blossom all in a moment, like someone is about to wave a magic wand or give you a bewitching love potion.

If something (or rather someone) special is destined to enter your life in the early months of 2009, much depends on your good sense of timing.

TRAVEL

By taking a proactive approach you can do much to make life more varied and interesting. As already suggested, this is going to be an action-packed month with more than enough to keep you on the move, so it's unlikely you'll be stuck in a rut! Travel is high on the agenda, even though you might not actually be going far from familiar territory. It's more likely that you'll be clocking up a high mileage because you have a full diary of meetings, appointments, invitations and visits. Whatever happens, there'll be plenty this month to satisfy your need for fresh experience and mental stimulation.

MONEY

Don't get complacent about money and business affairs early in the month. Much depends on keeping a fairly tight control on the situation if you're to avoid undue expense.

Once Mars takes leave of the money area of your solar chart on the 4th you'll soon begin to feel that you have a firmer handle on your immediate financial interests.

Although recent events have forced you to restructure things on a practical level, this has certainly not proved disastrous for you. On the contrary, it means that you're in a position of greater strength.

Lucky dates

4th, 8th, 13th, 27th

March

Jupiter's movement around the Zodiac gives a clue to where opportunities are most likely to arise. It also indicates how such opportunities will be used (or abused). As Jupiter is your ruling planet it has added significance, and throughout 2009 you are likely to find that enrichment of life comes in the shape of new ideas, or meetings with people who stimulate your mind and make you see things from a broader angle. You might also find that a relative, perhaps even a close neighbour, plays a rather fortunate role at some point in the proceedings. In March you'll discover that a change to your usual routine proves lucky.

LOVE

In the weeks ahead experience will teach you that love can be rather fickle. This is nothing that you won't be able to handle, and in fact it could be your own changeable feelings that introduce an element of uncertainty.

The presence of Venus in a romantic area of your solar chart throws a potentially pleasing light on amorous attachments, and taking a longer view the prospect appears highly attractive.

Venus switches to one of those apparent reverse movements early in the month, and what it means for you personally is that a romantic affair is about to go through an important transition that will either make or break the relationship in question.

Much depends on being honest about your own feelings rather than trying to keep up appearances. However, it would be a mistake for you to force issues or jump to conclusions. Be patient and be prepared to give it a fair chance.

TRAVEL

The pace of life continues to gather an exciting momentum, with special highlights forecast around the 4th and 13th.

A message you receive could call for a quick change of plan and a journey taken at a moment's notice. Whether this has to do with immediate business issues, social interests or spare time activity, there seems to be an element of luck written into the script at these times. In one way or another you can expect that a journey, visit or chance encounter stirs up your mental energies and enables you to make the kind of on the spot decision that could change your life.

HOME

It's essential that you don't lose sight of matters closer to home during March. Your social life and other activities will keep you on the go, which is something you'll relish at the start of March. However, from the middle of the month onwards you're advised to devote more time and attention to domestic and family interests - otherwise you can expect the atmosphere to get very tense.

Even if you live alone, neglect or carelessness in regard to your homebase could lead to problems. Check electrical appliances for faults before they arise. On a more positive note, an element of disruption may be justified if you decide to push ahead with a property deal or wish to give your home a makeover!

> A chance encounter stirs up your mental energies

Lucky dates
4th, 13th, 22nd, 31st

April

With Mars and Saturn at odds with each other early on in the month you're advised to slow things right down and stick to familiar territory. Not only might your health be put in jeopardy by keeping up the break-neck pace of recent months, but there's also a danger of upsetting someone close to you. An element of change and disruption may be hard to avoid in view of prevailing cosmic trends, and much now depends on taking a mature attitude and keeping a firm handle on what's most important. If you're feeling bored or unappreciated at work, hang in there rather than losing your cool. The situation will soon improve.

LOVE

It would be in your best interests right now to adopt a policy of non-interference and let a romantic affair develop in its own good time. If it all fizzles out by late month, it won't amount to a huge melodrama. It's more likely you'll end up feeling that you've had a narrow escape!

In some ways this is a month when any naivete concerning intimate relationships is sure to leave you feeling a bit deflated. Although you're unconsciously always seeking the ideal romance, you may have to realise that in the usual course of experience what you end up with is anything but ideal. Don't lose heart. Once Venus begins to smile on you again later in the month something more in line with your deeper wishes and desires is likely to emerge.

There's a hint that you'll be given a second chance to get acquainted with someone you met briefly earlier in the year.

HOME

This is likely to be the most significant month in 2009 for Sagittarians who are aiming to pull up roots and move to a new address. The underlying theme suggests a break with the past, or the end of a chapter followed by a new beginning. The situation may be disruptive, perhaps stressful at times, but it seems you'll be firmly in control of the situation and can expect everything to fall into place by late April or soon afterwards. If you're into DIY, be extra careful around mid month and be prepared to admit defeat and call in the experts if it all goes terribly pear-shaped!

MONEY

You'll need to exercise patience if your work situation or income leave much to be desired.

It would be unwise to rock the boat at present so make the best of what you've got. You'll only be wasting emotional energy by complaining that your career is in the doldrums or that you've become a prisoner of dull routine. OK, so you're feeling a bit restless. This is quite normal for a Sagittarian. The good news is that this rather frustrating scenario is due to give way to something more exciting, and it's the experience you're gaining now that will finally prove a genuine asset.

Lucky dates

4th, 9th, 16th, 24th

May

So far this year progress has probably been rather slow and in some ways life has been an uphill struggle for you. It's likely you've been obliged to shoulder added responsibilities and push your own interests into second place. From the middle of May onwards you'll begin to see light at the end of this particular tunnel, as pressures ease and obstacles fade into the background. Your creative energies are about to be given a kickstart as changing events bring fresh encouragement and enable you to get back in control of your own destiny. It's a month when your past efforts finally begin to come up with the goods.

LOVE

Amorous experience is liable to reach a peak of passionate intensity in the coming weeks and attractions will be irresistible and instantaneous. Well, if you think this sounds too good to be true, at least suspend your scepticism until later in the month when events are likely to make you see things differently. It promises to be a magical month if you're hoping to meet someone who has the answers to your heart's desires.

Stirring encounters are forecast as both Venus and Mars come together in an area of your solar horoscope that the old astrologers entitled the House of Courtship (these days we'd say lovemaking). Anyway, you get the gist of what's implied here! It all points towards the kind of scenario that you usually associate only with daydreams, but it could turn out to be a time when you learn some excellent lessons in the arts of love.

TRAVEL

If possible, try to deal with urgent matters relating to business and travel arrangements early in the month. With Mercury doing a bit of backpedalling from the 7th May onwards, other people are liable to be elusive and unreliable, and you'll find minor misunderstandings could leave you carrying the can. It's no use getting uptight if an awkward change of circumstances obliges you to rethink plans or postpone an important project.

This could in fact give you much-needed breathing space that allows you to reorganise your thoughts and get a clearer take on exactly which direction you wish to take in the future.

Events later in the month present you with a lucky break

MONEY

Material and practical interests are under an easier trend from the middle of the month onwards. After a rather slow pace and a feeling of uncertainty it looks as if your main aims and ambitions are about to take a turn for the better. It might not amount to a quantum leap, but at least you'll begin to feel that things are moving more steadily in the right direction.

Activities that engage your creative energies show interesting financial potential at this time - which is good news if you're aiming to push a spare time activity into a more professional bracket.

Events later in the month present you with a lucky break. Be sure to watch out for low value investment opportunities as it's not always the biggest risks that pay out.

Lucky dates
2nd, 10th, 21st, 26th

June

Now that Saturn is taking a more positive direction you can expect that the going gets easier and you can trust that the Fates are giving all the right cues. If you've done your homework and built up a solid basis of experience over the past year or so, you'll definitely be in a position to manoeuvre things to your advantage from this month onwards. Whatever you are aiming to achieve, this is where you begin to feel a greater sense of empowerment. Provided you feel confident in your abilities and are not tempted to go beyond your level of competence, your efforts are about to reap a rich harvest. Enjoy the rewards!

This is not a month when you can take too much for granted, particularly if a romantic attachment is fairly new. To put it rather coldly, this could be a testing time when you'll find out if feelings really are mutual.

Under prevailing cosmic trends it's likely that your love life has lifted you to the heights of euphoria and bliss. There's no reason why this pleasing scenario shouldn't continue, but you might find that there's a noticeable change of temperature around mid June. This is when rose-tinted spectacles are liable to crack and you're brought back down to earth with an uncomfortable thud.

Perhaps it's all been a mad infatuation, and maybe you've deliberately chosen to ignore what a friend has pointed out. At best, however, it's likely that after the initial high you now begin to discover that love is more than simple lust.

A steady improvement in your fortunes is forecast from June onwards, and this does not just mean financial improvement. There is much to suggest a welcome change in your work situation. The presence of Saturn in the top sector of your solar chart favours those who aim for a position of greater authority. It's the experience and knowledge that you've gained in the past that stand you in good stead.

If you're dissatisfied with your present employment, now is the time to do something positive about it and go for what you want.

TRAVEL

Now that you are free from last month's fiasco you'll be able to get things back on track.

The presence of Mercury in your opposite sign in the second half of the month ensures a quick and positive response from others - particularly if business agreements and negotiations are a priority.

During the third week a journey brings you in touch with people and places that have an inspiring influence. It's even better if you are taking a far-flung trip or vacation.

Lucky dates
3rd, 7th, 18th, 30th

July

What you experience in July is likely to set the pattern for important developments over the next six months or so. With Saturn gaining momentum it looks as if you'll be giving serious attention to very practical matters such as employment, career and other aims that are pivotal in your scheme of things. It's as if you're being empowered to give a more definite shape to your lifestyle and will be more determined than ever to push ahead with longer-term aims and ambitions. Saturn's negative and frustrating elements can be avoided by adopting a more realistic philosophy and knowing your limits.

LOVE

This is perhaps the most auspicious month in 2009 for those taking the plunge into matrimony. If this is something you envisage for a later date, it's likely that events taking shape during these weeks help to dispel your doubts, remove obstacles and make you feel confident about finalising plans.

Established couples are especially privileged in view of prevailing astrological influences. From both an emotional and material angle a feeling of increasing harmony and contentment surrounds you at this time. If there are underlying tensions, this is a prime time to address the issue, maybe have a heart-to-heart talk and establish a deeper level of understanding. It's a bright picture too for singles, with promising encounters forecast around the 8th and 19th. What seems like a flirtation may be destined to change your life, so expect the unexpected!

MONEY

The eclipses in July warn you not to take any risks and to make sure you have a reserve fund in case of unforeseen expenses. Provided you stick with a realistic policy and avoid get-rich-quick schemes, you can be sure to land firmly on your feet. Keep your wits about you if a contract is under consideration or you wish to realign your investment portfolio. Jointly held resources are brought into focus and might need attention at some point. No major traumas are forecast, but you can do much to head off problems by taking your time and staying within the realms of the possible. This is not a time for unrealistic expectations.

Promising encounters are forecast for singles in July

TRAVEL

Around the middle of the month an unexpected message throws your plans out of gear. You should be prepared for some last minute reshuffling of plans if an old friend calls you up or needs your assistance.

A journey or visit around this time will add a touch of the exotic to your usual agenda. You'll have the chance to re-establish old contacts and catch up on all the news. Something that's been a mystery to you for ages may finally turn out to have a pretty ordinary explanation after all.

Basically, this seems to be a month when information that comes to light is precisely that - enlightening!

Knowledge is power so take this new found information and use it to your advantage.

Lucky dates

2nd, 10th, 19th, 29th

August

A situation may arise in the first half of August that puts you in a quandary. Should you abandon an existing project for the sake of something that offers greater reward but which contains an element of uncertainty? Or should you stick to familiar ground and take a more laid-back attitude to life? It all depends on what's at stake, but if you're a fairly free agent you'd be asking for regret to let an exciting opportunity pass you by this month - even more so if this involves a journey overseas or the chance to push a major ambition on to a different level. You are by nature an adventurous soul, so make the best of it!

LOVE

You're advised to tread carefully with your loved one during the third week, when there's potential for conflict and disagreement over something of a very practical nature.

If you've been acting selfishly recently this is when you'll get to know about it in no uncertain terms. You'll only have yourself to blame if a relationship suffers. Do something to show you really care early in the month, and be prepared to reflect more deeply on the effect of your own behaviour on the person closest to you.

Meanwhile, romantic spirits who hope to find a dream lover are heading in the right direction in the third week. If a journey or holiday is on your agenda, this could provide you with a passport to bliss. But be careful not to rush into a situation where an obvious rival is lurking in the background.

TRAVEL

There are indications that you'll be revisiting a place that puts you in a nostalgic mood around mid month. This could coincide with the renewal of an old friendship and perhaps the revival of a mutual interest. There's a subtle energy of transformation coming into force during these weeks and it'll be through links with the past that changes could be sparked off. It's an excellent month for those interested in tracing their roots and ancestry. This could end up taking you on a real journey of discovery.

MONEY

Ambitious and career-minded Sagittarians can expect welcome developments under prevailing trends.

Mercury joins forces with Saturn, making this a prime time to give serious attention to upgrading your special skills, improving your qualifications and perhaps doing a bit of strategic string-pulling.

Financially the prospect looks good, so if you're aiming to boost your earning potential, trust your instincts and be ready to act quickly. You might not be about to make an instant fortune, but your determination and sense of realism will enable you to cover a lot of ground.

Lucky dates
6th, 13th, 16th, 20th

September

Sagittarius ↗

Compared with recent weeks, Sagittarians will find the going gets much easier throughout the coming month. Now that Mars has taken leave of your opposite sign, pressures ease and relations with everyone around you will be much improved. Any differences of opinion are now resolved and obstacles that have stood in the way of your progress fade into the background, leaving you with more room to manoeuvre. Instead of feeling like you're doing a balancing act and being obliged to dance to other people's tunes, you'll now find it easier to get your own act together and regain your real centre of gravity.

LOVE

A journey or invitation enables you to forge sympathetic links with kindred spirits, especially when Venus is strongly activated around the 7th and 16th. Romance beckons on a far horizon, and if you suddenly feel a magnetic attraction towards someone of a different nationality you can take this as a good omen.

It could even be that the object of your desires is visiting from overseas.

The proverbial holiday romance is a pretty obvious scenario, but this is unlikely to be something that's here today and gone tomorrow; out of sight out of mind. On the contrary, in view of prevailing planetary trends there is more than just a fifty-fifty chance that you meet a long-term soul mate on your travels.

In one way or another, all close ties of love and friendship somehow benefit via a change of routine and a change of scenery. There's a honeymoon feeling in the air, so you should make the most of it this month!

MONEY

Your determination to improve your earning potential and career status begins to have a positive and satisfying impact from this month onwards. Both personal and joint financial interests are under a progressive trend, which makes this a prime time for taking fresh initiatives and giving serious attention to long-range issues such as pension schemes, investments, loans and mortgage arrangements. The only proviso is to steer clear from obviously risky ventures and keep investments on a relatively modest scale if you're to avoid getting too deeply into the red.

TRAVEL

As already hinted, travel has a highly romantic flavour in the month ahead. Apart from the obvious significance of this

term, it could also mean that you are liable to fall in love with a destination you visit or perhaps read about.

Being a Sagittarian you have a natural affinity for far away places, and often dream of what it would be like to live far from your place of your birth. During September you'll be particularly sensitive to the charms of foreign countries, so perhaps if you're taking a far-flung vacation it'll end up changing your life. Well, at the least, it will prove highly inspiring and spiritually exhilarating. If you haven't planned a trip, it's time to get down the travel agents and make that booking!

> Love and friendships benefit from a change in routine

Lucky dates
7th, 11th, 12th, 29th

www.predictionmagazine.co.uk • horoscopes 2009 **131**

October

Your ruling planet, Jupiter, gathers a more positive energy from the middle of October onwards. After several months of hard slog and of having to run faster simply to stay on the same spot, you should soon begin to feel that things are moving forward. On an everyday level you'll be able to make your life more convenient, and instead of having to improvise or muddle through as you have done in previous months, you'll find it much easier to arrange things to suit your own purposes. The good news for Sagittarians is that you're able to break with old routines and introduce a feeling of greater freedom into your lifestyle.

LOVE

Both friendships and romantic attachments are highlighted in the second half of the month, but in the meantime don't jump to conclusions just because someone attractive smiles at you or says hello.

Astrologers often describe Sagittarius as flirtatious and fickle, so if you wish to avoid getting a reputation for playing loose it would be in your interests to stay cool. Allow things to take a more natural course, with maybe a little gentle encouragement. Once Venus changes signs on the 14th you're likely to feel less insecure in your feelings and more certain that a mutual rapport is real.

Someone you've been on nodding terms with for several months may appear in a more attractive light, and a chance meeting with this person late this month promises the fulfilment of your hopes and wishes.

MONEY

Over the past couple of years the dominant influence of Saturn has increased your motivation to improve your abilities and establish sound credentials. There may have been times when the going got tough and you felt that various commitments were cramping your style. Now that this planet is moving on you'll begin to realise that the hard slog has been very worthwhile. What this means to your financial and career status is a steady rise in success. The sky might not as yet be the limit, but you can expect to feel more confident about future prospects.

HOME

The shift of Saturn also takes the lid off various restrictions that have forced you to make compromises in domestic arrangements over the previous two years. Although there are indications of change and disruption in this area, by late October you'll begin to get a firm handle on the situation.

A long-standing difficulty relating to property or family issues is finally resolved, giving you much more room to manoeuvre when it comes to improving and enriching your living space. Welcome news concerning a relative or member of your own household is forecast later in the month.

Lucky dates
4th, 10th, 13th, 29th

November

Events that sometimes lead to major changes in life are often hardly noticed at the time, and it's only in retrospect that their significance is seen. This is an apt description of what's about to happen in November, when the Fates are weaving threads behind the scenes. It's during the third week of the month that you're likely to get a hint of what's going on. It could be that a chance meeting or certain information that comes to light sparks off a new way of thinking and eventually leads you to make a decision that changes the direction of your aims and objectives. Basically it's a month for developing a new vision.

LOVE

Love is likely to move into the shadows from the second week onwards and there may be an element of secrecy connected with new romantic developments. This is not to imply that you're about to get tangled up in a clandestine affair, though it has to be said that there is some danger of this around the 19th!

It could be that you have a very ardent but secretive admirer and perhaps you'll hear something through the grapevine that flatters your vanity. Maybe you simply prefer to keep your most private and personal affairs under wraps, rather than blazoning it to the world. At best, it's a month when amorous experience gains an added dimension and puts you in touch with your deeper feelings. Provided you make an effort to resist any temptation to venture on dangerous emotional ground, it's a time when your dreams will be realised.

TRAVEL

Matters of a private or confidential nature need discreet handling in the first half of November. Information might be a bit misleading, so try not to ignore details even if at first glance they seem to be trivial and irrelevant.

If you feel that someone is being evasive, insist on clarity. With Mercury in your own sign from the middle of the month onwards, communications at all levels gather a more positive momentum, and if something has been a source of puzzlement or worry to you in recent weeks all will be revealed. The company you're drawn into later in the month gives you a chance to air your views and develop a lively dialogue.

> There's a danger that over-working will take its toll

HEALTH

Lunar trends at the start of the month advise you to take greater care in matters of your health. You'll probably be feeling rather sensitive around this time and could be liable to over-react if someone appears to be criticising you.

There's a danger that over-working will finally take its toll. Even if this does not appear to be having a negative effect physically, it could mean that you feel ratty and appear to be operating on a short fuse. Perhaps this is your cue to do something positive about getting your work-life balance in better alignment.

Later in the month be prepared to play the ministering angel for a friend who is feeling under the weather. It could just be a case of making yourself available to talk when needed.

Lucky dates
5th, 10th, 23rd, 26th

December

It looks as though you will be in popular demand as the festive season approaches, which is bound to have an exhilarating effect and put you in the right mood for the coming merriment. The presence of Venus in your own sign most of the month ensures pleasant and congenial interaction with everyone you encounter at a day to day level. As you're a naturally companionable person and a born raconteur, you'll have ample scope for self-expression in the coming weeks. Altogether it looks as if you'll be in your element and drawing a whole new bevy of friends into your fascinating orbit. Enjoy being the centre of attention this month.

LOVE

Venus is, of course, the planet of love, so it's likely that December is going to be a special month for romantics.

Intriguing developments are forecast during the first week, when a secret admirer suddenly makes an ardent declaration of undying love. Don't be surprised if this turns out to be a proposal of marriage. At first you might find it hard to take this situation seriously, but by the third week you'll realise that something special is taking shape.

For those already married or in partnerships, the gentle influence of Venus enables you to establish a more intimate rapport with your loved one. Make sure you're in agreement about arrangements for late month, otherwise frictions could arise. Apart from this small proviso, the year ends on a note of harmony and understanding for Sagittarians.

MONEY

Mercury comes to your rescue if you need to deal with a financial problem early in the month. Just when you thought a business deal was in the bag, a minor detail threatens to put a spanner in the works. If you act quickly, and if necessary, get professional advice, everything should be back on course by the second week. Just keep a clear head and don't let well-intentioned others

try to tell you that there's a quicker profit to be made elsewhere. If you stick to what you know best and are fairly flexible in your approach, success is with you all the way.

TRAVEL

Events contrive to pull you away from familiar territory and chances are you'll decide to spend the festive season away from home. Your ruling planet Jupiter makes a significant conjunction with Neptune on the 21st, giving more than just a hint that far horizons are beckoning. Even if you are staying put, it's likely that your thoughts will be dwelling a on future excursions or exotic vacations for the year ahead.

Distant links are highlighted as the year draws to a close, with much to suggest that at least one visitor has come a great distance to be with you.

Lucky dates
3rd, 11th, 16th, 21st

For your fantastic weekly & monthly cash, career and romance and forecasts
Call 0905 515 0046
Starlines are updated every Tuesday. BT calls cost 60p per minute and last about 5 minutes. Cost from other networks may be higher. SP: Eckoh Herts HP3 9HN

Capricorn
december 22 to january 21

Zodiac fact file

Planetary Ruler: Saturn

Quality & Element: Cardinal Earth

Colours: Brown, black

Metal: Lead, pewter

Wood: Yew

Flower: Fuschia

Animal: Goat

Gem: Jet

Fabric: Hessian

January

You greet the New Year in a proactive frame of mind and will be wasting little time in pushing ahead with fresh initiatives. The presence of Mars in your sign throughout the month guarantees good progress and gives you the motivation to overcome obstacles and get to where you want to be. What takes shape during the early weeks of 2009 will set the pace for the months ahead and point you in a direction that is guaranteed to improve your status. You're now in a position to make optimum use of the opportunities heading your way, so if you've done the necessary groundwork a successful year is guaranteed. Go for it!

LOVE

The energising influence of Mars sets the pattern for amorous experiences early in the New Year, making this an unusually eventful month for those hoping to meet the kind of partner who really turns you on. The forces of attraction are greatly intensified and your personal magnetism and libido tremendously enhanced.

If new romance is about to materialise, it'll happen swiftly and almost take you by surprise. But please note that often when Mars is the instigator of passion there's a pretty high risk of quick burnout. In other words, it might turn out to be one of those wild infatuations that may be wonderful at first but ends up as a battle of wills and finally leaves you feeling emotionally wrecked! The heart has its reasons that leaves your head clueless, and at least there'll be no dull moments for lovers in the coming weeks.

MONEY

With Jupiter moving into the money area of your solar horoscope early in January it promises to be a year of opportunity with regard to material interests and your personal economy. Before getting too complacent about the situation, you are advised to keep your wits about you during the second half of the month, when what seems like an insignificant glitch could turn into a major problem.

Potential difficulties can be minimised by focusing on details and taking your time if faced with a difficult decision concerning investments or commercial transactions.

TRAVEL

Although the pace of life will keep you on the move, there will also be plenty of scope for leisurely interludes and a change of scenery.

Visits to or from friends and relatives provide a pleasant ambience during the third week, and a message you receive around the 23rd is sure to contain welcome and perhaps unexpected news.

Keep arrangements flexible late month and be ready to change your plans. An invite from an old friend, gives you a chance to take a break and add zest to your social life.

Lucky dates
6th, 11th, 16th, 24th

February

Positive trends early in the month enable you to tie up any loose ends and finalise various plans that have been on the drawing board since December. You may feel that events have been moving ahead faster than you can comfortably deal with, but now that the dust is settling you'll have far more time to get organised. Psychologically you're feeling stronger within yourself and therefore much more confident in how you approach the world at large. If certain events made you feel a bit vulnerable in the past, what happens in February puts you firmly back on your feet and helps you to move forward with all guns blazing.

LOVE

If a recent romantic attachment seems to be developing a few fault lines this is perhaps not such a bad thing. Rose-tinted spectacles can produce some wonderful effects, but there comes a time when the cold light of day makes its presence felt.

This is not to say that you are about to experience a total disillusion, though there does appear to be a make-or-break episode looming in the second week of February.

Basically this is not the easiest of months for intimate affairs. There's a kind of sifting process going forward and relationships are being put to the test.

Much depends on the level of maturity you're coming from. If you plunged into an affair on impulse and with your eyes closed, nemesis may be seeking you out in order to restore your natural good sense. You're usually cautious and realistic, but lately perhaps this has slipped. Get your thinking head on and you'll restore your judgement.

MONEY

With no less than four planets activating financial and material interests, this is sure to be a month of important developments, especially if you're involved in high-powered business initiatives and crucial negotiations.

You'll have reason to feel confident about an ongoing situation, and it's your own initiative and enterprise that gets the desired results. There might be some pressure on you to do some strategic restructuring if jointly held resources and long-term investments are to be kept on course. On the whole the prospect is bright and your fortunes are on the rise throughout 2009.

HOME

Venus begins an unusually lengthy sojourn in the lower sector of your solar chart, putting the focus on domestic and family interests from early February onwards.

If you have it in the back of your mind to make changes in your immediate living space, it's essential to take your time and make sure that everyone concerned is in full agreement. This applies even if you want to do something simple such as change the furnishings and the colour scheme of your home.

Venus is, after all, the planet of beauty and harmony, so if you wish to create the right ambience (and impress your friends at the same time!) now is the time to set your mind to it. Once you've consulted, decide on the way forward and stick with it.

> February is not the easiest month for intimate affairs

Lucky dates
2nd, 12th, 17th, 24th

Do your best to get important plans finalised and everything in place if you wish to avoid unnecessary stress in the coming weeks. From the middle of the month onwards the pace of life gathers a rather hectic momentum, leaving you with precious little time to rethink a project that's already up and running. Provided you are adaptable and are not afraid to think on your feet, great things can be achieved, and you'll arrive at the end of the month well ahead of your game. Getting hung up about minor setbacks or annoyances is a waste of your time during March as what you lose on the roundabouts, you'll gain on the swings.

LOVE

If you're having second thoughts about an existing romantic attachment this doesn't mean that you have to be insensitive. It's likely that you're going through a psychologically tricky phase that's all part of a pattern of inner growth and maturing.

There's some discrepancy between what you expect from an intimate relationship and the actual reality of the situation. Maybe you've been trying too hard to fit your love life into an image dictated by convention or media hype rather than allowing it to evolve naturally.

Whatever happens, this is going to be a decisive month for relationships and at present it is hard to say which way the winds of change are blowing.

At a level that you may not be conscious of, it seems that your instinct is guiding you in the right direction, so if in doubt don't force any issues.

MONEY

Although there might be times when you have to work hard to keep your act together, the underlying trend is highly supportive as far as your material fortunes are concerned. Initiatives taken recently continue to have a progressive and expansive effect on financial and business interests, but make your best efforts in the first half of March if you are aiming to put things on a more efficient and streamlined basis. It's a time of great opportunity, which is good news if you're seeking a job that gives better scope for expressing your potential - and with a decent pay packet!

TRAVEL

You may need to loosen up mentally early in the month if you are not to get the reputation of being hidebound and lacking imagination.

Even if you don't entirely agree with the views of a friend or colleague, this is no reason to get over-defensive simply because something doesn't support your own theories. By cultivating an open mind, you'll find that life becomes infinitely more interesting.

From mid month onwards the pace of life move into the fast lane, and this is precisely where you'll need to cultivate a flexible mental energy.

Lucky dates
5th, 11th, 22nd, 31st

April

You may get the feeling that everything hangs in the balance, but it would be unwise to make any new commitments until after the middle of April. From then on you'll find that the mists clear and new light will be shed on a seemingly contradictory situation. You may be forced to realise that sometimes it's not what's out there but rather the way you are looking at it that's the main source of difficulty. There's no doubt that your outlook on life is going through some interesting changes, and perhaps it's the influence of a new friend in your life, a therapy you're interested in, or an unusual experience that provides the key.

LOVE

There might not be any dramatic amorous encounters in the weeks ahead, and you may not feel the earth move, but what happens around the middle of the month gives you a hint that something good is flickering into focus.

What's helpful is that your social life becomes more inviting and interesting from the second week onwards, and this is perhaps just what you need to pull you out of the doldrums. If love is destined to enter the picture it's likely to come via a chance invitation, a short journey or a last-minute change of plan.

An element of serendipity, synchronicity and coincidence could work the right kind of magic for Capricorns, and romance appears just when you're not really looking for it.

Meanwhile, for established couples (whether married or otherwise), there's a more relaxed feel later in the month and you will have a chance to show those close to you that you do think highly of them.

TRAVEL

Avoid hurrying around if you need to travel on the 6th and 15th of April. In many ways these are two of the most critical dates in the entire year for Capricorns.

There's an indication that there's a breakdown in communication, and this could mean that your travel is disrupted because the car breaks down or there's some glitch in other forms of transport. If possible, aim for the second half of April if an important journey is on the agenda.

From a different angle, it's an excellent month for educational interests and your recreational activities. You might also find that what is currently a spare time hobby could be shifted onto a more productive - and eventually more profitable - level.

Take the time to explore the possibility of expansion.

It's an excellent month for educational interests

HEALTH

The tricky dates already mentioned contain a health warning. This can be summed up in one word - accidents!

It would be in your interests to take things slowly and not put yourself under any unnecessary pressure at these times. Avoid doing anything too strenuous, and if you're handling power tools or cutting instruments take extreme care! If you're a sports fan and eager to get yourself in shape for an event, remind yourself that this cannot be achieved in a moment. Work towards ultimate fitness one step at a time otherwise you'll do yourself an injury.

Lucky dates
9th, 19th, 25th, 28th

May

You're the kind of person who likes to feel in control of your own destiny rather than leaving things to chance, and now that Saturn (your ruler) is gaining force, the desire to clarify your views and develop a more structured sense of purpose is greatly strengthened. Throughout most of the year this planet indicates a thoughtful and perhaps a more philosophical frame of mind. You're more inclined to reflect on your experience and seek a deeper or spiritual dimension to life. The upshot of this is that your lifestyle, your personality and your relationships are given added value; think quality rather than quantity.

LOVE

Relationships that engage your deeper emotions are likely to become a source of reflection during May, particularly if your experience of amorous attachments has not been exactly easy in recent months.

Maybe you're finally beginning to realise that love is not something that comes in the shape of a ready-made package deal, custom designed to suit your own interests. At best you're a very loyal person, but there's always the danger that you look upon your loved one as a part of the furniture. If this sort of attitude has caused problems in the past, you now have an excellent chance to change the parameters and widen your spectrum of sensitivities.

Perhaps you should reflect on the fact that if you don't learn from past mistakes then you're bound to repeat them until the light finally dawns.

HOME

The main centre of events appears to focus on matters closer to home throughout May. If you were hoping for a bit of peace and quiet, forget it! Whether you like it or not you'll have to cope with more than your usual quota of visitors. Friends and relatives are likely to ask favours of you, such as looking after their kids while they're otherwise engaged, or helping out with various domestic chores.

Nevertheless, it's a splendid month for having a blitz on your own living space, getting rid of excess clutter, refurbishing the place and arranging things in line with your changing tastes.

MONEY

If you've been working within a fairly tight budget in recent months, pressures are about to ease and in the coming weeks your fortunes are being steered in a more positive direction.

A powerful link between Jupiter and Neptune towards the end of May brings more than just a hint of welcome opportunities and wider scope for upgrading your earning potential. Restrictions are about to dissolve, giving you much more leeway for spending on the things you really desire. It's a lucky omen if you're intent on enhancing your domestic lifestyle.

Lucky dates
4th, 11th, 17th, 30th

June

Whichever way you look at it, the astrological pattern for June is decidedly promising. Early in the month there's good news concerning current aims and objectives, and it seems that ideas you've been juggling with since the start of the year suddenly take on a definite shape. Something that up to now has existed in the realm of theory can at last be translated into practice, thanks to the goodwill and useful suggestions of friends or colleagues. It's looking particularly promising for business ventures. Altogether you'll experience an easier flow of energy and be able to tap into a fresh source of creative inspiration.

LOVE

This promises to be a month of spectacular developments for romantically inclined Capricorns. Something you have long wished for finally enters the realms of possibility, and before long you'll be riding the crest of a wave.

Now that you've put the past behind you and (hopefully) know how and why a previous attachment finally fizzled out, the future takes on a rosier glow. This doesn't mean that you can jump to conclusions, and if romance does begin to beckon in the coming weeks it's essential that you let it develop in a natural sort of way, rather than attempting to lasso it for your own personal convenience!

The stage is set for something extra special, and the chance of meeting a future marriage partner is high; but there are certain sensitivities to be taken into consideration; so don't go and blow it by wading in and immediately trying to take control.

MONEY

Whatever you're aiming to achieve, it's almost certain that you'll be covering a lot of ground in the coming weeks.

Events taking shape early in the month enable you to pull strings in your favour and develop a productive dialogue with those who are able to support and advise you in your efforts.

Capricorns are ambitious by temperament and you are at your best and happiest when you have a clearly defined goal in view.

It seems therefore that you'll be in your element and have plenty of scope for expressing your best potential throughout the whole of June, all of which is sure to have a positive impact on your financial status.

> The stage is set for something extra special

TRAVEL

Information that comes to light around the 7th June enables you to get a clearer take on a situation that's been riddled with ambiguities lately.

Something you've found hard to understand recently finds a perfectly rational explanation, which is good news if you've been struggling with a course of study and attempting to pull ideas into a more coherent shape.

From the middle of the month onwards your mind is focused on matters of a practical nature and you'll get the desired results if dealing you are with officialdom or seeking advice on matters that are at presently high on your list of important issues.

A joint trip could be on the cards for adventurous Capricorns. Don't immediately dismiss friends' suggestions.

Lucky dates
3rd, 9th, 17th, 28th

July

A lunar eclipse in your sign on July 7th signals a subtle shift in your feelings and a change in the way you approach your aims and interests. This is unlikely to amount to any major traumas, but it might worry you that the level of enthusiasm you previously felt for a certain activity begins to lose momentum. Perhaps you're having second thoughts because something more absorbing and inspiring has recently taken away your attention. If you feel it's time to bow out gracefully, wait until the end of the month before expressing your intentions to do so. Once this is done you'll probably breathe a huge sigh of relief.

LOVE

A solar eclipse on the 22nd puts the focus on personal relationships. There are indications of a paradigm shift, though this is not something to get alarmed about.

If an existing romantic attachment has cooled, you can expect this date to mark a major turning point. After a great deal of soul searching the situation becomes clear to you, and if you decide on a parting of the ways you'll soon realise that it's the right move. It's unlikely there'll be any hard feelings in this scenario, and chances are you'll remain on friendly terms in future.

Married Capricorns might find the emotional climate threatens to get a bit turbulent later in July, but you'll only have yourself to blame if you've been taking your partner for granted. Make a point of lavishing more care and attention on your loved one!

TRAVEL

Mercury's swift flight through your opposite sign between the 3rd and 17th signals a lively exchange of ideas and a chance to establish contact with people on your own wavelength. Discussions, meetings and interviews are highlighted and it's almost certain that you'll win through if it's a case of having to get your message across and convince others that you're the right person for the job.

If you're into research and need to do a bit of detective work, what you discover later in the month brings fresh insight and enables you to make the right connections.

MONEY

Your material fortunes continue to flourish under the expansive influence of Jupiter. Watch your step, though, when Mars is adversely placed around the 6th, when you might be tempted to take risks and throw money away on crackpot schemes. Generally you're a cautious person when it comes to money, but there are times when your urge to get one better and score points over others can trip you up.

As far as career interests are concerned you should find that things come up to your expectations. Think carefully if a job offer comes up late month.

Lucky dates
2nd, 10th, 19th, 25th

August

If relations with other people have caused tensions recently, you'll have no difficulty pouring oil on troubled waters in the coming weeks. The gentle influence of Venus ensures that harmony prevails and a little goodwill goes a very long way. In regard to practical and everyday activity, the going could get tough during the second week of August, but it seems that you're the one that's turning up the pressure and raising the bar. OK, Capricorns are the kind of people who thrive in a challenge and are never happier than when aiming high, but you should bear in mind that sometimes by doing less you will actually achieve more.

LOVE

Your love life gets into the right groove this month and brings a feeling that everything is for the best in the best of all possible worlds. OK, so this could be a bit of an overstatement, but the fact is that with Venus moving through your House of Partners you're likely to experience moments that are either magical, blissful, memorable - and probably all three at once!

If you're planning on taking a far-flung vacation or journey with your loved one, a honeymoon atmosphere surrounds you all the way. Incidentally, this is perhaps the most favourable month in 2009 for those who are taking the plunge into matrimony - or at least thinking seriously about it.

If various obstacles have made you rather cautious about making this kind of commitment, the prospect now brightens considerably and the future begins to look decidedly attractive for would-be brides and grooms.

TRAVEL

Honeymoon or not, this is an excellent month for getting away from familiar routines, chilling out, or letting your hair down. After a strenuous phase of activity in recent months you'll be able to take a break without feeling anxious about work, business interests or other mundane preoccupations. The accent on wider horizons applies also to the mind. Efforts geared towards improving your knowledge and skills prove highly stimulating at this time, and if you're on a spiritual quest and wish to meet those of like mind the Fates are definitely guiding you in the right direction.

HEALTH

Your energy level is given a boost throughout the month, and perhaps it's a change of routine that acts as a tonic to your vital spirits. Prevailing trends favour those intent on getting in good shape physically and achieving optimum fitness.

Having tried all kinds of faddish diets and exercises in the past, you'll probably now discover that the answer is staring you in the face. It's a case of getting back to basics and taking a serious look at your lifestyle and the quality (or lack of it) of food you eat. This is where your typical determination and common sense enable you to produce the desired result. After a while the new regime will become second nature so hang in there in the early stages when it may seem more painful.

> Your energy level is given a boost throughout the month

Lucky dates
7th, 16th, 18th, 27th

September

What takes shape in the coming month could mark a significant turning point in your ongoing scheme of things. At last it seems that you will be breaking free of a situation that's perhaps cramped your style in recent months. Metaphorically speaking, there's a confrontation between the old and the new, which of course could mean that you have to deal with a rather tense phase of experience, particularly in the days leading up to the new Moon on the 18th September. From then on the way forward gets easier, any doubts and misgivings fade, and there will be a feeling that you've definitely made the right decision.

LOVE

The presence of Mars in your opposite sign could make this a potentially explosive month when sensitivities are liable to wear rather thin. If there are underlying tensions within a relationship, you'll only make matters worse by pretending that all is well, or simply telling your partner to snap out of it.

The worst thing you could do is seek an intellectual solution to an emotional problem, as this is bound to create further misunderstandings. Sensitivity is the name of the game, but also a willingness to be absolutely open and honest about your feelings. By talking things over in a direct way instead of pretending a problem doesn't exist, relationships are sure to be greatly strengthened. At best this is an excellent month for clearing the air and establishing a deeper understanding with your nearest and dearest.

MONEY

Appearances could be deceptive and therefore you need to stay alert for potential pitfalls, especially in dealing with business and commercial transactions. If a fundraising venture runs into difficulties in the second week, be prepared to hold your horses and do a bit of serious rethinking. Be ready to step in with your practical good sense if you feel that someone close to you is getting

carried away with unrealistic schemes or dubious business dealings. There's good news, however, about an important job interview.

TRAVEL

Be careful if you're delegating tasks to other people in the first half of the month, as this is unlikely to have the desired effect of speeding up a job. Also, resist the temptation to cut corners or be pushed into making a decision concerning your career or other important aims and objectives.

As for travel, the final 10 days of the month favour leisurely trips and holidays, but be prepared for minor disappointments if your journey is for business reasons. If officialdom and legal red tape are creating frustrations, there's light at the end of the tunnel late month.

Lucky dates
2nd, 12th, 17th, 29th

October

Your best strategy is to cultivate the gentle art of allowing things to emerge rather than attempting to force issues through impatience or because you feel the need to score points over others. By being too upfront and demanding you'll only put others on the defensive and antagonise those who could actually be helpful to you later on. Relax, you don't need to get uptight right now about proving or improving your status, getting the better of competitors and being top dog. Now that your ruling planet moves into the upper sector of your solar chart, success will come easily - but it will come in its own good time.

LOVE

If something has been creating a rift between you and your partner recently, you can expect to be moving into calmer waters during the coming month. Be warned, though, that sparks could still fly until the middle of October, after which the fiery planet Mars takes leave of your House of Partners.

Perhaps a relationship has become a bit dull and stagnant in the past and emotional readjustments have been called for in recent weeks.

If you've managed to avoid a complete bust-up, the prospect brightens considerably and your love life is moving from strength to strength.

It's a brighter picture, too, for those hoping to marry in the near future. Obstacles that have stood in the way to your heart's desires should finally be a thing of the past and

maybe this is why there are indications of a celebration towards the end of the month.

MONEY

Under the changing pattern of planets not only will your aims and ambitions take on a clearer outline, but also your inner sense of direction and purpose will put you on track to a welcome steady rise in your status over the next couple of years.

This helpful trend is programmed to carry your financial and material interests forwards and give you a feeling of being firmly in control of your destiny.

A fortunate turn of events happening around the middle of October gives Capricorns a hint of the future potentials and opportunities, all of which puts you in an extremely positive and optimistic frame of mind approaching the end of the year.

> There are indications of a celebration at the end of the month

TRAVEL

A great deal of your mental energy is focused on matters of immediate practical importance throughout the whole of October.

If you're faced with a major decision concerning your career or some other significant activity, be prepared to weigh up carefully the pros and cons.

A hasty move could land you in a position that's just beyond your current level of competence and what at first seems like a lucky break could in fact become a burden.

It would be better to keep your aims at a modest level at present, while at the same time looking into the various possibilities for upgrading your qualifications, improving your skills and widening your vision. Don't rush things and keep your end goal firmly in view.

Lucky dates
6th, 10th, 13th, 29th

November

Lunar trends at the start of the month stir up your gregarious and pleasure loving instincts and surround you with a feeling of well being. People you arrange to meet socially around this time stimulate your mind and complement your own interests, which is particularly good news for those involved in the fields of creative activity, sports, or entertainment. The pace of life becomes less demanding and gives you some much-needed breathing space to catch up on neglected interests and make up for lost time in regard to leisurely activities, spare time interests and whatever makes life more worthwhile for you.

LOVE

A chance encounter in the first week has all the makings of a perfect romance, but you might need to bide your time until the third week before the real action takes place.

Over the past couple of months you probably had the feeling of wandering in the wilderness or being a member of the Lonely Hearts Club. Suddenly the picture changes, so don't despair if previous experience left you feeling a bit cynical about finding happiness. There's an increasingly friendly aura around you throughout November and it certainly looks as if you'll be moving in wider social circles. It's a time when new friends gravitate into your orbit and you establish contact with kindred spirits. Links are being forged and your cherished hopes are on the way to realisation.

MONEY

Jupiter, planet of luck and expansion, continues to gather a positive momentum, signalling a potentially successful month financially and a tremendous step forward for those engaged in commercial and business activity. A project that's been incubating in the back of your mind for several months gets the green light and quickly translates into a useful source of extra income. By being more experimental and enterprising, great things can be achieved and obstacles to the improvement of your fortunes easily overcome. If you're working in line with a partner, progress will be made.

TRAVEL

Journeys have the unexpected and delightful effect of enriching your social life and putting you in touch with those on your own wavelength.

Involvement in group activities and anything that depends on teamwork are guaranteed to come up with the goods and give you a platform on which to express your practical ability and talent for organisation. Prevailing trends in the second half of November favour those interested in occult, mystical and alternative studies. Keep a dream diary and take more notice of intuitive hunches.

Lucky dates
2nd, 7th, 15th, 26th

December

Events taking shape in the background generate a feel-good influence in the weeks leading up to the festive season. Relations on all levels run smoothly and even if antagonisms do arise you'll have the necessary presence of mind to defuse a confrontation before it gets over-heated. Uranus is strongly activated and gives more than a hint of unexpected (and welcome) changes in your day-to-day routines. It might mean that you have to be more adaptable than usual and prepared to think on your feet, but there's absolutely no excuse for feeling bored in the month ahead! It's all systems go from this point onwards.

LOVE

December is one of those months when appearances prove deceptive and just when you think love has passed you by, it's liable to take you by surprise and crash in on you like a revelation.

Something secretive is indicated and perhaps you'll be obliged to exercise discretion if there's a danger of upsetting a third party. In other words, make sure there are no lingering ties to previous romantic attachments and be wary of entering into a new relationship that might be open to misinterpretation.

Apart from these provisos, the chances of finding your elective affinity are greatly enhanced this month, and when Venus finally enters your sign on the 25th there's every indication that it'll turn out to be a truly memorable occasion.

Towards the end of the month an unexpected and enjoyable meeting with an old flame could have intriguing consequences in the coming year. Keep your mind open and go with the flow.

HOME

If you plan to remain on home territory in December there's much to suggest a pleasant atmosphere surrounding the domestic arena. This is helped greatly by the arrival of visitors who had almost achieved the status of strangers in your current scheme of things.

A return of old friends into your orbit is likely, which will certainly contribute to making the festivities something extra special. If you're entertaining guests later in the month, the presence of Venus in your sign endows you with the necessary ease and grace and gives you a feeling of being truly appreciated as the year comes to a close.

> There will be a return of old friends into your orbit

MONEY

Throughout 2009 your financial status has on the whole moved along a steadily rising trajectory. Limitations have eased and this has given you a greater incentive to expand your personal economy and take a more ambitious approach to business and money-making activities.

This trend continues throughout December and into the New Year, and with Jupiter and Neptune once more joining forces on the 21st of the month, there's a promise that very soon you'll get the kind of lucky break that you've been hoping for. In addition, it looks as if you're unlikely to be short of funds for lavishing gifts and goodies on close friends and family. You're going to be a very popular figure this December!

Lucky dates
6th, 10th, 21st, 25th

For your fantastic weekly & monthly cash, career and romance and forecasts

Call 0905 515 0047

Starlines are updated every Tuesday. BT calls cost 60p per minute and last about 5 minutes. Cost from other networks may be higher. SP: Eckoh Herts HP3 9HN

Aquarius

january 22 to february 18

Zodiac fact file

Planetary Ruler: Uranus

Quality & Element: Fixed Air

Colours: Electric blue, bright pink

Metal: Lead, pewter

Wood: Pine

Flower: Pansy

Animal: Fox

Gem: Garnet

Fabric: Crepe

January

With just about every planet hovering in and around the sign of Aquarius, an exciting prospect comes into view as the New Year arrives. With Jupiter taking up residence in your sign from early January onwards you are among the astrologically privileged throughout 2009! What makes it particularly interesting is that this fortunate planet joins forces with Neptune and points strongly to a widening of your horizons in coming months. The keyword is opportunity, and together with an increasing urge to break free of your restrictions, Aquarians can look forward to an unusually eventful time ahead.

LOVE

With such an unusually powerful pattern of planets, it seems that your expectations and emotional needs are undergoing a kind of tectonic shift. You might not be consciously aware of this subtle inner change immediately, but you're likely to get a hint of what's going on through your experience of new or newish amorous attachments early in the year.

Being an Aquarian, you're never entirely happy in a relationship that's one dimensional and based only on the most obvious attractions. What you actually crave is a feeling of deeper affinity that includes the physical and mental as well as spiritual dimensions.

This might sound like an unattainable ideal, but really all it means is that personal relationships must be genuine friendships if what you want is something more meaningful and lasting. However, bear in mind that whatever it is you're seeking may already be on its way to you!

MONEY

Pressures are easing throughout the month, giving you better scope for updating your personal economy and improving your earning potential. If money has seemed to drain away at an alarming rate over the previous couple of months, by the middle of January you'll be back at the controls.

The helpful influence of Venus ensures that cash flow gains a more satisfying equilibrium and enables you to overcome any existing problems with ease.

An unexpected bonus is winging its way to you later in the month, and at last you'll have the wherewithal to splash out on the good things of life and give yourself a real treat.

Make the most of it and indulge your retail fantasies. You never know how long it will be until the next opportunity comes around.

What you're seeking may already be on its way to you

TRAVEL

Although you probably won't experience any major setbacks, you can do much to head off potential hassles by tying up loose ends and arranging schedules well in advance. A decision that's still hanging fire may need your prompt attention early in the month, particularly if this has to do with a business proposition or a new job offer.

From mid month onwards you'll be saving yourself a lot of irritation by keeping to a fairly strict agenda and accepting that other people are liable to be absent minded. Also, you should be careful not to put too much faith in verbal agreements.

Lucky dates
2nd, 7th, 19th, 24th

February

An unusually eventful month is forecast as no less that four planets activate your sign. The winds of change are rising considerably and what takes shape in the coming weeks will determine the direction of your interests, probably for several years ahead. Fresh initiatives taken will meet with the right opportunities and enable you to put aims and objectives on a broader and more ambitious basis. What it all adds up to is a month when you get the kind of break that seems to be tailor made especially for you. This is definitely not a time to be over-modest about your potential. Believe in yourself and reach for the stars.

LOVE

There seems to be a dramatic twist to events during February, and perhaps this will be most evident in the sphere of romantic encounters. This is not to imply that everything is destined to run smoothly or that your ideal lover is about to appear on the scene.

The presence of fiery Mars in your sign from early month onwards signals a phase of intense passions and irresistible attractions. Of course, this kind of scenario can cut both ways and there's no saying how the situation will finally pan out. Whatever happens, this is not going to be a dull month for romantically inclined Aquarians.

Even if you do experience emotional turbulence, this is not necessarily a bad thing. What it means is that you begin to see clearly the difference between genuine love and momentary lust. Keep flirtatious impulses in check around the 6th!

HEALTH

The recent solar eclipse in your sign could mean that your vitality is on something of a roller coaster during February. The energising influence of Mars helps to offset this potentially negative trend, but it also means that there's pressure on you to live life in the fast lane, leaving you with little time for relaxation. There's a danger of ending up feeling totally wiped out by the end of the month. Forewarned is forearmed, so try your best to create a suitable balance between work and play, and be prepared to take a firm line with those who may make unreasonable demands on your time and energy.

TRAVEL

As just hinted, there's plenty to keep you on the go in the coming weeks, and you'll relish this upsurge of activity.

Provided you can hold your act together it promises to be a progressive month, offering you plenty of scope for varying your interests and establishing contact with people who stimulate your mind. Travel is bound to play a key role in this scenario. In the first half of the month this is likely to be more a duty than a pleasure; but from midmonth onwards anything that takes you away from familiar territory will prove fun.

Lucky dates

7th, 12th, 22nd, 23rd

March

A conjunction of Mercury and Mars in your sign certainly gets the month off to a lively start! There may be a sense of urgency you will have to contend with and a snap decision will have to be taken. You'll definitely have the necessary presence of mind to deal with this, but be careful not to antagonise someone who does not share your unconventional way of tackling a problem. Positive trends in the first half of February put you in a forward-looking frame of mind and give you the needed motivation to push right ahead with fresh initiatives and make your presence felt where it's most needed and has the correct impact.

LOVE

Although there's no guarantee that love will be all sweetness and light in the coming weeks, you'll certainly not be lacking in admirers. Your psychic aura has the quality of an electromagnet under the prevailing cosmic influence, endowing you with an almost magical ability to attract both friends and lovers into your orbit. Someone you chance to meet in the first half of the month will have special appeal, probably because he or she has an unconventional style and is involved in an area of work that has a touch of glamour.

Though romantic experience will be exhilarating and exciting there's still nothing to promise a lasting attachment. Strangely enough, this does seem to suit your temperament at present simply because you're not so keen to make any special commitments as yet. However, you should be careful not to play too blithely with other people's feelings.

Someone you meet in the first half of the month has appeal

MONEY

If you've been complaining of a shortage of funds recently, or feel that there's an inverse ratio between your effort and reward, you can expect a very positive change for the better from mid month onwards. Commercial and business interests are due to take a quantum leap forward and you'll be in a much better position to upgrade your targets and diversify your outlets. Efforts and initiatives aimed at improving your earning powers will meet with speedy success, so keep your wits about you if you're not to miss out on a likely opportunity. Take a bold approach and turn your assets to maximum advantage.

TRAVEL

People you have arranged to visit or who have promised to pay you a call may be in the habit of changing their minds at an inconvenient moment during March.

It could be that certain relatives are liable to lead you round in circles and mess up your well-laid plans, so you must try to adopt a flexible strategy if your nerves are not to start unravelling.

The situation improves from the middle of the month onwards, when you'll have much more time for pleasing yourself and perhaps taking an unexpected short break from usual routines.

Later in the month it seems that messages are flying to and fro and there's a possibility that a speedily arranged meeting throws you into delightful company.

Lucky dates
4th, 5th, 13th, 31st

You're likely to be devoting a great deal of energy to re-organising your lifestyle at a very practical level during April. Metaphorically speaking, you have an urge to tear down the old order and replace it with a new and improved model. You might suddenly realise that there's a need to get rid of excess baggage in order to give yourself more space to breathe. Your attitude to material things does appear to be changing during 2009 and you're definitely becoming more sensitive to the difference between your real needs and those endless wants that we're constantly being conned into believing we must have.

LOVE

Affairs of the heart are not exactly high profile at present, but this does not mean that you're completely out on a limb. If a previous romantic episode has left you feeling a bit cynical, maybe you need time to regain your inner equilibrium and get back in touch with your inner feelings.

You're not the easiest person to please when it comes to finding the right partner and at times there's a feeling of being caught in a repeating cycle of boom and bust. Take heart, because there is new light on the horizon and someone you get acquainted with later in the month may be the one who helps you to break through the manic-depressive pattern of previous experience.

Maybe there won't be any instant miracles, but you're on the right path.

MONEY

Material and financial interests may call for fairly radical measures in the first half of the month, but this is no reason to give way to impatience if certain obstacles appear to be reluctant to shift. There's pressure on you to bring things up to date and do some radical restructuring in areas such as business, investments and longer-term financial interests.

Definitely take your time if you're thinking of splashing out large sums on new technical gadgetry or vehicles. If in doubt, put things on the back-burner for a while, and focus on consolidating your existing resources.

HOME

During the second and third weeks of April, matters closer to home gather a lively momentum and you can expect more visitors than usual. Most of these will be very welcome and give you a chance to catch up news.

Aquarian parents are advised to keep youngsters under close surveillance in the second week if mishaps are to be avoided. If you're planning to go ahead with major home improvements, be prepared to shop around for a few quotes before plunging into action.

Later in the month don't get careless about matters of security and make sure your insurance policy is up to date.

Lucky dates
2nd, 9th, 19th, 28th

May

If experience since the start of the year has obliged you to change direction and reorganise your plans, an undercurrent of invincible optimism has enabled you to win through and deal successfully with problems as they arise. From this month onwards you'll have reason to feel especially optimistic, probably because a long-standing obstacle is finally overcome and you are now finally free to get on with your life in a way that suits your current aims and objectives. With Jupiter and Neptune joining forces in your sign later this month, your need for increased freedom is now given wider scope for expression.

LOVE

Temperamentally you are not the kind of person who usually gets carried away by your emotions. In fact, people often experience you as being rather cool, detached and aloof. Maybe this actually does an injustice to your deeper feelings, which are always a pretty true guide when it comes to closer and more intimate connections.

The thing is, you don't like pretence and are always very aware of the difference between truth and illusion. This is why you rarely go overboard when it comes to romance, and take a long time to feel totally at ease with another person. Granted, you always project a friendly aura towards others, but underneath you are extremely discerning about what is and is not genuine friendship. There's no lack of amorous opportunities in May, and you might be pleasantly surprised at your change of feeling before the month is over.

There is no lack of amorous opportunities in May

TRAVEL

The pace of life gathers a hectic momentum at times during May, but on the whole you'll find this is a trend you will welcome.

Events taking shape in the affairs of relatives or friends are likely to keep you on the move, and though you might find it hard to comply with everyone's wishes at times around the middle of the month, it's unlikely this will amount to any major disagreements.

A journey you were forced to cancel a couple of months back can now be put back on the agenda, and it seems that a change of routine later in May provides the ideal opportunity for making new friends and having fun.

HOME

From the middle of the month onwards you'll need to do a bit of quick rethinking if proposed changes to your living space are under consideration.

Matters relating to property – whether you're considering buying, selling or upgrading – need careful attention if you are hoping to keep plans on schedule. You should be prepared for a few minor setbacks and delays if you're dealing with the legal side of things, such as planning, building, or getting a Home Information Pack prepared.

From a different angle, a relative or a close friend may confide in you concerning a difficult emotional situation, and this is where your ability to point out certain truths helps to clarify matters for them. Don't underestimate your ability to help them.

Lucky dates
5th, 17th, 24th, 27th

June

This promises to be one of the most fortunate and expansive months of the year for Aquarians, especially if you're aiming to develop your creative potential and establish a broader base for expressing your skills and talents. Your social life gathers a pleasing momentum, especially in the third week of the month when you'll find plenty of scope for getting involved in purposeful group activities and social events. It promises to be a time when new and perhaps influential friendships are established. Especially favoured are those campaigning for a cause or charity, or interested in environmental and community affairs.

LOVE

It seems that a process of emotional transformation is coming full circle as the summer solstice approaches. This is where your love life takes a marked turn for the better, and after several months of doubting your own ability to find happiness, it's now time to accentuate the positive.

The close link between Venus and Mars in the second half of the month suggests a new chapter is about to open, and this will appeal to your romantic hopes and desires.

Meanwhile, for those who are married or have an established partnership the prevailing trend is equally encouraging, especially if you are hoping to improve your lifestyle at the domestic level. Obstacles to your happiness fade into the background, giving place to a feeling of increased togetherness.

MONEY

Now that Saturn is gaining a more positive momentum, any long-standing restrictions that have stood in the way of financial or business interests loosen their grip. Both personal and joint money matters come under a steadying trend, and now that you're gaining better control over these matters you'll be more inclined to focus your mind on the potential for upgrading your portfolio. Finance is closely woven with domestic affairs throughout June, making this an excellent time for property transactions or spending money to enhance your lifestyle.

HOME

An unusually powerful accent on all things domestic ensures that good progress is made in your efforts to bring about desirable changes.

You can expect a flurry of activity around your own home in the second half of June, with a spate of visitors keeping you amused as well as busy.

Any bright ideas you have for altering and refurbishing your living space should definitely not be left to languish in the realm of theory. Now that your material fortunes are on the upgrade, there's no reason that you should continue to accept second best or deny yourself a luxury or two.

Lucky dates
3rd, 11th, 18th, 29th

July

As Jupiter and Neptune continue to be the dominant force in your astrological pattern, it's your natural imagination and broadness of vision that enables you to enrich your life at many levels in the weeks ahead. Whether you're striving to further an ambition, embark on a voyage of discovery or spiritual quest, you're certainly on the right wavelength throughout July. Being one of the so-called 'higher octave' planets, Neptune benefits those who take a serious interest in mystical explorations, alternative therapies and anything that is geared towards the cultivation of the soul in the deepest sense of this term.

LOVE

Although you might not be aware of it, events taking shape over the past couple of months have woven you into a pattern of wider sympathies and brought you in touch with at least one person who is destined to play a central part in your life.

If you're seeking a soul mate the stage is set for sweet encounters in the coming weeks. You're likely to be feeling more extrovert, inclined to get out and about and strike up new friendships. An improvement in social life is almost certain to have a delightful spin-off that comes in the shape of a new romantic partner.

You're definitely on the right wavelength for amorous developments in the second half of July, and it's something that will enter your orbit as if by magic. It could be one of those odd twists of events, a kind of synchronicity, that finally provides you with the key to your heart's desires.

MONEY

Apart from an unexpected glitch early in the month that may force you to do a bit of quick rethinking, you're now in a good position to organise and update your budget to suit current needs and necessities. From the middle of the month onwards a forward-looking trend kicks in, signalling increased incentive and motivation to those who wish to launch an enterprising venture or put a spare time interest or hobby on a more lucrative footing.

You're tapping into a deeper source of creative energy at this time and can feel confident that your initiatives and decisions bring the desired results, and even better, they bring them fast!

It's time to pay some attention to your personal image

HEALTH

Your energy and vitality are in abundant supply most of the month, but there are a couple of dates, notably the 7th and 22nd, when you're advised to take a step back, ease the pace and just chill out.

If you're travelling far and wide or taking a holiday, a discerning approach is called for if you're intent on sampling the local exotic culinary delights. You may regret being quite so adventurous.

On a more positive note, you can make the most of prevailing trends in July by making a conscious effort to tone up your system and get yourself in optimum shape physically and psychologically.

It's time to pay some attention to your personal image and give yourself a serious makeover. Go on, you'll actually enjoy it!

Lucky dates
2nd, 8th, 16th, 19th

August

A lunar eclipse in your sign early in the month warns you not to count your chickens before they're hatched. This is especially so if you're involved in a competitive or sporting event. Over-confidence could have an effect which is the precise opposite of what you expected! During the second week a fine balance needs to be struck between your urge to push ahead with an ambitious project and the need to keep other people on your side. It'll be only too easy to get on your high horse, ignore the needs and sensitivities of others, and end up feeling that the world is against you. Try to avoid the dangers of becoming complacent.

HOME

What takes place in the first half of August sets the scene for a romantic encounter, either now or in the near future. Amorous relationships go from strength to strength and by the end of the month your thoughts are likely to be moving in the directions of marriage. Even if it doesn't amount to this, you're likely to be feeling more secure in your feelings.

You're naturally attracted towards people whose interests and lifestyle are off the beaten track and rather unconventional. If this describes someone you chance to meet in August then you can certainly take it as a good omen. As this is the traditional month for taking a vacation, perhaps you'll meet a kindred spirit when you're away from home. Whatever happens, romantic developments come via unusual paths.

MONEY

There's a positive focus on career interests throughout the month, which bodes well if you're seeking the kind of job that does proper justice to your best abilities and potentials. Prevailing trends ensure good relations with colleagues and bosses, and if you have any bright ideas concerning current arrangements now is the time to discuss the issues. Whether you're working at a corporate level or taking a more independent line, it's your ability to develop a broad vision and to think out of the box that enables you to boost your status and your income in the month ahead.

TRAVEL

Journeys taken in the early part of the month have a vitalising effect and give you scope for convivial interaction. Even if you're not going far it's likely that you'll bump into the kind of people who share your views and your sense of humour.

Your ordinary routines could give rise to some interesting meetings and encounters, so don't always think that commuting to and from work has to be a ritual of grim endurance. In fact there is a decidedly romantic element written into a seemingly insignificant trip during the third week. Life has some surprises in store, so keep an open mind.

Lucky dates
6th, 13th, 17th, 31st

September

A powerful link between Uranus and Saturn in the middle of September suggests an important turning point for Aquarians. Both planets are strongly associated with your sign, so if you get the feeling that the Fates are taking a hand in your affairs you won't be far wrong! Circumstances that have perhaps cramped your style over the past year or so are about to dissolve, and though this might entail elements of disruption the final result is bound to please. A conflict of loyalties may be felt, but if you're intent on gaining greater independence it would be unwise to let this window of opportunity pass you by.

LOVE

The transit of Venus through your opposite sign weaves an aura of harmony and understanding around intimate relationships. If an undercurrent of tension has generated negative vibes lately, the gentle influence of this planet now gives you a chance to reconcile differences of opinion and develop a more sensitive rapport with your loved one. A brighter prospect comes into view for those who have been undecided about going ahead with a wedding. Aquarians are a bit wary about this kind of commitment, but in view of prevailing astrological trends it's an option that now appears highly attractive.

The good news is that certain obstacles that have stood in the way of your hopes and wishes are due to disappear, and a happy ending is in sight. For singles, there's an equally bright prospect especially if you're seeking a long-term relationship.

MONEY

The Saturn-Uranus link indicates something of a watershed in your material fortunes. What takes shape around the middle of the month is destined to have important repercussions on your career, and what this means is a steady improvement in your financial and worldly status over the next year or so.

You might need to restructure your finances, particularly in regard to investments, pension schemes and jointly held resources, but by taking firm action now you can do much to minimise potential problems in the future. Basically, this is a time to get serious about finance and build a more secure base.

Clever planning is the key to your success this month

TRAVEL

Make sure you don't delay if you need to deal with legal or official matters early this month. Likewise, you'd be doing yourself a great favour by finalising various plans especially if this involves a fairly lengthy journey later in September. Leaving things to chance will be to invite a whole lot of unnecessary hassles, so be warned!

Even with the best of intentions you may be obliged to go over the same ground twice due to either your own or maybe other people's absent-mindedness.

However, by adopting a fairly flexible policy, especially in the third week of September, you can do much to prevent frayed nerves and stay on good terms with others. Clever planning is the key to your success.

Lucky dates
1st, 2nd, 12th, 29th

October

A rather changeable pattern of experience over the past few months becomes much more focused during October. It's as if a phase of preparation is finally coming full circle allowing you to get a firmer handle on your future aims and aspirations. With Jupiter starting to gather a positive momentum in your sign, luck accompanies your efforts and you have it in your power to create your own opportunities. A wider horizon now beckons, giving you greater freedom to do your own thing, explore new ideas and establish the kind of lifestyle that's more in tune with your deeper needs. Your needs are being answered this month.

LOVE

Passions are liable to be strong but unfocused in the first half of the month. A new romantic affair might give you the impression that everything is fine, but there is perhaps a hidden agenda that you won't be able to ignore. Things may not be what they seem and there's a danger that someone is simply playing games.

A friend is likely to put you wise soon after the middle of the month, so be prepared for some fireworks. It's an entirely different picture in the second half of October, when Venus throws a favourable angle to your sign and promises something more genuine and satisfying. Be careful not to sabotage your own happiness by dwelling on a previous emotional liaison. It's time to give yourself a clean slate and get on with your life.

MONEY

Over the past months financial matters have probably been something of a juggling act, but from October onwards an easier trend prevails and you'll have reason to feel confident that your fortunes are moving in the right direction. There's a decidedly expansive trend coming into force, and now that Saturn is changing signs you're shaking yourself free of past restrictions and beginning to benefit from previous efforts and initiatives. Career interests gather a more definite momentum after what has probably been a time of difficult decision making. From now, you're in the driving seat.

TRAVEL

The theme of wider horizons puts a special highlight on long-range journeys for Aquarians and the urge to get away from familiar territory.

Whether it's for business or for pleasure, travel proves highly rewarding at this time and opens at least one new window on the world.

Everything is programmed to enrich your experience and broaden your horizons, making this an excellent month for educational interests and upgrading your credentials. It promises to be an inspiring month for those interested in alternative paths of knowledge and the development of a more spiritual outlook on life.

Lucky dates
7th, 13th, 17th, 27th

November

Saturn's change of sign helps you to give clearer shape to your future plans and brings a more serious edge to the philosophy of life for Aquarians over the next couple of years. The need to widen your range of knowledge, either through travel or higher educational interests, will become more highly focused, and what you learn is sure to have a maturing influence on your mind and soul. Basically, you're entering a new chapter in your life when inner personal growth becomes a higher value in your scheme of things, and this could lead you in a direction that completely alters your outlook on the world. It's an exciting time.

LOVE

With Mars starting a lengthy sojourn in your House of Partners, what takes shape in November is likely to begin a process of realignment in the way you approach intimate relationships. Existing romantic ties are liable to be thrown into a state of transition and there'll be times when your emotional poise is knocked slightly off balance.

You need to readjust your attitudes in order to break out of what threatens to become a rather negative cycle of experience. Valuable lessons in self awareness are written into this changeable scenario. If you've fallen into the habit of taking another person for granted, be prepared to meet with criticism and confrontation.

If you come to feel that a relationship has been outgrown you'll be saving yourself and your partner a lot of stress by confronting the issue now rather than hanging on until later.

HOME

Lunar trends help you to achieve a feeling of increased contentment within the home and family circle early in November. After a rather unsettled phase you'll now begin to feel more relaxed and be more inclined to devote time and attention to improving your current living space.

For those who have recently moved house or set up home for the first time, this is an excellent month to organise a house-warming party. Prevailing trends show that you are more sensitive to your immediate surroundings and therefore more inclined to make improvements and bring things in line with your changing tastes.

Confront an issue now rather than waiting until later

MONEY

Experience gained over the previous two years will prove invaluable if you're intent on furthering your existing career or feel the need for a change of direction.

Whatever your aims and objectives, this could turn out to be the most eventful and decisive month of the year for Aquarians. Not only are you likely to get all the right breaks, but you'll actually be in the right place at the right time if opportunities do arise. The realisation is dawning that perhaps you've been underestimating your potential and you're now discovering that you don't always have to tread the conventional path.

Success comes through using your imagination broadening your perspectives. You'll be amazed at just what you can achieve.

Lucky dates
3rd, 7th, 16th, 23rd

December

For the third time this year Jupiter and Neptune join forces in your sign, and with your ruling planet turning direct, your experience is likely to contain an element of the unexpected. You'll be pleased to know that there's also an element of luck written into this script and it's bound to raise your spirits and put you in the right mood for the festivities. What's also bound to please you is the way that certain kindred spirits seem to gravitate into your orbit exactly when you most need them. Friendship, co-operation and wider social interests are all under the spotlight and will have special appeal to your natural Aquarian instincts.

LOVE

You might have noticed that friends often play a significant role in your life, almost as if they are somehow fated to change you and awaken you to experiences that you had not previously thought about.

In December there is every indication that a friend, either directly or indirectly, sets you on a path that leads to the realisation of your romantic hopes and wishes. Your social life is about to acquire a more interesting aspect giving you greater scope for widening your circle of significant friendships. It's a chance encounter around mid month that holds the key to something much deeper. Quite by chance, a friend or perhaps a casual acquaintance introduces you to someone who sparks the kind of chemical reaction that really makes your eyes light up and it won't be long before everything clicks into place.

TRAVEL

Around the 7th a journey or a message you receive contains something of a blast from the past. Either you bump into an old friend quite by accident, or someone renews contact after several years of silence. This is sure to put you in a reflective and nostalgic frame of mind, but you'll also be intrigued and delighted by what you learn. At a more mundane level, you are advised to get a second opinion if something private needs to be sorted out. Later in the month hang loose if minor irritations are to be avoided.

MONEY

An unforeseen twist of events early in the month could have an unexpectedly fortunate impact on current financial and business interests.

You might find that several threads can be usefully woven together to produce something more creative, and profitable. Here, too, friends appear to be an important influence, and if you're aiming to drum up support for a fundraising venture you'll be pleasantly surprised at the response.

In fact this is a time when corporate activity and team spirit enable you to raise your game to its highest level and put your aims and objectives on a more streamlined basis.

Lucky dates
1st, 11th, 17th, 28th

For your fantastic weekly & monthly cash, career and romance and forecasts

Call 0905 515 0048

Starlines are updated every Tuesday. BT calls cost 60p per minute and last about 5 minutes. Cost from other networks may be higher. SP: Eckoh Herts HP3 9HN

Pisces

february 19 to march 20

Zodiac fact file

Planetary Ruler: Neptune

Quality & Element: Mutable Water

Colours: Soft silvery blues & greys

Metal: Platinum, tin

Wood: Cedar

Flower: Lupin

Animal: Fish

Gem: Carnelian

Fabric: Chiffon

January

A central feature of your experience in 2009 focuses on the need to strike out in a totally new direction and to develop the kind of lifestyle that more truly reflects your many-faceted personality. You might find that the going gets tough at times and perhaps feel that the whole world seems to be thwarting your efforts, but by trusting your own intuition and by being true to your inner self, you'll exercise a kind of magic and eventually transform your ideals into realities. Everything depends on your ability and willingness to combine the old with the new and to take a less conventional approach without giving way to total rebellion.

LOVE

After a rather secretive and uncertain state of affairs, your love life finally settles into a more harmonious pattern as the New Year begins.

The good vibes generated by Venus in your own sign ensure that harmony prevails and a closer rapport is established between you and your loved one. It's a good omen for single Pisces who may have been languishing in an emotional wilderness lately and going through a phase of storm and stress. Events taking shape soon after mid month throw a new light on the situation and restore your faith in the power of love. The influence of Venus not only enhances your attractive qualities, but also you'll be in greater demand socially. An unexpected encounter around the 23rd makes you realise that miracles can happen.

TRAVEL

Make sure you have a fairly well organised agenda for the early weeks of 2009 and do your best to stick with it and avoid unnecessary distractions. If you've neglected certain matters over the past month, this is when it will all pile in on you and threaten to create chaos. Try to take one thing at a time rather than attempting to muddle through. In the second half of January you're advised to steer clear of controversial issues and keep your thoughts to yourself. Exercise care and discretion in dealing with matters of a private nature. Keep calm; by late month you're in the clear!

MONEY

You might not be immediately aware of it, but an undercurrent of good fortune comes into effect early in January and continues to gather force throughout the year ahead. It's as if there's an underlying back-up system that provides you with the right answers just when you most need them. There's a potentially successful trend in your affairs, particularly in the sphere of finance and career interests.

You'll find that success and progress come via corporate activity and your ability to work closely with like-minded people. Altogether it's an encouraging start to the year!

Lucky dates
3rd, 9th, 23rd, 30th

February

A pivotal date this month is the 5th, when Uranus in your own sign links forcefully with Saturn. This is when you're most likely to feel some tension between your need for greater freedom and the necessity to stick with business as usual. By nature you are a long-suffering sort of person who doesn't mind making sacrifices, especially if there's a goal in view. You may, however, be feeling dissatisfied with the status quo and wish to change the parameters. The best advice is to allow things to emerge rather than force the issue this month. It's a time for reflection rather than action, so there's no need for you to get anxious.

LOVE

The powerful influence of both Uranus and Saturn during 2009 suggests that your attitude to personal and intimate relationships is going through a fairly radical transformation.

This could give rise to elements of tension if you're married or have an established partner, and this is something that's likely to emerge in the first week of February.

If you feel hemmed in or restricted because of an existing relationship, it's no good suffering in silence and simply putting up with things as they are. It's better to confront the issues openly now rather than waiting until later, otherwise the whole thing could develop into a battle of wills and even a total breakdown in communication in the worst case scenario.

For those seeking a soul mate it's not until the final days of the month that you're likely to see any real action. It all sounds a bit vague at present, but don't despair, it will happen in good time!

MONEY

Although there are indications of change in your pattern of work, this is unlikely to have any negative impact on your current financial interests.

Cash flow may appear to slow down after the middle of the month, but this is no reason to think that your personal economic situation is about to go into recession.

The presence of Venus in the money sector of your solar chart ensures that your fortunes remain buoyant and that you have something left over to spend on leisure and pleasure. Besides which, it looks like you'll have a chance to do some advantageous manoeuvrings later in the month.

> Cash flow may appear to slow down after mid month

HEALTH

You'll probably experience an unaccountable drop in your energy levels, especially around the lunar eclipse on the 9th February. It's in your best interests not to ignore any warning signals or attempt to keep up the usual pace if you're obviously feeling below par. It is in fact an excellent month to take a more conscientious approach to your own health and well being. If you're not feeling on top form during February, maybe it's your deeper self sending up signals that it's time to reorganise your diet, get yourself down to the gym, and completely overhaul your current lifestyle.

It may not sound inviting right now, but there's no doubt you'll reap the rewards from the final result.

Lucky dates
2nd, 12th, 17th, 25th

March

A situation that's been in a state of limbo over the previous couple of months is finally brought out of the shadows and steered in a more productive direction. In addition, what happens in the second half of the month will help pave the way to a more dynamic trend in your affairs. Not only does it look as if your confidence level is about to take a quantum leap, but this is nicely complemented by the enthusiasm and the inspiring influence of people you get to know at this time. On the whole, you can expect to become more creatively engaged and you will get to feel that you're back in the driving seat during March.

LOVE

This may turn out to be a month of contrasts for romantically inclined Pisceans, though it's unlikely this will amount to an emotional trauma. Keep your wits about you and tread tactfully, especially after mid month when there's a danger of arousing jealousy and rivalry from a certain quarter.

A relationship that' s been carried on at a platonic level for some time might flare up into something more passionate. This is where sensitivity and discretion could be blown to the winds, and before you know what's happening you'll be entangled in all kinds of unwanted and unsuspected emotional complications.

Before giving way to your deeper feelings and longings, make sure you're going into the situation with your eyes open. You can then be sure that by late month it all falls into place.

MONEY

It's not until later in the month that financial and commercial interests gather a more progressive momentum, but in the meantime you can do much to improve your prospects by doing some extra homework and sorting out priorities. Any attempt to push ahead to quickly, either through your own impatience or the misplaced enthusiasm of another person, is sure to leave you carrying the can. Most of all, watch your step if dealing in second hand items as appearance could be deceptive and you might be rather susceptible to the dubious persuasions of smart-talkers. Get wise!

TRAVEL

The swift flight of Mercury through your own sign in the month ahead helps give clearer shape to your thoughts.

Mentally you'll be in good form, which is good news if you're attending an interview or need to express yourself in a convincing manner. There's something unexpected linked with a journey or chance meeting around the 22nd. Whatever happens, it'll be inspiring and perhaps give you the answer to something that has puzzled you. You might also come across information that's meant just for you!

Lucky dates
5th, 8th, 14th, 22nd

April

Although the energising influence of Mars in your own sign inclines Pisceans to take a more forceful approach to life, you'll need to keep a weather eye on how others are reacting to your behaviour. Tricky dates are the 6th and 15th April, when there's a danger of getting at loggerheads with other people, and you'll only have yourself to blame if an otherwise friendly relationship hits the rocks. Leave important initiatives until the second half of the month, when you'll see the way ahead more clearly and be less likely to antagonise others through impatience, short-sightedness or by unintentionally giving mixed messages.

LOVE

Between the 12th and 24th April, Venus returns to your sign, giving you a welcome and unexpected window of opportunity to rekindle a flame you thought had been completely extinguished.

Chances are that you will have second thoughts and perhaps a few regrets about a previous romantic attachment that never really seemed to get past the starting post. What happens under this odd transit of Venus could actually throw an entirely new light on the whole situation.

The simple fact of the matter is that you're given a second chance and will be pleasantly surprised how easy it is to pick up the old threads and weave them into something more truly fulfilling.

Established ties of love and friendship are also favoured for Pisceans, and here too there are strong indications that the emotional atmosphere can be made more vibrant. Make the most of this unexpected opportunity to make up for lost time.

MONEY

Anything to do with buying, selling and trading will get positive and speedy results early in the month, but if you're looking for a bargain don't think about it too long, just go for it! It's your own energy and initiative that carries you forward during April and this is sure to get you where you want to be if it's a new job you're after or a fundraising scheme you wish to get off the backburner.

Towards the end of the month your cash flow threatens to get a bit over-heated, but provided you avoid risky ventures and don't get carried away by over-confidence you'll land on your feet.

TRAVEL

The pace of everyday life quickens from the second week of April onwards and it looks as if you'll be on the move. Journeys might not take you far from familiar territory, but you'll nevertheless be clocking up the miles.

It might be preferable if you can stay put on the 15th of the month and not venture far from home, but from then on you're unlikely to experience any major glitches while in transit. Later in the month you'll welcome the chance to break away from your familiar routines for a day or two. Thanks to a last-minute invitation from an old friend, you'll suddenly find yourself in congenial company and catching up on all the latest gossip. You'll soon wonder why it took you so long to make the effort.

> Your energy and initiative will carry you forward this month

Lucky dates
5th, 12th, 17th, 28th.

May

The transit of Saturn through your opposite sign indicates that 2009 is a year when Pisceans should not expect everything to be handed to them on a plate. This planet is often described as a hard taskmaster, usually signifying the kind of experience that somehow tests your strength and ability. From the middle of May, this rather sombre planet shows a more positive face and signals the easing of restrictions. A long-standing obstacle is finally overcome and from now on events carry you forward instead of standing in your way. Later in the month luck comes your way via a flash of inspiration or an unforeseen twist of fate.

Staying on the theme of Saturn, obstacles that have stood in the way of your hopes have perhaps caused you to postpone a wedding in the past 12 months. From an emotional point of view everything is fine, but it's probably certain pragmatic considerations that have obliged you to delay. The good news is that this frustrating state of affairs is about to loosen its grip, and by late month plans can be finalised and celebration is called for.

Throughout 2009, Saturn indicates a changing attitude towards intimate relationships. You're getting more serious and perhaps more discerning about the kind of partner you choose, and it's unlikely you'll be inclined to rush into marriage. It might mean that romance seems to be a scarce commodity at times, but the end result will bring happiness.

MONEY

Financial and business interests gather a pleasingly progressive momentum throughout the coming month. It's a time when you can combine initiative, imagination and a touch of diplomacy to get the desired results. Don't be afraid to act quickly if an opportunity crops up in the third week; it could be just the break you've been looking for. The incentive and motivation to boost your earning powers is greatly increased, but don't let success go to your head by blowing money on luxury items. Extravagance could undo all the good work!

HOME

Be prepared to make small sacrifices if a member of your family needs your attention in the second week.

Arrangements may have to be altered, especially if you've invited friends around for a special get-together or wish to get away for a few days. This uncertain state of affairs gives way to something far more positive at the new moon on the 24th May.

What takes shape later gives you a chance to make good what's been neglected, resolve a disagreement, and create the kind of domestic ambience that soothes your soul.

Lucky dates
9th, 10th, 21st, 27th

June

Lunar trends generate positive vibes in the second week of June, when you're likely to be feeling pleased with yourself because an important task is finally brought to completion. Whether this is something to do with your career, a home renovation project or maybe passing your driving test, it will put you in an optimistic frame of mind. The pace of life gets quite hectic at times during the month ahead but this is unlikely to cause any problems for you. On the contrary, you'll probably welcome the opportunity to diversify your interests, get yourself out and about and feel more actively engaged in what's going on around you.

LOVE

There's an element of serendipity woven into a new amorous encounter in the coming weeks. In other words, romance is liable to take you by surprise, in circumstances where it's least expected.

There's much to suggest that a short journey, invitation or last-minute change of plan provides the essential key to your heart's desire. If it's going to happen, it'll happen quickly! With Venus and Mars coming together around the 21st it's as if feelings that have been locked up are suddenly given an open door, and maybe you'll realise that up to this point you haven't been firing on all cylinders.

Passions are liable to get very intense, and perhaps friends will shake their heads and say you've changed, but maybe this is a time when fairytales come real and you'll

look at life from a more positive angle. If it doesn't quite work out like this, it'll certainly turn you on!

TRAVEL

Apart from having a distinctly romantic flavour, journeys of all kinds have a pleasing and invigorating influence in your scheme of things most of the month. A chance to take a break from usual routines should definitely not be missed, especially if you've been complaining recently that social life is dull or you felt trapped in the rat race.

A change of scenery, even for a just a couple of days, will be an ideal soul therapy at this time.

People you happen to meet and talk with on your travels have a positive influence on your mind and make you realise there's far more to life than getting money and spending it.

> Someone close to you may announce a surprise wedding

HOME

Something you were obliged to postpone can be put back on the agenda early this month and you'll be in the clear if you wish to make changes to you immediate surroundings.

In the third week of June, events in the affairs of relatives or close friends throw you into a flurry of sudden activity and something quite unexpected could mean that you have a rather full house later on in the month. You shouldn't be surprised if someone close to you announces a surprise engagement, wedding or something else wonderful that calls for celebration.

On a more mundane level, you can expect to get speedy results if employing a workforce around the house in the second half of June. This is the time to get the house in order and carry out repairs.

Lucky dates
3rd, 13th, 17th, 28th

July

Y ou're advised to keep alert for any unforeseen problems early in the month and be ready to negotiate around obstacles that you hadn't anticipated. In other words, take nothing for granted and don't attempt to bury your head in the sand. The good news is that the rather hectic pace of recent weeks gives way to something steadier from the second week of July onwards. This will give you much-needed breathing space to recoup your energies and get your priorities in clear perspective. The underlying message here is to be careful that misplaced enthusiasm or impatience on your part doesn't lead to any premature action.

LOVE

It would be a mistake to feel that an existing romantic affair is about to fizzle out simply because of a disagreement.

You're likely to be going through one of those unpredictable changes of mood that often make the Piscean character so hard to understand. It's essential that you avoid getting into a downward spiral of negative thoughts in which you end up wallowing in self-pity and unworthiness. If there are issues to be discussed with your partner, all you have to do is trust that it's better to get it all out into the open rather than getting stuck in a groove of misplaced guilty feelings.

It's not the easiest of months for love, but that doesn't mean that all is lost. There's no need to overreact, get suspicious, or turn your relationship into a stage on which you can act out your fantasies.

HOME

Venus sheds a harmonious light on domestic affairs most of the month, and if you're intent on making changes to your living space, your efforts are guaranteed to have the right effect. Visitors in the first half of July provide a congenial atmosphere and give you a chance to exchange thoughts with a sympathetic soul. The fiery planet Mars enters the frame from mid month onwards, signalling good progress and speedy results in all that concerns property and home renovation. If you're considering a change of residence, now is the time to get the ball rolling.

MONEY

If a lack of funds has been the main obstacle to realising your objectives, you can expect a change for the better.

Something you've been obliged to deny yourself will now become possible. Whether it's to do with your home, the purchasing of state of the art technical equipment or the launch of a business venture, events are at last contriving to point you in the right direction. Job seekers are advised to weigh up the pros and cons late month. What sounds wonderful in theory may not be so in practice!

Lucky dates

2nd, 10th, 19th, 29th

August

Be prepared to shoulder some extra chores and responsibilities during the second week of August. A friend or colleague is likely to ask a favour, and there's a chance that this will give rise to a conflict of loyalties for you. However, you can count on others to show sensitivity and understanding, and in the end you'll be highly appreciated. As a Piscean you have a kind of inborn instinct for wanting to help other people out and play the caring angel. What happens early in the month will therefore give you an ideal opportunity to express this side of your nature and make everyone (including yourself!) feel good.

LOVE

Something promised in the previous month is likely to gather a satisfying momentum in the weeks ahead, and by the end of the month it looks as if you'll be riding the crest of a wave.

The prevailing cosmic pattern makes the month of August a highlight of the year for romantically inclined Pisceans, and after a rather uneventful or disillusioning phase of experience you can look forward to something that answers to your ideals and dreams. Even better, it's not only the younger generation who are destined to feel this heart-warming vibe.

Pisceans of more mature years are especially favoured at this time, and whether you're single, divorced or otherwise unattached, a chance meeting at some time in the coming month could end up changing your life.

If an existing relationship has seemed a bit lacklustre recently, a break from your usual routines provides the required tonic.

TRAVEL

Whether you're travelling on business or simply for the fun of it, everything is guaranteed to meet with and perhaps exceed your hopes and expectations. Recreation and leisurely activities are highlighted, making this a splendid month for doing your own thing and indulging your pleasure-loving instincts.

Prevailing astrological trends couldn't be much more apt for what is traditionally the holiday month! If you're seeking something that gives you a sense of adventure or contains an element of sport and skill, you'll certainly have plenty of scope to express yourself and impress others.

MONEY

Work-related interests are under a helpful trend but be careful not to make too many promises or commitments around the 12th. It's an excellent month for cultivating the right kind of dialogue with those who are in a position to help further your aims.

If you're in doubt about career prospects or aspects of your current employment, don't waste valuable time worrying about it. By taking action now and seeking professional advice you'll be pleasantly surprised how easy it is to sort things out. Towards the end of the month an unexpected urgent repair job may be more expensive that initially anticipated, so make sure you budget for a reserve fund to cover any unforeseen costs.

> An urgent repair job may be more expensive than anticipated

Lucky dates
6th, 13th, 17th, 24th

September

Your creative energies are given renewed vigour in the month ahead, and if you're aiming to promote your special talents and develop a broader field of self-expression this is when you're most likely to make an important breakthrough. Your social life gathers a more interesting momentum and opens a wider scope for meeting people on your own mental and spiritual wavelength. Psychologically your confidence is at a high and you're expressing a more extrovert attitude to life. If you're involved with the arts, sports or the world of entertainment, now is the time to get out there and blow your own trumpet!

LOVE

This could turn out to be a month of surprises, with dramatic encounters forecast when Mars is strongly activated around the 13th and 22nd.

Emotional reactions are liable to be intense and perhaps there'll be a tendency to swing to extremes, but at least there'll be no dull moments and what you experience will make you realise that you still have much to learn in the art of love.

The forces of attraction are decidedly electric later in the month as Venus moves into your House of Partners and draws new admirers into your orbit. A chance encounter could mark the start of a passionate episode, though it's a bit hit and miss whether this is destined to stand the test of time. Whatever happens, you'll realise what it means to meet someone who lights your fire!

MONEY

Do your best to clear any outstanding debts early in the month, and likewise don't leave any loose ends dangling if a business agreement is under consideration. Procrastination will invariably lead to further hassles later on, so it's in your best interests to focus on getting finances sorted out. From the second week onwards don't take too much for granted or leave anything to chance where commercial transactions and jointly held resources are concerned. Don't attempt to cut corners or kid yourself that there's an easy way around the red tape.

TRAVEL

With Mars giving a boost to your energy and vitality, this is a prime month for seeking distant horizons and going places that make you feel extra vibrant. A change of scenery will be a kind of soul therapy during September, stirring your imagination, bringing you fresh inspiration and making you appreciate the wider world.

On a more mundane level, you'll need to exercise patience as well as keeping your wits about you if seeking special information or wanting a definite decision on an important issue. Don't allow others to coax you into making a financial commitment if you're not totally convinced.

Lucky dates
4th, 12th, 22nd, 30th

October

Events taking shape in the background are programmed to have a helpful influence on your life in the near future. You might not be immediately aware of it, but there's a hint of significant change that's geared towards expansion and enrichment. It's as if a fairly lengthy phase of preparation is coming full circle and from now on you are able to develop a more focused sense of direction. It's not always easy for Pisceans to decide on what they want to do with their life. Often there's a kind of stalemate and you're pulled in two directions, but you'll be pleased to know that from late October there's a clear way ahead.

LOVE

Venus throws an aura of harmony and sympathy around close ties of love and affection most of the month. This is especially good news for established couples, and even better if you're taking the plunge into matrimony during October or hope to take this step in the near future.

The really good news is that Saturn finally takes leave of your House of Partners late in the month. Long-standing obstacles and restrictions that have stood in the way of your happiness are due to fade into the background, and from now on it's plain sailing for those aiming to put a relationship on a more secure basis.

For singles the prospect is equally encouraging, because it suggests that the rather disappointing experience of the previous couple of years is about to give way to an easier trend. One thing's for sure, you're unlikely to repeat your old mistakes!

MONEY

If there's been a question mark hanging over a joint financial venture recently, you can expect the situation to be resolved soon after the 10th.

A decision that's been pending falls into clearer perspective, giving you the necessary confidence to push ahead with a new project. From the middle of October onwards fortune smiles on you as an added bonus arrives and welcome extra cash comes your way via a rebate, gift or lucky windfall.

Also there are indications that the good fortune of someone very close to you puts you in a cheerful mood and maybe there'll be cause for a joyful celebration later in the month!

> **You have confidence to push ahead with a new project**

HEALTH

Prevailing trends continue to give Pisceans an energy boost and make you feel more integrated mentally, emotionally and physically.

The general pattern of events generates a positive and optimistic state of affairs, but if you feel there's something missing in your life, now is the time to address the issue. Maybe you allowed yourself to be railroaded down a track that no longer fits your developing needs and potential? Whatever it is, face the situation head on. The relief when it's resolved will be worth the effort.

Positive trends coming into force in the middle of the month give you the incentive to dissolve any lingering malaise and encourage you to make contact with your deeper creative energies.

Lucky dates
4th, 10th, 17th, 27th

November

Over the past couple of years there have been times when life seemed to constantly put you in an ambiguous position. The urge to move forwards and make desirable changes has perhaps been a struggle against the odds and in the end you've been obliged to compromise or simply put up with second best. It all changes now that Saturn has shifted from your opposite sign. This gives free reign to the influence of Uranus, and what this means is that from now onwards you're empowered to change and transform your lifestyle to fit your changing needs and express your true self. It's time to put yourself first for once!

LOVE

The pattern of change indicated by Uranus not only has an impact on your material aims and interests. Even more significantly it means that your deeper emotional needs are about to take a paradigm shift, perhaps quite unexpectedly.

In the past unpredictable feelings have probably turned your love life into a roller coaster (or carousel). You met someone, felt irresistibly attracted and got deeply involved, then you realised that this is not what you wanted at all. This abrupt turnaround ended by creating an atmosphere of bewilderment. Yet after a short while the whole cycle started again.

If this describes your experience, it looks as if you're outgrowing this pattern and have learned some valuable lessons. What takes shape in November puts you on a more satisfying road.

MONEY

Saturn now begins to focus on both personal and joint financial interests, giving a feeling of increasing stability and a determination to get your act together once and for all. There's much to suggest a change in the direction of your main aims and objectives that's bound to have a positive impact on your financial status between now and the end of 2010. It's likely you've been going through a transition phase careerwise and perhaps you've felt a bit uncertain about your work situation. An opportunity around mid month is likely to solve your dilemma.

TRAVEL

You've made a good choice if there's a long-range or leisurely excursion on the agenda for the coming weeks. Travel contains an element of surprise around mid month and perhaps you'll bump into a long lost friend while away from home.

For business-minded Pisceans, what takes shape in the first half of November has the effect of broadening your horizons and putting you in contact with the right kind of people. Be prepared to take seriously a proposition put to you by a friend or colleague, especially if it means making more productive use of one of your neglected talents.

Lucky dates
4th, 7th, 16th, 26th

December

With Jupiter now heading towards your own sign you're likely to get some good omens as the festive season approaches. The underlying cosmic influence is highly supportive, generating an undercurrent of luck and inspiration. You may be realising by now that 2009 has been something of a year of destiny for you, in the sense that you are now in a position to see exactly the direction you're aiming to take in the coming twelve months. After a lengthy phase of experimentation, and perhaps a few false turnings along the way, you have gained enough experience to know what exactly it is that you do and do not want.

LOVE

Established ties of love and friendship continue to benefit under the prevailing pattern of trends. Now that various obstacles and restrictions that were in your way are becoming a thing of the past, you'll be feeling a great deal more positive about pushing ahead with the desirable changes you have in mind.

If one such change entails marriage, you can be sure that this is the right decision. Your wish to give a firmer foundation to a relationship will work like magic and enable you to transform your ideals into realities.

It might not be the most eventful month for single Pisceans who are hoping to meet their affinity, but there are indications that a sympathetic link is being forged during the final days of December. You may have to make up your mind, however, if you're still living under the shadow of a previous romantic attachment. Do yourself a favour, let go of the past. It's time to move on!

HOME

Sensitivities within the family circle are liable to wear rather thin in the early days of the month. If you have children, be prepared for minor skirmishes and mishaps, but don't rise to the bait if they're deliberately trying to wind you up and create a drama.

On a more positive note it looks as if your home is the focus of a very friendly and convivial state of affairs from mid month onwards. This trend sets the scene for what turns out to be a truly memorable occasion. Much to your delight, you'll have plenty of scope for making friends, exchanging gifts, and ensuring that a good time is had by all.

HEALTH

You're tapping into a high energy source at present and are feeling more harmonious within yourself. The only proviso comes later in December when you're advised to ease the pace and don't allow other people to bully you into taking on more than you can deal with. It's important that you keep up your resistance at this time, otherwise an untimely seasonal ailment could well spoil your fun.

From a different angle, you can expect to receive good news concerning the health of someone close to you who has perhaps been under the weather recently. Your initial worries prove unfounded and quickly fade into the background. All in all, it's a positive end to the year.

> **Don't allow others to bully you into taking too much on**

Lucky dates
3rd, 11th, 21st, 30th

The Orient Psychic Service

Love, Health, Career
Family, Spiritual Problems.

Genuine, Honest, Accurate, Friendly,
With 30 years Experience.

Please Contact Ki-Lin for
appointments.

07818 050673

Donation Only

LIVE **LISA MORGAN**

Famous psychic featured
in magazines & radio.
Specialising in heart
breaking situations.
Will you be back together
again?

Love - Career - Finance

0906 120 2724

ALL CREDIT & DEBIT CARDS ACCEPTED

0845 050 1895

Calls cost £1.50 per min from BT landline.
All calls recorded. 18+. Sp Abs BCM2714

THE WESSEX
ASTROLOGER

For a wide range of astrology books and
products. Astrological consultations
available by appointment. For more
information visit our website at

www.wessexastrologer.com

or contact us at:
The Wessex Astrologer
4A Woodside Road Bournemouth
BH5 2AZ Tel +44 (0)1202 424695

Heart 2 Heart

A little reading goes a long way

Need Guidance In Your Life? Need To Contact Someone In Spirit?

Choose From Our Gifted Psychics:

Tarot, Mediumship and Clairvoyance

♥ **Romance** ♥ **Career** ♥ **Finance** ♥

£20.00 for 30mins £12.50 for 15mins

New Services: Just For You

Credit/Debit Hotline Call 0845 644 3320
£1 goes to British Heart Foundation.

Get A Free **Email Reading@**
www.heart-2-heart.co.uk

Ellie Marie
And Richard
Leading Psychics

We Offer Live Phone Readings
No Birth Dates asked or Tarot Used.
26 years Experience and we are not a
company.

We are Genuine you will see why so
many clients return.
When you call you will only speak
direct with us.

0800-01903-69

As seen in Media and Magazines.

24 hour service/7 days
All readings are payable on your
credit/debit card.

SPELLS CAST

By experienced
witch/psychic
For details send
problem and SAE to:-

Susan Collins
145 Waverley Avenue,
Nuneaton Warks
CV11 4RZ

Brilliant new children's fantasy book
for 7 to 10 year olds with a powerful
and inspiring nutritional theme.

TG and the Rainbow Warriors
Gripping, funny and endearing, TG and the Rainbow Warriors
lends itself beautifully to being read to children, giving many
opportunities for discoveries, discussion and enjoyment.

Adults love it too!
The ideal way for parents and teachers to help children gain
confidence to make the best choices for a healthy, happy future.

To place your order of TG and the Rainbow Warriors go to
www.balancedhealththerapies.co.uk
Price £7.99 (£5.99 + £2.00 p&p)

The Tarot year ahead

Talented Tarot reader, **Xanna Eve Chown**, consulted three cards for each month of the year to see what's hot in 2009 for the UK

January
Knight of Coins ®
Five of Wands
Six of Coins

The year gets off to a slow start with the first card drawn: the reversed Knight of Coins. This Knight is steady and can't be rushed, even in urgent circumstances. He represents stability, but when the card is reversed, this stability becomes more of a stubbornness.

However, the second card drawn, the Five of Wands, suggests that a hotly contested debate will soon get things moving, as this card is all about struggle and competition.

There are always more than two sides to an argument under the influence of this card. Often, the main quarrel is made up of lots of smaller points and disagreements, with several players adding their ideas to the main drama. Although the contests that this card brings are ones that can bring out the best in the people involved, this is certainly not going to be the case now.

The main argument will become diffused as the month wears on, with the influence of the reversed Six of Coins. This card also represents quarrels, but when reversed they are like petty disputes rather than healthy debate.

The appearance of this card also shows that the situation has been driven by greed and envy. It suggests that the matter involves an inappropriate handling of funds.

Two Coins cards so early on in the year already highlight a bias towards financial situations being high on the agenda for the future.

February
Knight of Cups ®
Hierophant
Three of Wands ®

The Knight of Cups that appears in February is reversed, to show that someone in the public eye is not all that he seems. As a person, this Knight is full ☛

of deceptive charm that actually masks an inner insecurity.

This is a card that can refer to a damaging childishness of disposition, and often points to a destructive romantic relationship or divorce. A high-profile case of infidelity may hit the headlines this month.

The first Major Arcana of the year follows, the Hierophant card, which suggests that traditional values are being challenged by this Knight, and that many people are shocked by the revelations that are being revealed.

The Hierophant is ruled by the astrological sign of Taurus, which is the second sign of the zodiac. Taurus loves to be surrounded by luxury and is concerned with accumulating wealth and prosperity, and can be a formidable opponent when its path is crossed.

The final card for February is the reversed Three of Wands, which is sometimes seen as a card that represents pride and arrogance. It can even suggest a large betrayal of a friend or partner.

Under the influence of this card, someone has convinced themselves that the ends justify the means. They're not concerned with friendship, but rather with staying in the spotlight for as long as possible.

March

The Tower
Two of Coins ®
The World ®

March looks set to be an interesting - and also disruptive - month, with three cards that all refer to different aspects of change.

The Tower is sometimes considered to be one of the most feared cards in the Tarot pack as it usually suggests a bolt out of the blue, a major change or catastrophe that leads to a complete rethinking of a situation. This situation can lead to a breaking of the protective barriers that we put up to guard ourselves from reality and often causes shock and confusion for those involved. However, the changes that result from the events of this card can be positive, allowing for a greater sense of freedom and transformation.

The reversed Two of Coins, sometimes called the card of change, suggests that this upheaval will be concerned with

material and financial concerns. There will be a time of uncertainty leading up to a modification and change in priorities.

The World card appears reversed to suggest regret and disappointment. When it appears the correct way up, this card refers to the completion of a cycle. However, when reversed it describes the failure to reach certain important goals. It shows that there are big lessons that need to be learned, and that people's attitudes need to adapt in order to learn them properly. However, this may turn out to be more of a struggle for some people than for others.

April

Seven of Cups
Nine of Wands
Ten of Coins ®

April starts with an interesting card, the Seven of Cups, which in many decks shows a number of goblets with many different things inside, symbolising choice. There are lots of possible reactions to the current situation, and lots of different ideas and solutions being offered all at once.

This card warns us not to be tempted by illusions. The people making the choices must be careful to look closely at all their options before making a decision that is sure to affect many people other than themselves.

The card that is drawn next, the Nine of Wands, suggests that people are looking for ways to defend themselves, and taking extra precautions to look out for those around them. This is a card that refers to people making a show of strength. People are remembering past attacks and expecting the worst from a situation. The positive side of this card is that it encourages people to stand together against a common problem or cause in group situations.

The reversed Ten of Coins is a card that often highlights a squandering of material resources. There may be a sudden rush to spend public money without due care or attention at this time. Although the outward suggestion is that this is for the greater good, this card points to a fear of loss of reputation, which is not usually the strongest or best reason for action.

May

The reversed Knight of Coins reappears in May. It was the first card that appeared in January, and suggests that a similar situation will come about this month. As court cards are often character cards, it could show that the same person will be hitting the headlines again.

The reversed nature of the card suggests that this character is not being seen in the most positive of lights. This card often represents stagnation or perceived laziness when action is required or expected. Of the 11 court cards that appear this year, nine are reversed.

The card drawn next, the Three of Swords, is sometimes called the card of heartbreak. In Tarot decks inspired by the influential 1910 Rider-Waite deck, the design is of a large heart pierced by three long swords. In more general terms, the appearance of this card can point to unsettling

noise or the revelation of a truth that is painful to hear. People affected by this news need understanding and compassion as well as a fair discussion of events.

However, the reversed Judgement card points to an inability to bring matters to a quick conclusion. The Judgement card is ruled by Scorpio. This is the sign that presides over the eighth house of the zodiac. It's a sign of well-kept secrets, but it also shows a desire to look inwardly to find out where to place blame or heal.

June

The Three of Swords appears for the second month running, showing that the consequences of the previous month's situation are overlapping into June. This is backed up by the appearance of the Ten of Swords. Swords usually stand for conflict, and this is no exception.

The Ten of Swords points to the aftermath ☞

of a conflict, the sense of sadness that sets in after the fury or excitement of the actual battle. It suggests that a considerable amount of force has been used to reach this point. However, on a more positive note, this card suggests that this conflict is fully at an end. This means that it is time to start picking up the pieces and moving on.

Happily, these two cards are closely followed by the Nine of Coins, a card of good luck in material affairs. This card often shows a confident, elegant woman standing in a garden. She wears rich clothes and the vines behind her sprout grapes and coins in abundance. It is a card that suggests a time of financial contentment or investments.

July
Nine of Cups
Queen of Coins ®
Queen of Wands®

The positive trend of the previous month continues into July with the Nine of Cups, a card sometimes known as the wish card or simply called the card of happiness. This card brings a feeling that peace of mind is achievable. Leaders appear to be more in tune with the feelings of the general public under the influence of this card, which leads to a sense of well being.

Two Queens appear this month: the queen of material wealth and the queen of energy and power. When two Queens appear in the same month, it suggests that there will be a certain amount of gossip in the air, with an undertone of rivalry. Both women are skilled and successful at manipulating the public interest, but in totally different ways.

The reversed Queen of Coins is a woman who is accustomed to putting on expensive displays of wealth. Although she is a generous hostess, these displays are more about her status than a desire to make others happy.

The reversed Queen of Wands is a card that symbolises a passionate woman who gets what she wants by using her sensuality. Look out for headlines this July when these two Queenly personalities collide. All three of these cards appear in subsequent months, showing that these situations could form a repeating pattern.

August
Six of Wands
Nine of Coins ®
Page of Swords ®

The summer continues with the appearance of the Six of Wands, the victory card. Many decks show a man on horseback holding up a laurel wreath and wearing another one as a crown. A laurel wreath is an ancient symbol of victory and success. This card herald the resolution of an important matter, and a general sense of satisfaction at what is perceived generally to be good news. However, as the saying goes, you can't please all the people all of the time.

The Nine of Coins makes its second appearance in this year's reading, but this time the card is reversed and its message is subtly altered. Now this card is associated with an erosion of security and stability, often in the financial arena.

The reversed Page of Swords signifies the approach of an unexpected challenge. Someone is trying to gain attention by positioning themselves against the system and public feeling.

As a character, this Page is a young person, who is quick-thinking and very clever with words. He has too much confidence in his own ability to be taken seriously, and may be perceived as untrustworthy and creating an unnecessary diversion to meet his own ends.

September

The High Priestess ®
Queen of Coins ®
Nine of Cups

All three cards drawn for September appear more than once in this year's spread. The reversed High Priestess, who appears again in the final month of the year, is a card of deception. Don't trust everything that you read or hear in the news this month: all the evidence is not yet in.

The High Priestess is ruled by the Moon, and is intuitive and sensitive. This card suggests that

someone is setting out to deceive, so fully that they are also seen to be deceiving themselves.

The reversed Queen of Coins, who we met once in July, is coming back as a major player this month. A wealthy woman, who is far better at spending money than saving it, this star is surrounded by people who shield her from criticism. They tell her everything she does is good, meaning that she lives in a bubble and is unable to see things the way that they are. However, she is being deceived into seeing things the way that she wants them to be, making for an interesting month in the gossip columns.

The month ends with the Nine of Cups, a card that appeared for the first time in July.

October

Three of Swords
Queen of Cups
Ten of Wands ®

October starts with the Three of Swords, and it

is possible that a funeral will make the news this month. Heartbreak and grief feel more painful when they are unexpected, but this card suggests events could be prepared for, or been anticipated for a while.

The Queen of Cups suggests that the person making the news was a much-loved figure, an older person who had a long, varied career and was respected for their spirituality and grace. In a more general sense, this is the card of flexibility. Often, the more flexible we are, the easier it is to live in the world. This doesn't mean being a pushover, but trying not to always react to situations in the same way through habit. Instead, approach each new situation on its own merits.

The reversed Ten of Wands appears towards the end of the month. Wands are concerned with energy and power, and this card warns against a leader taking on too much power when it should be shared out. This is a card of burdens and may depict a man weighed down by a bundle of wands that he struggles to carry. This card can suggest a lawsuit making the headlines, as one of the ☞

people involved has some large losses to deal with.

November

The nights are drawing in and the reversed Nine of Coins appears for the third and final time in this year's reading. Although it seems that there have been many reversals in this year's spread, it's half and half.

The Nine of Coins can refer to bad luck or dishonesty in financial dealings - and also to a snobbish attitude towards these problems.

The reversed Queen of Wands describes someone who will do anything to get what she wants and this may be causing her downfall. The person referred to by this card refuses to take the blame, even when public opinion turns against them. They are domineering and believe that their position or wealth will keep them out of harm's way. However, the shadow caused by this

episode clears towards the end of the month with the light of the Sun, one of the most positive cards.

One meaning of this card is that brighter days lie ahead. Another meaning is that the 'light' of this card reveals things for what they are. This month will reveal some of the secrets from earlier in the year and bring them to the public attention.

December

The year ends with three strong cards, two character cards from the Tarot court and the second appearance of the reversed High Priestess, the strong feminine spiritual principle. This card could suggest that the world is being guided too much by masculine thoughts and ideas. In many ways, a balance between the two paths (feminine/masculine, yin/yang) is the way to reach a deeper level of contentment.

The Page of Swords

appears reversed, for the second time. This Page often brings malicious gossip to the fore, although the stories are often titillating for the people not involved in the scandal.

The final card of the year is the Queen of Cups, another strong example of the feminine principal. In some decks she is shown as Persephone, a goddess associated with fertility and a new beginning.

This year will be balanced between the positive and the negative. Just as there is an equal number of reversals and cards the correct way up in this year's reading, so there is an equal number of cards from the suits of Swords, which relate to conflict - and Cups, which relate to emotions. ❖

further info

This delicious Tarot deck features images from the Middle Ages and Renaissance and is finished with a sumptuous golden edge. £16.99 from: www.tarotchest.co.uk

Astromagic.org

E-mail a question and pay by Paypal. No waiting on the phone.

Astrology
Natal Reading — £12.99
Compatibility Profile — £12.99
Transits — £12.99

Numerology
Numerology Profile — £8.99

Tarot
One Card Reading — £4.99
Celtic Cross — £9.99
Hopes and Dreams — £9.99

Runes
Odin's Rune — £4.99
Three Rune Reading — £8.99

For all your psychic needs.

eLLa's gifteD PSYCHICS
09051 630 532
50 P PER MIN

CREDIT/DEBIT CARDS: 0800 0439866

All calls recorded fyd online M1 1FB 20 mins only £10

CALON KORE

Literally means Heart Maiden.
An elite sisterhood of healer
priestesses each expert in
several healing arts.
Contact us via:

www.calonkore.co.uk

IRIS
FAMOUS
CLAIRVOYANT/MEDIUM

Caring. Honest. Accurate
and Genuine. Working with
Spirit Guides and Crystals.
As seen in Media. 36 years
experience.

I ANSWER ALL CALLS PERSONALLY

Credit and Debit Cards welcome

01843 232 638

Or Pay by Phone

0907 128 6912

Calls cost £1.50 per min recorded 24S
PO Box 567 LS2 7WP

FAITH

*GIFTED CLAIRVOYANT. PSYCHIC.
MEDIUM. HEALER AND SPELL CASTER*

0208 451 8876 (Credit Card)
0906 661 2779 (Calls cost £1.50 min, recorded)
MOB: 07765 821 131 (Info on spells and healing)

*ACCURATE. AND SINCERE READINGS.
CARRIED OUT WITH THE HELP AND
BLESINGS OF MY GUIDES TO GUIDE YOU.*

TEXT FAITH TO **78887** (£1.50 per question)
THREE QUESTIONS £10

BOX A386, PREDICTION, LEON HOUSE, 9TH FLOOR, 233 HIGH ST, CROYDON CR9 1HZ

Text our psychics!
Text PREDICT & qn to 81007

Pay by phone:
09063 442 102
Pay by card:
08006 121 154

Calls to 0906 numbers £1.50 p/min. Mobile costs may vary.
Calls recorded. Text replies cost £1.50. You may get 2 replies.
Ralph Riley Ltd. PO Box 37157 London E4 7YW.

Whispering Spirits

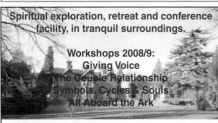

Spiritual exploration, retreat and conference
facility, in tranquil surroundings.

Workshops 2008/9:
Giving Voice
The Couple Relationship
Symbols, Cycles & Souls
All Aboard the Ark

Purley Chase Centre, Purley Chase Lane, Mancetter, Warwickshire, CV9 2RQ
For further information please contact either Anne or Sally on:
Tel: 01827 712370 or
Email: enquiries@purleychasecentre.org.uk
www.purleychasecentre.org.uk

PURLEY
CHASE CENTRE

Blue Storm
why have just one witch
when we give you the whole coven
CustomSpells cast for most situations
there are none more powerful
psychic/tarot readings by post £10
Po Box 60 Isle of wight PO36 8YQ
www.blue-storm.org 07500 596088

SUBSCRIBE TO

AND GET A FREE GIFT- THE INCENSE BOX

Plus save up to 20%

When you subscribe to Prediction magazine today you can SAVE OVER 20% - PLUS you will recieve The Incense Box, absolutely FREE!

The healing power of incense has been used for thousands of years. Scent stimulates a part of your brain that can produce strong physical, emotional and psychological effects and can alter your mood dramatically. Incense calms anxiety and stimulates your energy levels.

The Incense Box contains three delightful fragrances to soothe and revitalise your mind, body and spirit:
● Sandalwood
● Rose
● Frankincense

The 48-page book describes the traditional use of the three fragrances and how to get the best from each. There are meditations, visualisations and affirmations, plus snippets of incense lore. An attractive black ceramic incense burner is also included.

Don't Miss Out, Subscribe Today

CALL NOW!

✆ 0845 676 7778

www.predictionmagazine.co.uk/ipdcl

Subscription Hotline. **Please quote code 37A** Phone lines open seven days a week, 9am–9pm. Please have your payment detail ready when you call or subscribe online at: www.predictionmagazine.co.uk Offers closes September 30th, 2009.

prediction

prediction
better than ever

Great features in *Prediction* every month:

★ **Magical ways to attract love, luck, money and happiness**

★ **Psychics, astrology, ghosts...**

★ **The answers to life's mysteries!**

Prediction, your monthly mystical guide to life, love and the future, is bursting with fascinating features on psychic phenomena, tarot, dreams, spiritual topics and absorbing real life stories. We have the answers to life's mysteries! If you want to be in the know - don't miss out on this wonderful offer!

Direct Debit Guarantee This guarantee is offered by all Banks and Building Societies that take part in the Direct Debit Scheme. The efficiency and security of the Scheme is monitored by your own Bank or Building Society. If the amounts to be paid or the payment dates change IPC Media Ltd. Will notify you at least ten days in advance of your account being debited or as otherwise agreed. If an error is made by IPC Media Ltd. Or your bank or Building Society you are guaranteed a full and immediate refund from your branch of the amount paid. You can cancel a Direct Debit at any time by writing to your bank or Building Society. Please also send a copy of the letter to us. Direct Debits can only be paid through a Bank or Building Society. Your Direct Debit price will stay the same for 1 year from start date.

YES! I would like to subscribe to Prediction and recieve the incense box for absolutely free!

❑ 6 monthly Direct Debit - £15.30 saving over 20% off the full price of £19.18
OR
❑ Full 1 year Cheque/Credit Card - £32.50 saving over 15% off the full price of £38.35

OVERSEAS READERS: to save 25% and recieve your Prediction by priority airmail, please call our hotline on+44 845 676 7778 and quote code 37B. (Please note we are unable to send gifts overseas)

Complete this coupon and send with your payment to: Prediction Magazine Subscriptions, FREEPOST CY1061, Haywards Heath, West Sussex, RH16 3BR (No stamp needed)

YOUR DETAILS

Title _____ Surname _____

Address _____

_____

_____ Postcode _____

Telephone _____

Would you like to receive messages to your mobile from IPC and Prediction containing news, special offers, product and service information and take part in our research? If yes, please include your mobile number here:

Mobile _____

If you would like to receive emails from Prediction and IPC containing news, special offers and product and service information and take part in our magazine research via email, please include your email address below:

Email _____

PAYMENT DETAILS

❑ I enclose a cheque for £ _____

made payable to IPC Media Ltd

I wish to pay by ❑ Mastercard   ❑ Visa
❑ Amex   ❑ Diners   ❑ Delta   ❑ Maestro

❑❑❑❑❑ ❑❑❑❑ ❑❑❑❑ ❑❑❑❑ ❑❑❑

Expiry Date ❑❑ ❑❑ Issue No. ❑❑ ❑❑ (maestro only)

Signature _____ Date _____

I am over 18 ❑

For office use only:
Originators Reference - 764 221

DIRECT Debit

A/C No ❑❑❑❑❑❑❑❑❑

Name of Bank _____

Address of Bank _____

Postcode _____

Account No ❑❑❑❑❑❑❑ Sort Code ❑❑❑❑❑❑

Name of Account Holder _____

Instructions to your Bank or Building Society: Please pay IPC Media Ltd. Direct Debits from this account detailed on this instruction subject to the safeguards assured by the Direct Debit Guarantee. I understand that this instruction may remain with IPC Media Ltd and so, details will be passed electronically to my Bank or Building Society.

Signature _____ Date _____

I am over 18 ❑

All subscriptions will begin with the first available issue. Offer only available to new UK subscribers and the 6 monthly offer is only available in the UK by Direct Debit. Our free gift is subject to availability and will be delivered seperately within 28 days after your first payment is received. IPC Media Ltd reserve the right to send an alternative gift of equal or higher value. In the event that you cancel your subscription within 12 months, we will refund you the value of the undelivered portion of your subscription but IPC reserve the right, in our absolute discretion, to deduct the value of your free gift from any amount refunded. The offer closes 30th September 2009. For enquiries please email: +44 (0)845 676 7778, fax: +44 (0)845 123 9010 or e-mail: ipcsubs@quadrantsubs.com Prediction, published by IPC Media Ltd., (IPC) will collect your personal information to process your order. Prediction and IPC would like to contact you by post or telephone to promote and ask your opinion on our magazines and services. Please tick here if you prefer not to hear from IPC ❑. IPC who publish Prediction would like to send messages to your mobile with offers from carefully selected organisations and brands, promoting and researching their products and services. If you want to receive a message please tick here ❑. IPC may occasionally pass your details to carefully selected organisations so that they can contact you by telephone or post with regards to promoting and researching their products and services. Please tick here if you prefer not to be contacted ❑.

37A

MEDIUM CLAIRVOYANT PSYCHIC TAROT

Are you enthusiastic and motivated? We need experienced people to join our Psychic Team.

Excellent Rates of Pay

Work From Home

Flexible shifts (Between 7am and 2pm)

We are also currently recruiting for night shifts

Applicants will be working with our existing, well established high profile clients. You will have proven experience working on the telephone as well as face to face with clients.

A strong desire to achieve high standards is essential. We are a constantly expanding company with a successful team. We offer a range of telephone services both premium rate and credit card, as well as work on SMS. There may also be the opportunity for work in TV.

If you are interested and think you have what it takes to be part of our team then please call Amy on 0870 609 5503
(Confidentiality assured)

Pronto Media Ltd. Office 4, Corunna House Business Centre, 42-44 Ousegate, Selby, North Yorkshire YO8 4NH

The MagikThread

With over 200 different tarot and oracle decks with 25% off the normal retail price. The Magik Thread is the place to buy for all your future need.

Use the code **FUTURE** and get an extra 5% off when you order online.

0115 939 4777

www.themagikthread.co.uk

The Psychic

Gift Discover your Future

Call Alethea's family of caring psychics now

0906 110 0965

For payment on your phone bill. All calls recorded £1.50 per min from BT land lines

0800 915 2345

Free call for credit card payment

Text "Gift" & your question to a live psychic on 84184 £1.50 per reply.

www.thepsychicgift.com

Helpline 0808 156 0022

www.gailkeenan.co.uk

Need immediate answers?

Our gifted psychics will give an accurate reading relating to any issues you may have

Credit/Debit: **0207 111 6076** Pay on Bill: **0906 539 0181**

Text: **gail** to text **88818**

18+ • calls recorded • 0906 = £1.50 per minute • £1.50 per text

REGENT STREET • LONDON • W1B 2QD ENT ONLY

LUCY CREEN

Psychic, Medium and tarot card reader

0844 888 0559

Credit/debit card readings call

0870 128 7245
0844 848 1480

20-30 mins £25-£35

For phone billed readings call

0906 110 5942

calls recorded and cost £1.50/min from a BT Landline

Eire +44 13 23 439339

10am to 10:30pm

"Transnet" M25 1PS

www.lucycreen.co.uk

Sharon Brush

at Silver Sun

International Renowned Clairvoyant

As Seen on TV

30 Years Professional

Amazingly Accurate

Call Me On

01621 843 992

Switch/Credit Cards

Or one of my Readers on

0906 110 8425

Text SILVER followed by any question to **84184**

Readings cannot be guaranteed Calls cost £1.50 per min from a BT landline & recorded PO Box 7388, CM9 6WA

Sky Redferne

Tarot, I Ching, Runes and Angel Card readings. £20

Spell Candles

Available shortly The Hedge Witches Diary 2009

Or join our heal the earth initiative.

www.skyredferne.co.uk

PO Box A424, 9th Floor Leon House 233 High Street Croydon, CR91HZ

For postal readings make cheques or postal orders payable to Fearn Thomas

---

CORA

Psychic/Tarot/Crystal Ball

Over 30 Years Clairvoyancy

RELATIONSHIP AND LOVE READINGS

020 8924 3703

10 am to midnight 7 days

All major cards accepted

Weekly predictions for everyone

Expert astrologer **Peter West** examines
the cosmic patterns in 2009 that will affect all
of us in the months ahead

Jan 1 - 4

There are four changes of astrological sign in the first few days of the year. This suggests you should feel your way forward and not try to take charge and go with the natural flow. Your romantic life is about to become more meaningful.

Jan 5 - 11

Work related matters could seem a little bit on the bumpy side this week but it's nothing to worry about. This is a time to use your social skills and any intuitive feelings you have to bring people around to your way of thinking.

Jan 12 - 18

Mercury has now moved retrograde so it is time for you to be on the ball. This week favours study more than on-the-spot action. Beware others dragging up events from the past. Make sure you stick to your guns and go for what you want, not what other people want you to do.

Jan 19 - 25

As fast as you try to get one task under way, somehow or another, it all seems to unravel. Things just won't go the way you want. You're better off dealing with one thing at a time and leaving long term affairs alone. Perhaps concentrate on DIY or outstanding jobs.

Jan 26 - Feb 1

Social and business affairs become interlinked as amazing gains in one area may be marred by some big changes in the other. Financially, make sure all is well and that you have reserves to see you through. It's all about keeping a healthy balance in your life. The police or military forces may be in the news.

Feb 2 - 8

Communication and transport matters pick up. People are inclined to be unhelpful and family members try to off-load their responsibilities on you. Help out but you have to draw the line. Put down roots but also make sure you get out and about and have some fun. Spruce up your social life.

Feb 9 - 15

Oh dear! Those involved in secret affairs could be discovered and some may have to look for alternative employment as a result. The New Moon in Leo shows young people will take centre stage and might need to be dealt with promptly.

Feb 16 - 22

A much better time for everyone and it all appears to be bright and bubbly. The social scene moves up a notch as does the emotional side of things. People closely involved with others may find that their lives become more meaningful. Some may travel abroad or book a welcome holiday. Don't try to change anything but do accept the changes that come your way.

Feb 23 - Mar 1

Expect an air of importance as things speed up. You may find business matters developing mostly in your favour. This will suit those working in public relations, advertising and the communication industry generally. New ideas with mobile phones or computers may be announced. Family members share a get-together in harmony.

Mar 2 - 8

Travel and money matters seem to take on greater importance. People tend to be a little finicky, restless or ill-at-ease especially if they can't get their own way. The

women could become obsessed with their personal image while the men incline towards being more macho in their dealings with either sex.

Mar 9 - 15

Be wary of health and diet and, if out and about, be selective when choosing somewhere to eat and drink, especially if you're on unfamiliar ground. Elsewhere, people may be inclined to try something different. A few will show this in a new-found freedom of self-expression.

Mar 16 - 22

Those into sports might be tempted to show off their skills. Be careful of a communication breakdown in the work place. You may have to show your independence and do your own thing if people refuse to help out. You're more than capable of getting things done and dusted on your own.

Mar 23 - 29

Business, legal matters and possible career changes are under close scrutiny. None of these areas are favourable - especially on Monday. However, sexy social affairs and new romance are on the top of the agenda. This will be a red-hot smouldering week for single and married people alike. Bring the passion back into your life.

Mar 30 - Apr 5

There is general feeling of relaxation and consideration both at home and at work. Now is a good time to commit to agreements, sign documents and make promises you intend to keep. Messages or mail from far-away places or remote family members stir up a few memories.

Apr 6 - 12

The first part of the week could seem a little accident prone. An unusual event might leave a mark on everyone. Local councils might be more fanatical about recycling or wanting to make changes. Diet and health regimes are in the air but don't rush into anything willy-nilly.

Apr 13 - 19

Bank Holiday Monday may have more than its fair share of transport problems and the police may have to deal with a particularly nasty crime or incident. An increased vigour will be apparent with spring in the air. People are more assertive but the more practical the ambition, the better the chance of success.

Apr 20 - 26

Love is blooming, you might find you only have eyes for your favourite person at this time. With the Full Moon culminating in Taurus, you should careful when looking at your finances. Think about how you and your partner want to take your relationship to the next step.

Apr 27 - May 03

Practical considerations of all kinds will be up against emotional feelings. There could be disagreements in anything from personal relations to how things should operate in the working arena. Envy or jealousy, warranted or not, may stop things running as smoothly as they should. Think carefully before you react or choose to release your inner demons.

May 4 - 10

Look out for some power struggles behind the scenes this Bank Holiday Monday. And with Mercury turning retrograde in Gemini there will be clever-clogs everywhere trying to show the world they are right. Don't be taken in by people trying to pull the wool over your eyes.

May 11- 17

Back to work with a vengeance! This could be a week to make appointments and get them out of the way. Then you can knuckle down and get things done with no distractions. Anyone that comes across a bit pompous could be in for an unwelcome surprise. Indulge yourself - but not too much.

May 18 - 24

Relationships may need a little more work so give your partner some extra tlc. On the plus side, the business world seems to speed up a bit and there may even be a major break though. Look out for fresh, new innovations. You may also hear some welcome good news at some point this week.

May 25 - 31

In yet another Bank Holiday week people can't bear to be stuck inside. Get out and about, organise a game of rounders with friends or perhaps a giant water fight. Politics may be up in the air and someone might deliver a speech of real importance. Heavy machinery firms may be in the news with a take-over or merger.

Jun 1 - 7

All is well with the world now Mercury is moving direct again. You can put your feet up and relax as everything should come together swimmingly. Those of you striving for a position of power should be able to get ahead. The athletics world will be admiring the incredible ability of the best performers we've seen yet.

Jun 08 - 14

Jupiter turns retrograde this week, which means there could be some tricky decisions ahead. This is especially true for those in the legal profession or in a position of authority. You can't please all of the people all of the time but try to be as fair as possible. Keep your money in your pocket and stay away from the casino.

Jun 15 - 21

People who journey far and wide could come up against unexpected problems. Passports and visas may be hard to obtain or travel could meet with silly little hold ups. The rebels are there will be tempted to let loose and blow off steam this week.

Jun 22 - 28

What may seem serious at first will soon fade away into the wind. Certain emotional entanglements may seem to get serious very quickly but be careful, they might not last very long. Strange things may happen over these few days. Think seriously if you're planning any joint financial ventures.

Jun 29 -

Jul 5

Four major planets are retrograde in these first few days of July. It would best to keep a low profile and let others do their own thing. New leadership or changing the rules could leave people a bit dazed and confused. Take the time to put things across nice and clearly.

Jul 6 - 12

Anything can happen! This is generally a nice happy week where you can get lots done with the right attitude. Those involved with the arts, entertainment and corporate business dealings do very well. Trying to convince your partner that you really do need that luxury cruise abroad could prove to be a bit of a feat. Make sure you sell it in the right way.

Jul 13 - 19

Overall, a rather eventful period, quite lucky for money matters. Don't be scared to go for that risk or take the odd chance here and there. You may be called upon to help out younger people with their affairs. A great time for outdoor pursuits, short distance travel, self-expression and perhaps an indulgence or two.

Jul 20 - 26

The total solar eclipse in Cancer will have a positive affect on home life. You may find that quite a few people are moving house as well. Personal relationships take on a new meaning and couples will become closer in their

understanding of each other. For some of you love birds, the gentle sound of wedding bells may not be too far away.

Jul 27 - Aug 02

You may be tempted to splash out on some extravagances. Love and sex will also be high on the agenda. Selfishness and a lack of consideration for others will also be apparent so don't be afraid to point this out. At work people try to usurp the system and use their position for personal gain.

Aug 03 - 09

The lunar eclipse in Aquarius implies a busier than usual social life probably involving the old and the young. There could also be a hint of a rebellious streak lurking in the background. Some people do their best

to get a better deal for themselves. Make sure you're involved in every level of the negotiations.

Aug 10 - 16

Be on your toes and look out for potential hazards. Concentrate and use your energy wisely and it will all work out perfectly. Keep at it even during sticky moments. Adventure and sporting issues play a major part this week.

Aug 17 - 23

For most this will be a period of self-indulgence. The temptation to get out and have fun and splash a little cash could lead you to lose touch with the consequences. There could be some mixed feelings with business and pleasure. More than one office romance may begin this week. Will suit people in the performing arts.

Aug 24 - 30

This week it feels like everything is picking up speed. You might struggle to keep up with everything that's going on right now. Don't panic, a cool head will help you to stay ahead of the game. As the weekend gets closer travel may be a problem in some areas. Sudden temper flares are likely to be commonplace perhaps from the last people you would expect. ☞

Aug 31 - Sep 06

Bank Holiday Monday should be relatively trouble free except for the mischievous weather forecasts. Later in the week you may have to face up to someone and discuss their issues. It could be someone trying to undermine your opinions and what you stand for. Avoid too much extravagance. Children could get on your nerves this week.

Sep 07 - 13

There could be a confusing couple of days where you just can't make up your mind. Take some time out to find your focus, perhaps make a pros or cons list or do some meditation. Mercury retrograding in Libra will bring delays in decision making in many areas of life. You'll notice it especially when it comes to partnerships, the law and money matters. Don't let people take too long to make up their minds or opportunities could slowly fade away.

Sep 14 - 20

Somehow, secrets slip into the public domain and can cause havoc. Be careful to bite your lip if you've been entrusted with big news. Those who work on at sea or people from abroad may have a hard time moving around or getting to where they want to be.

Sep 21 - 27

Opportunities to increase personal responsibilities at work or within the family circle won't come quite as easy as you may first think. Be prepared to work for them and prove yourself. If you're on a health kick or concentrating on your personal well being, don't be scared to ask advice from those in the know.

Sep 28 - Oct 4

Mercury moving direct eases pressures all round. This is a bright, happy, positive week. Travel and communication issues go smoothly and people may sign agreements without too much worry. Love and romance are also highlighted nicely.

Oct 5 - 11

One of those occasional periods where people play hard and lose fast at every opportunity. Don't be drawn into it. The rebel streak gets into us all at one time or another - and this is it! Feel free to be adventurous and burn off some steam, just don't throw the cash around.

Oct 12 - 18

There may be a favourable government statement regarding the NHS and, in particular, the dental service. A news item about a couple whose love affair has caught public imagination could prove to be quite helpful. Educational matters, children and their needs may have to be properly addressed and rearranged.

Oct 19 - 25

It's all systems go and, when it comes to promotions, may the best man or woman win. There could be some travel on the cards related to your job or business. However, be on your toes and look out for those out to deceive you. If you make the wrong deal could cost more than just money.

Oct 26 - Nov 1

Generally, the accent is on family values, your social life and getting along with other people as best you can. However watch out for someone trying to take over and dominate events. This behaviour could lead to break-ups, changes and emotional upsets we can't always control properly. Prepare to act as mediator.

Nov 2 - 8

The Full Moon in Taurus is a reminder that you must keep your financial affairs fluid and pay bills promptly. Joint monetary matters may have to be looked at. People may have to settle for less than expected if they're waiting on an insurance pay out. Travel abroad is indicated. You might take off on a romantic trip away, honeymoon or even a break with your friends.

Nov 09 - 15

Love, sex and romance will be in the air. It feels like spring has come again with the way some people act. The ambitious ones among you will make good progress. People that work with the arts, entertainment and luxury goods will flourish.

Nov 16 - 22

Much of the last week's activities may be carried over into the work place so, if you want privacy, be discreet! In business issues the more practical, shrewd-thinking people seem to come up with a few good ideas worth putting into practice. However not everyone will be happy about it.

Nov 23 - 29

A government body may fall under scrutiny due to pleasure seeking activities.

You may want to step away from too much self-indulgence yourself and instead focus your attention on other people. News of someone fiddling the books may also be one of this week's headlines.

Nov 30 - Dec 6

All forms of partnerships, formal or emotional, suffer setbacks as one partner plays games the other one doesn't understand. Yet again, secrets leak out creating quite a few red faces in the process. Important matters that are not for general consumption become common knowledge. There could be a few disgruntled people this week.

Dec 7 - 13

As we near holiday time, strong leadership abilities will be recognised. Other people will also be forced to recognise this. It's a good idea for people involved in sport, games or dancing to organise young people to put on demonstrations or public displays. Definitely a week for festivities and fun.

Dec 14 - 20

The business world turns to face the entertainment fields as a more established kind of sponsorship is announced. The New Moon in Sagittarius suggests that

you might have to do some serious thinking. Especially when it comes to looking after knowledge and personal development. Perhaps it's time to sit down and organise how young people will further their education in the New Year to come.

Dec 21 - 27

Young people spending Christmas with their partner's family for the first time will have to be on their best behaviour. Practice the art of diplomacy, especially with tempers rising as the celebrations are organised. However everyone will soon settle down and it'll be a lovely, warm time where families come closer together.

Dec 28 - 31

Everyone should be more truthful with each other. This is a time of fresh new beginnings and you should leave the past behind. Let people know what your intentions are - you'll be surprised at the positive response and support you will receive. ❖

Reiki

healing energy for mind, body and spirit

Release feelings of stress and exhaustion, emotional and psychological blockages and accelerate healing of injuries and chromic pain.

Opening the body's energy channels (meridians) and major nerve centres (chakras) falicitating your natural ability to heal yourself.

0777 404 1941
or email energyhealing@ymail.com
sessions and attunements available

Robert West
reiki master/teacher

Why not!
have a phone reading with Aileen
0208-830-6118
(my clients say I'm the best)

independent reader/ 24 hrs

25 yrs professional

Readings cannot be guaranteed

FREYA

DO YOU BELIEVE IN MAGIC?

Inspired Psychic Predictions & Powerful Spells!

Love Money Career

Health & Family Concerns

For Every Problem There Is A Solution!

01843 868999

Exclusive Credit & Debit Card Service

www.freyawitch.com

The Ending of the Words
Magical Philosophy of Aleister Crowley by Oliver St. John and Sophie di Jorio

THE ENDING OF THE WORDS

MAGICAL PHILOSOPHY OF
ALEISTER CROWLEY

The Ending of the Words examines the thought and philosophy of the English magician Aleister Crowley through the lens of practical research. With an in-depth presentation of the source Tradition, the book introduces Thelema, the Law of the New Aeon declared by Crowley, to a modern readership. Fully illustrated, with a comprehensive glossary of essential Egyptian, Qabalistic and Thelemic terminology.

Available from major book retailers or direct from the author's website:
www.lulu.com/oliverstjohn   http://www.lulu.com/oliverstjohn

DON'T TELL US, WE'LL TELL YOU

ARE YOU SICK OF CALLING PSYCHIC LINES AND BEING ASKED ALL THE QUESTIONS?

Because you won't find that with Psychics That Know. We'll tell you what's going to happen, when & even how it will happen. Plus, we'll reveal secrets about you and your loved ones. Get the answers you need from the best psychics in the world. Guaranteed answers or your money back - that's our promise.

THOUSANDS OF REPEAT CALLERS CAN'T BE WRONG

PAY BY CREDIT CARD, CALL:

CALL US NOW

0870 249 1509   0905 0090 505

"My future astounded me". D. Jones, London.

£1.50/min. Readings for guidance only. Customer Service: 0870 9222 220.
Infodial. All Calls Recorded. 24 Hours. **Web: PsychicsThatKnow.com**

UK Premium Rate
0907 128 80 80
Credit Card
0844 544 154
Eire Premium Rate
1580 939032

Text **HIGHWAY** to **84010**

The Psychic Highway

www.thepsychichighway.com

0907 calls cost £1.50/min. 1580 calls €2.40/min (mobiles & pay-phones more) Text replies £1.50 each. You must be 18+ with bill payers permission. All calls are recorded. Service Provider: 24 Seven PO Box 567, Leeds LS2 7WP.

KATY BRADSHAW
MEDIUM & AUTHOR

YOUR QUESTIONS ANSWERED

YOUR DESTINY REVEALED

01639 831164

DEBIT/CREDIT CARDS ACCEPTED

TO PAY ON YOUR PHONE BILL

0906 400 7510

£1.50 PER MIN

'Readings are for guidance only'

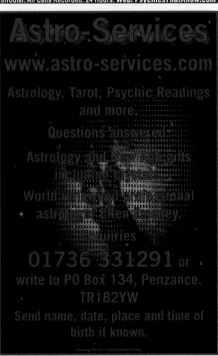

Astro-Services

www.astro-services.com

Astrology, Tarot, Psychic Readings and more.

Questions answered

Astrology and New Age gifts including crystals

World renowned, professional astrologer Ellen Tiernen

Enquiries

01736 331291 or

write to PO Box 134, Penzance. TR18 2YW

Send name, date, place and time of birth if known.

Readings for recreational purposes only

predictionmagazine.co.uk

Your online guide to angels, tarot, horoscopes and more...

Discussions

Stay up-to-date and have your say on the latest mystic news and trends. We cover news stories on anything supernatural, psychic, planetary, astrological and more!

Horoscopes

Daily horoscopes coming soon!

Blogs

Inside the spiritual, paranormal, psychic and downright crazy world of the *Prediction* team!

Events

Your guide to spooky and spiritual happenings across the UK

www.predictionmagazine.co.uk